Jan(

WOMEN, MEN AND EUNUCHS

GENDER IN BYZANTIUM

WOMEN, MEN AND EUNUCHS

Gender in Byzantium

Edited by Liz James

London and New York

First published 1997
by Routledge
11 New Fetter Lane, London EC4P 4EE

Simultaneously published in the USA and Canada
by Routledge
29 West 35th Street, New York, NY 10001

© 1997 selection and editorial matter, Liz James; individual
chapters, the contributors

Typeset in Garamond by
Ponting–Green Publishing Services, Chesham, Buckinghamshire
Printed and bound in Great Britain by
Biddles Ltd, Guildford and King's Lynn

All rights reserved. No part of this book may be reprinted or
reproduced or utilised in any form or by any electronic,
mechanical, or other means, now known or hereafter
invented, including photocopying and recording, or in any
information storage or retrieval system, without permission in
writing from the publishers.

British Library Cataloguing in Publication Data
A catalogue record for this book is available from the British Library

Library of Congress Cataloguing in Publication Data
A catalogue record for this book has been requested

ISBN 0–415–14685–2 (hbk)
ISBN 0–415–14686–0 (pbk)

CONTENTS

CONTENTS

PLATES AND FIGURES

CONTRIBUTORS

Charles Barber is Assistant Professor of the History of Art, University of Notre Dame.

Leslie Brubaker is Senior Lecturer in Byzantine Studies at the University of Birmingham.

Averil Cameron is Warden of Keble College, Oxford, and was formerly Director of the Centre for Hellenic Studies, King's College London.

Robin Cormack is Professor of the History of Art at the Courtauld Institute, University of London.

Antony Eastmond is a Research Fellow in the History of Art at the University of Warwick.

Barbara Hill is an independent scholar based in Toronto.

Liz James is Lecturer in the History of Art, School of European Studies, University of Sussex.

Dion C. Smythe is Research Associate on the Prosopography of the Byzantine Empire Project based at King's College London.

Shaun F. Tougher is Lecturer in Byzantine Studies, Queen's University, Belfast.

Ruth Webb is Assistant Professor in Classics, University of Princeton.

ACKNOWLEDGEMENTS

This volume grew out of a seminar series, *Gender in Byzantium: Still an Issue?*, organised by Charles Barber and myself at the Institute of Classical Studies, London. I would like to thank the Director and staff of the Institute of Classical Studies for their support, both of the original series and of the plans for publication. I would also like to thank the participants, both speakers and audience, in that series for their contributions and their patience as regards this, the end product.

Liz James

ABBREVIATIONS

B	*Byzantion*
BHG	*Bibliotheca Hagiographica Graeca*, F. Halkin, ed., 3 vols in 1 (Brussels, 1957)
BMGS	*Byzantine and Modern Greek Studies*
DOP	*Dumbarton Oaks Papers*
JÖB	*Jahrbuch der Österreichischen Byzantinistik*
ODB	*The Oxford Dictionary of Byzantium*, 3 vols, A. Kazhdan *et al.*, eds (Oxford, 1991)
PG	*Patrologiae Cursus Completus, Series Graeca*, J.P. Migne, ed., 161 vols in 166 parts (Paris, 1857–66)
PL	*Patrologiae Cursus Completus, Series Latina*, J.P. Migne, ed., 221 vols in 222 parts (Paris, 1844–80)
PLRE 1	*Prosopography of the Later Roman Empire*, vol. 1: AD 260–395, A.H.M. Jones, J.R. Martindale and J. Morris, eds (Cambridge, 1971)
PLRE 2	*Prosopography of the Later Roman Empire*, vol. 2: AD 395–527, J.R. Martindale, ed. (Cambridge, 1980)

Spellings of proper names, places, etc. are based on those in the *ODB*.

INTRODUCTION: WOMEN'S STUDIES, GENDER STUDIES, BYZANTINE STUDIES

Liz James

This volume had its beginnings in a seminar series at the Institute of Classical Studies in London called *Gender in Byzantium: Still an Issue?* The term 'gender' was deliberately chosen, to make it clear that this was not a series of papers that dealt with individual Byzantine women or one that attempted to reconstruct what it must have been like to be a woman in Byzantium. Even if such biographies and reconstructions were conceptually possible, we lack the historical evidence to achieve them.[1] Rather, the series sought to explore the ways in which the surviving evidence might be used to build up a picture of the representation, the image, of women in Byzantium.

Previous work on women in Byzantium concentrated first on the rediscovery of individual women and then on the nature of women's lives. This fits the pattern of feminist research more generally. Early feminist studies established that the proper business of such research was women, both individually and collectively, as far as their lives could be recovered. Academic feminism in Britain, perhaps as a result of this, found its first home in, and has remained very much a product of, sociology, since sociological methods demand research on individual women or groups of women whom the researcher then places in their setting.[2] As sociology absorbed different theoretical approaches, so feminist research too focused on the lives of women, initially via a structuralist-Marxist methodology and then, more recently, through phenomenological, ethnographic and interactionist approaches.[3] It was political sociological feminism that conceived of women's studies as having a political agenda for change

xi

and that called for women to be included in academic research as a subject of research, not as a variable within that research.[4] Further, it was within sociology that the division between feminist studies, with its political dimension, and women's studies, which lacks such a dimension, was initially pointed out and debated.

The result of this has been that feminist research focuses above all on the interaction between the researcher and the actual women; this is seen in sociological disciplines through the concentration on the experiences of women, in historical disciplines in the excavation of the lives of women, and in literary disciplines in the reading of women writers. However, this legacy of feminist sociology works best in periods from the eighteenth century onwards; the closer to the present one is, the more evidence is available about actual women, including their own words about themselves. More problematically, it presumes that research can be seen to uncover and describe reality for practical purposes, a dubious assumption even in the present. Within historicising subjects such as history, art history, Byzantine studies and archaeology, the proposition that feminist studies should be the study of named, individual women is still more unlikely, though one that frequently underlies much research. It is not always recognised that the tools developed in the 'here-and-now' social sciences do not always work either where it is impossible to carry out first-hand, interpersonal research, and/or where the nature of the evidence does not allow an uncovering of a total 'reality'.

History itself is representational. In whatever form it survives, it offers partial and motivated accounts predicated upon a number of other partial and motivated accounts that have a complex relationship to the underlying events represented by the historical record. 'Facts', derived from these accounts, are themselves stitched together by the preoccupations and intellectual concerns of the historian, not of 'the past' itself. Above all, the traps of ahistoricity and anachronism have to be avoided. Sociological feminist analyses – indeed feminist analyses generally – have often failed to recognise this.[5]

Despite this, the development of feminist studies within disciplines such as history, art history, even, to some extent, literary studies, has tended to follow the pattern laid down in sociology.[6] There appear to be three basic stages: women in; women and the means of production; and beyond women alone – gender. The 'women in' approach searches for evidence of women in areas where received historical truth has assumed there is none.[7] In my own discipline, history of art, this has been encapsulated in the question asked by the nineteenth-century art historian Linda Nochlin, 'Why have there been no great women artists?'[8] Where were the women, specifically the women artists?

This question came at a time in the 1970s when much work was being done in literary studies and history to rediscover neglected or lost women and to incorporate them into the canons of study.[9] Feminist art historians made their own contribution to this through the compilation of lists and catalogues of women artists who did not form a part of the canon of works traditionally taught in art history degrees.[10] The work of these women was compared to and extolled over that of their male contemporaries, and the traditional definition of 'art' extended to take in 'crafts'. The 'shortcomings' of female artists were excused in terms of the political agenda outlining the tyranny of patriarchy: in the words of Germaine Greer, 'one cannot make great artists out of egos that have been damaged, with wills that are defective, with libidos that have been driven out of reach'.[11]

This focus on the empirical collection of data, the unearthing of the lives of individual women, was born out of the methods employed in sociology. It also derived in part from the agenda of political feminism, above all, the dictum that the 'personal is political', the belief that the recovery of individual women and their experiences is important. Nevertheless, when Greer made her statement in 1979, she was almost seven years too late. Even as Nochlin asked her deceptively simple question, so she too offered an answer and pointed out the trap. What is 'greatness'? How is it defined and by whom? In other words, whose definitions are we buying into? In the art historical canon, greatness, the Old Masters, is a construction of patriarchy. To use the term meant to define women in terms of already established patriarchal criteria for great art and genius. Several stories circulated, making this point. When believed to be by the eighteenth-century artist Jacques-Louis David, the *Portrait of Mlle Charlotte du Val d'Ognes* was hailed as 'a perfect picture, unforgettable'; when reassigned to Constance Marie Charpentier, it became apparent that 'its poetry, literary rather than plastic, its very evident charms and cleverly concealed weaknesses, its ensemble made up of a thousand subtle artifices all seem to reveal the feminine spirit'.[12] So, as Nochlin had herself pointed out, 'why have there been no great women artists (or, indeed, writers, politicians, generals)?' was not the right question to ask since it demanded an answer in terms of the already existing patriarchal status quo.

Of course it was necessary to restore women to the historical record, but the terms in which this was done needed to be redefined. The excavation of lost women tended to place these women in a relatively untheorised 'real' world. Thus Greer could talk in a universalising way of damaged egos and defective wills; the portrait of *Mlle Charlotte du Val d'Ognes* could be constructed in relation to the 'real world' of the eighteenth century, where, depending on one's perspective, either David was the supreme artist or Charpentier displayed all the characteristics of the eighteenth-century woman. Women were merely added in; the empirical corpus extended. Where once there were no women artists, writers, saints, politicians, now they abounded. What such an approach overlooked was that these women, these representations of women, whether defined as texts, images or actions, were themselves biased and very partial. Simply to be descriptive, to say that there were women painters and this is what they produced, that there were women saints and this is what they did, was, and is, quite frankly, boring. It was also an approach that could readily be accepted by the patriarchal establishment, for it merely extended and refined traditional working procedures. Thus feminist studies could become women's studies and we could all safely 'do women'.[13]

Stage Two feminist methodologies, sought to deal with this. The 'why' became important. Why did women artists paint as they did? Why did they paint rather than sculpt? Why did they paint the topics they did – why horses rather than children?[14] Why were female saints fasting visionaries rather than reforming bishops,[15] reformed prostitutes rather than stylites, virgins rather than missionaries?

Feminist thought branched off in two directions, the essentialist and the marxist. Art history, borrowing again from literary studies and from psychoanalysis, sought to establish a 'feminine aesthetic', an artistic equivalent to '*écriture féminine*', a hierarchy of qualities applicable to women which makes their work distinctive from men's work. Women's art, like their literature, is gentle, graceful, nurturing, at one with the natural world; men's is rugged, strong, virile, about events. Women's art is decorative; men's narrative. This position is, of course, simply a reversal of the David–Charpentier position. *Mlle Charlotte du Val d'Ognes* looks as she does because a delicate poetry is the hallmark of Charpentier's creative, feminine genius. A virtue is made out of a necessity; those qualities previously seen as defects are upheld as better than anything any man can produce. Such an approach is a form of biological essentialism at its best, wherein qualities are defined as eternally 'feminine' or 'masculine', but it is one that has received academic approbation. The semiotician Norman Bryson attempted to distinguish between still-life paintings by male and female artists on the grounds of their inherent pictorial qualities.[16] Still lives by women reflected their private inner sphere; those by men the outside world, a familiar public/private dichotomy. This allowed Bryson to note, for example, that whilst Paul Cézanne's aesthetic compositions owed nothing to the natural placement of objects, in the case of Paula Modersohn-Becker, 'the hand which balances the formal composition is also able to reach out and pour the tea'.[17] This notion of a universal feminist aesthetic has also been supported by such notable post-modern feminists as Julia Kristeva and Luce Irigaray.[18] The feminist aesthetic's construction of the essentialist, unchanging nature of women creates problems for the historian. This universalising essentialism is itself a temporal construction. Its assumption is that, throughout history, 'woman' has remained the same, displayed the same qualities, possessed the same intrinsic psychological make-up. This lack of historical specificity and anachronism serves only as a feeble justification for the rediscovery of lost women.

The alternative was to look at the means of production, at the social, political and economic circumstances surrounding these women – of how Charpentier might have come to produce *Mlle Charlotte du Val d'Ognes*. Marxist–feminist art historians such as Griselda Pollock rephrased Nochlin's original question in terms of Nochlin's own answer. Nochlin observed that 'art is not a free autonomous activity of a super-endowed individual . . . but occurs in a social situation, is an integral element of social structure and is mediated and determined by specific and definable social institutions'.[19] In her early writing, *Old Mistresses* (1981), with Rozsika Parker, and *Vision and Difference* (1988),[20] Pollock approached women artists from this perspective of their socio-economic background and the effect this had on their work, whilst discounting the subjective element of 'greatness'. So, where initially monographs on women artists had hailed their rediscovery and praised their work, the discipline moved on to set that work into the social context of its time whilst continuing to privilege the individual female practitioner – the legacy of sociology.

Consequently, this approach represented merely another, more subtle, reworking of Nochlin's original question. It served to tie the art so closely to the artist, to the individual and the way in which her socio-economic situation affects her creative powers, that it offered no way out beyond the figure of the individual artist herself. In this way, feminist methodology comes full circle and, in art historical terms, creates a feminised echo of the dictum of the great traditional-ist art historians. Pollock might, with Sir Ernst Gombrich, have claimed that 'there really is no such thing as art, there are only artists'.[21]

This same two-stage methodological pattern is apparent in re-search into women within Byzantine studies. Individual women have been excavated. Steven Runciman paid lip-service to what he called 'these days of female liberation' by looking at that 'glamorous Athenian', the eighth-century empress Irene, at the 'pious but pert' poetess Kassia and at the unfortunate seventh-century empress Martina, of whose tongue-slitting he remarks crudely that 'it was perhaps the only way to stop her talking'.[22]

These women were then placed in their socio-economic context. Judith Herrin outlined her three avenues of approach for identifying the position, activity and authority of women in Byzantine society: the collection of chance references to female activity in (male) sources; the documentation of the ingenuity with which women exercised their limited legal rights; and the outlining of the signific-ance of ecclesiastical institutions and Christian beliefs for women – all collecting data about the 'reality' of women's lives.[23] Byzantinists have explored the legal positions of women, women's economic roles, women's relations to public life, women and monasticism, even women artists in Byzantium.[24] The overall aim has been to illustrate the practical reality of women's life in Byzantium. We now have some glimmerings of women's economic status, some hints of their legal position, an idea of their political role – who was where, doing what and what their status was.

This is important work, of which more remains to be done. Ruth Webb's chapter in this volume offers an example of the type of lower-class, less respectable women that Byzantine scholarship has so far tended to overlook. On the other hand, it is not the end of the story, any more than the discovery of women artists was the end. As Webb points out, the information that can be garnered is both partial and biased. This is the point, however, where the legacy of feminist sociology fails us. As I have already discussed, this type of methodo-logy depends above all on one thing: being able to recover individual women and something of their life histories. It works admirably for periods where names and biographies exist. It is not a method that works particularly well for Byzantine studies where so much evidence does not survive. There is no evidence for any named female artist in Byzantium; there is no evidence for any named male artist until the tenth century.[25] We know of a handful of women writers from Byzantium; we do not always know even the most basic things about them such as their dates of death and birth. This is the point where 'women aren't enough'.[26]

This is where gender becomes an issue. I see 'gender' as the third stage in the development of feminist research methods. As a tool for research, gender refers to the differences between men and women in terms of the differences created by societies rather than the biological difference of sex. In this way, it enables both women and men to be integrated into any subject; rather than treating 'women' as a special category, we can look to understand the social construction of femaleness and maleness. Gender invites us to see the world not in terms of 'men' and 'women', but in terms of 'masculinity' and 'femininity' and the social construction of appropriate roles for the sexes.

Joan Scott pushed this use of gender still further by suggesting that we look beyond the social construction of gender to its meanings, above all as a metaphor for many human relations and activities. She defined gender as a 'primary way of signifying power'.[27] Women may not always be present in the historical record. Gender, however, is, and can be used to explain something of the construction of these absences. Women may not, for example, hold positions of political power or be represented in the Church hierarchy, so it is not possible to write about women bishops. However, their absence is a result of their gender: they cannot be bishops because they are women. In this way, the concept of gender allows us to look not just at women and their spheres of activity and not just at the social construction of masculinity and femininity, but to explore every field for the role and place occupied by 'gender'.[28] That which is absent can be used to define what is present and women's absences can be as telling as their presence. Moreover, the distinction between sex and gender need not be so simple; Judith Butler argues that gender has come to be seen as the expression of an inner, personal core, almost the spiritual equivalent to the simple biological sex. Rather, it should be viewed as performative. Male and female might be biologically determined; identity, however, is fabricated rather than essential and each physical body can be the site for a number of different genders.[29]

So gender can be used to explore the structures, the systems that keep women in their place – in other words, patriarchy. Judith Bennett has expressed it best in her account of how patriarchy has become the feminism that dare not speak its name in academic history circles. She argued the case for feminist history taking on the history of patriarchy.[30] Patriarchy is an historical phenomenon, changing and existing in many forms and varieties; feminist historians need to look at how patriarchy has changed and survived over time and place and at the patriarchal ideologies and realities that have assured women that there is power and safety inside and danger beyond. 'Gender' rather than 'women' offers a way into this.

A range of questions can be opened up. The concept of 'gender' allows us to break out from the stranglehold of personalities and individuals and to ask bigger questions about the ways in which the Byzantines structured their world. In art historical terms, the artist can be left aside. Byzantine images are, overwhelmingly, designed and created by men; they formulate and reflect a culture designed by men for women and for men; their images of women are men's images of women, a male response to women and a male response to the relationship between men and women.[31] In what terms should we study them? What messages did they carry for women? And this concerns not just pictures but texts also. Susan Ashbrook Harvey has shown how this works in hagiography. Rather than trawling saints' lives for what they tell us about women saints and the incidental depiction of women's lives, she shows how hagiography needs to be read in its own terms. It does not offer an historical reality of women's lives but depicts women according to its own purposes as symbolic literature.[32] The nature of hagiography means that women will be depicted in certain ways and as performing certain actions. It offers a cultural construction of 'woman', enabling us to see that a holy woman is not the same as a holy man for reasons beyond those of biological sex. What can be done is to look at the place of women in society, the roles of women, at the ideas and constructions of 'good' and 'bad' women, at the cultural construction 'woman', rather than simply the individual person, at what absences tell us as well as presences. This is why, in Byzantine studies at least, women's studies need to become gender studies.

Catia Galatariotou's 'Holy women and witches: aspects of Byzantine concepts of gender', published in 1988, is one of the earliest and most influential pieces written about Byzantine women, and one that engaged specifically with gender.[33] Galatariotou used the concept of gender in examining the writings of a particular man, the hermit monk Neophytos, who wrote for a specific, enclosed male world. She demonstrated how he employed the concept 'woman' to make ideological, above all religious, points, and she used Byzantine gender distinctions to understand Byzantine men and women and to explore the nature of patriarchy in twelfth-century Byzantium. Lynda Garland also attempted to go beyond collecting information on women's lives in a study of the ideology of 'womanhood' in Byzantium.[34] As Barbara Hill's chapter in this volume shows, this was brave but not entirely successful, thanks to an underplaying of the concept of 'ideology' and an over-literally minded reading of texts. Nevertheless, it was an attempt to see the bigger picture.

It is this broader picture, underlain by the concept of gender, that this book seeks to explore. Both Hill's chapter and Dion Smythe's chapter on Anna Komnene demonstrate that texts are enormously complicated: a text is never just a text; it tells things not as they were but from all sorts of angles influenced by the writer (and the modern reader of the same text). Smythe begins unpacking some of the multi-layered complexities that surround a text written by an imperial woman both within and outside the cultural system that was Byzantium, whilst taking apart still further the concept of 'writing as a woman'. Hill looks at the way in which male historians depict powerful women and the strategies that those historians implicitly report those women as using to maintain their accepted gender roles. Ruth Webb also considers the strategies used by writers, both Byzantine and modern, in dealing with the female body. She looks at how texts reveal polarities and what these polarities in turn reveal.

Leslie Brubaker and Antony Eastmond also examine the construction of gender roles and the potential transgression of these roles. They look at some of the ways in which 'correct' womanly behaviour is defined and the strategies employed if this behaviour is not seen as suitable. Both begin from a specific person – the empress Helena in the case of Brubaker and queen Tamar of Georgia in the case of Eastmond – but use these as jumping-off points to explore concepts and ideas. Eastmond looks at the idea of the female king and how gender affected the construction of kingship both in medieval Georgia and in the perceptions of that rule in later centuries. Brubaker explores the idea of female patronage: what it meant to commission art, to build buildings if you were a woman. She examines how the career, both historical and legendary, of the augusta Helena was employed as a template for correct ways of female behaviour, particularly in the specific circumstances of church building. Again, both of these pieces engage with the ways in which texts are constructed and the reasons why this might be so.

Robin Cormack also confronts issues about the construction of texts. He argues that, previously, historians have been too ready to take at face value the deeds and actions of women participants in the iconoclast dispute. He sees women's place, their presence and absence, in iconoclasm partly as a construction designed to make political and ideological points. In looking at women and icons, he moves the focus away from women, and individual, specific women at that, on to the symbol of 'woman' and how that symbol was used by both sides in the iconoclast debate to deal with the issue of religious images.[35] He asks how gender might be understood as a factor in interpreting the production and meaning of icons.

Most of the chapters consider the ways in which language is used in marking out gender. Averil Cameron pushes this beyond the ways in which authors write about women into a consideration of the very construction of language and its use in dealing with and describing abstract ideas and conceptions through gender.[36] She discusses how language itself tells us about attitudes to gender through an examination of Byzantine religious writings about God and the nature of divine love.

Moreover, it is not enough to look only at women and the construction of the feminine; we need also to see the Subject against which women appear as an Other. The study of gender allows the rigid distinctions between men and women to become more fluid. Roles can be played by both men and women and these same individuals can occupy different roles at different times. A female visionary may have powers over a layman that as a nun she does not possess in relation to her father-confessor; an imperial woman, as several contributors point out, can be both powerful and powerless, depending upon the role she plays. Gender allows for men who act like men and those who did not, for women who acted like women and women who 'became like men'. Thus Charles Barber's chapter attempts to begin to discover how masculinity was constructed in Byzantium. By understanding what was masculine, a clearer picture of the feminine may emerge. Further, as Shaun Tougher demonstrates, gender in Byzantium is not restricted only to male and female. Eunuchs were a major part of Byzantine society: as castrated men, were they gendered male, female or neither? Tougher examines how eunuchs and the concept of eunuchs fitted into Byzantine society.

An investigation of Byzantine women has to be undertaken in parallel with an investigation of Byzantine constructions of gender. We do need to continue to look at what women did in Byzantium. Once we have this empirical evidence, however, we must do something with it; we must look at how women function ideologically as image and symbol. We need to look not only at the idea that women were devoted (or not) to icons but also at how this devotion was used by the Byzantines to construct a world view about God and the place of art in society; not only at the fact that some women chose to be virgins but that the symbol of virginity was a perceptual statement about the nature of the world and humanity's place within it; not only that the empresses Zoe and Theodora were bad empresses but what the Byzantine historian Michael Psellos meant by saying this; not only that women were donors but what it meant to be a female donor, a female ruler, a dancing girl in Byzantium, how these roles were constructed. Women alone are not enough in understanding women's lives in Byzantium.

NOTES

1 D.M. Nicol, *The Byzantine Lady* (Cambridge, 1994), is a scholarly version of a method that more often produces works such as C. Diehl, *Figures byzantines* (Paris, 1909), or A. Bridge, *Theodora: Portrait in a Byzantine Landscape* (London, 1978), which look to recreate, or invent, characters and personalities.

2 L. Stanley and S. Wise, *Breaking Out Again. Feminist Ontology and Epistemology* (London, 1993), 2.

3 For the development of feminist sociology and the debates over 'correct' methodological practices, see Stanley and Wise, *Breaking Out Again*. The earliest influential feminist sociologists such as Juliet Mitchell were also Marxists.

4 Ibid., 6–9. A further positive contribution from feminist sociology was the insistence that the researcher could not stand outside of the research: she/he should no longer construct her/himself as a detached objective observer and recorder. J.M. Bennett, 'Feminism and history', *Gender and History* 1 (1989), 251–72, esp. 259–66, suggests ways in which the study of history can be given this political focus by defining itself in terms of the exploration of patriarchy and the ways in which patriarchy has changed through time.

5 See the discussion of this issue in Stanley and Wise, *Breaking Out Again*, 216–19. A debate about the representational nature of history and its significance for feminist analysis has been carried out by Joan Scott and Linda Gordon: see J.W. Scott, 'Gender, a useful category of historical analysis', *American Historical Review* 91 (1986), 1053–75; J.W. Scott,

Gender and the Politics of History (New York, 1988); and the pieces by Scott and Gordon in *Signs* 15 (1990), 848–60.

6 See Bennett, 'Feminism and history', 251–72, and 'Medievalism and feminism', in N.F. Partner, ed., *Studying Medieval Women* (Cambridge, Mass., 1993), 7–30; and Susan Mosher Stuard, 'The chase after theory: considering medieval women', *Gender and History* 4 (1992), 135–46, for a discussion of the same processes in history and again in medieval history.

7 Examples of this search are given both by Bennett, 'Feminism and history', 253–4, and A. Frantzen, 'When women aren't enough', in Partner, ed., *Studying Medieval Women*, 145.

8 L. Nochlin, 'Why have there been no great women artists?', first published in *Art News* 69 (1971); refs. here to the reprint in L. Nochlin, *Women, Art and Power and Other Essays* (London, 1991), 145–78. For feminist art history, see T. Gouma-Peterson and P. Mathews, 'The feminist critique of art', *Art Bulletin* 69 (1987), 326–57.

9 See, for example, among many, E. Showalter, *A Literature of their Own: British Women Novelists from Bronte to Lessing* (New Jersey, 1977); D. Spender, *Women of Ideas and What Men have Done to Them from Aphra Behn to Adrienne Rich* (London, 1982), and *Mothers of the Novel: 100 Good Women Writers before Jane Austen* (London, 1986), especially the introduction.

10 For example, and again among many, K. Petersen and J.J. Wilson, *Women Artists: Recognition and Reappraisal from the Early Middle Ages to the Twentieth Century* (New York, 1976); A. Sutherland Harris and L. Nochlin, *Women Artists 1550–1950* (New York, 1976); E. Honig Fine, *Women and Art, a History of Women Painters and Sculptors from the Renaissance to the Twentieth Century* (New Jersey and London, 1978). See also the account given in W. Chadwick, *Women, Art and Society* (London, 1990).

11 G. Greer, *The Obstacle Race* (London, 1979), 327.

12 The first comment is that of André Maurois, the second that of the art critic Charles Sterling; see Chadwick, *Women, Art and Society*, 22–3. In this section of the book, Chadwick details similar occurrences.

13 See above, n. 4. This also opened women's studies up to men, an area of considerable debate. See Frantzen, 'When women aren't enough', 147–9 (a male perspective), and Bennett, 'Feminism and history', 253–5. I do find it a problematic political concern.

14 Nochlin, 'Why have there been no great women artists?', 170–5, on Rosa Bonheur.

15 C. Walker Bynum, *Holy Feast and Holy Fast* (California, 1987).

16 N. Bryson, *Looking at the Overlooked* (London, 1988).

17 Ibid.

18 Kristeva's writings on art include 'Giotto's joy' and 'Motherhood according to Giovanni Bellini', both published in English in J. Kristeva, *Desire in Language*, T. Gora *et al.*, trs (Oxford, 1981), 210–36 and 237–71 respectively. Both Kristeva and Irigaray contributed long essays to the exhibition catalogue, *Le Jardin Clos de l'Âme: L'Imaginaire des religieuses dans le Pays-Bas du Sud, depuis le 13e siècle*, P. Vandenbroek,

ed. (Brussels, 1994). See the review by L. James in *Oxford Art Journal* 18 (1995), 143–7, for criticism of the conceptual problems of these pieces.

19 Nochlin, 'Why have there been no great women artists?', 158.

20 R. Parker and G. Pollock, *Old Mistresses* (London, 1981); G. Pollock, *Vision and Difference* (London, 1988). These are also the issues that Pollock saw as relevant in 'Women, art and ideology: questions for feminist art historians', *Women's Art Journal* 4 (1983), 39–47. Pollock's most recent published piece on feminism and art history, 'Theory, ideology, politics: art history and its myths', in the section 'Art history and its theories', *Art Bulletin* 78 (1996), 16–22, suggests that only feminism 'could release into discourse aspects of feminine desire for the mother and thus for knowledge about women' (17), implying a move towards essentialism, supported by her later statement about what she believes to be important in art history (20).

21 E. Gombrich, *The Story of Art*, 16th ed., revised and expanded (London, 1995), 15 (the first sentence of the Introduction).

22 For Irene, see S. Runciman, 'The empress Eirene the Athenian', in D. Baker, ed., *Medieval Women* (Oxford, 1978); for Kassia and Martina, see S. Runciman, 'Women in Byzantine aristocratic society', in M. Angold, ed., *The Byzantine Aristocracy* (Oxford, 1984), 10–22.

23 J. Herrin, 'In search of Byzantine women: three avenues of approach', in Averil Cameron and Amèlie Kuhrt, eds, *Images of Women in Antiquity* (orig. London, 1983, rev. ed. London, 1993), 167–89 in the revised edition.

24 Thalia Gouma-Peterson's *Bibliography on Women in Byzantium*, produced by Wooster College, Ohio, offers details of the bulk of material published on Byzantine women. As a small sample, see, among others, J. Beaucamp, *Le statut de la femme à Byzance (4e–7e siècles)* I and II (Paris, 1990 and 1992), on women and the law; A. Laiou, 'The role of women in Byzantine society', *JÖB* 31/1 (1981), 233–60, on women's economic position; A.-M. Talbot, 'Late Byzantine nuns, by choice or necessity', *Byzantinische Forschungen* 9 (1985), 103–17, on women and monasticism; A. Weyl Carr, 'Women artists in the Middle Ages', *Feminist Art Journal* (1976), 5–9 and 26.

25 Weyl Carr, 'Women artists'. *ODB*, s.v. 'Artist'.

26 The statement is Frantzen's: 'When women aren't enough', in Partner, ed., *Studying Medieval Women*, 143–70.

27 Scott, *Gender and the Politics of History*, esp. 2–4. On gender and history, see also L.J. Nicholson, *Gender and History. The Limits of Social Theory in the Age of the Family* (New York, 1986), esp. chap. 3, for an approach that tries to link gender theory with Marxism.

28 Bennett has pointed out some of the risks in this approach – the dangers of ignoring material reality, of intellectualising the inequalities of the sexes: Bennett, 'Feminism and history', 258. Nevertheless, Scott's approach can offer a fruitful way into those areas where women are absent in the historical record. G. Perry and M. Rossington, eds, *Femininity and Masculinity in Eighteenth-century Art and Culture* (Manchester, 1994), is an example from art history taking this wider perspective. My thanks to Nigel Llewellyn.

29 J. Butler, *Gender Trouble* (New York, 1990).
30 Bennett, 'Feminism and history', 260–6.
31 These questions were raised in relation to fourteenth-century Tuscan painting by Margaret Miles in *Image as Insight* (Boston, 1985), chap. 4.
32 S. Ashbrook Harvey, 'Women in early Byzantine hagiography: reversing the story', in L.L. Coon, K.J. Haldane and E.W. Sommer, eds, *That Gentle Strength: Historical Perspectives on Women in Christianity* (Charlottesville and London, 1990), 36–59. Evelyne Patlagean's work, on transvestite saints in particular, is also significant in this context: 'L'histoire de la femme déguisée en moine et l'évolution de la sainteté féminine à Byzance', *Studi Medievali* 17 (1976), 598–623.
33 C. Galatariotou, 'Holy women and witches: aspects of Byzantine conceptions of gender', *BMGS* 9 (1985), 55–96.
34 L. Garland, 'The life and ideology of Byzantine women', *B* 58 (1988), 361–93.
35 E. Cowie, 'Woman as sign', *m/f* 1(1978), 49–64, and reprinted in P. Adams and E. Cowie, eds, *The Woman in Question. m/f* (London and New York, 1990), 117–33.
36 For the significance of language in the construction of gender, see Scott, *Gender and the Politics of History*, and the Scott–Gordon debate in *Signs* 15 (1990). Averil Cameron, 'Virginity as metaphor: women and the rhetoric of early Christianity', in Averil Cameron, ed., *History as Text* (London, 1990), 181–205, and 'Early Christianity and the discourse of female desire', in L. Archer, S. Fischler and M. Wyke, eds, *Women in Ancient Societies. An Illusion of the Night* (London, 1994), 152–68, explores these topics in a similar way to her piece here.

1

SACRED AND PROFANE LOVE: THOUGHTS ON BYZANTINE GENDER[1]

Averil Cameron

Love bade me welcome; yet my soul drew back,
Guilty of dust and sin.
But quick-eyed Love, observing me grow slack
From my first entrance in,
Drew nearer to me, sweetly questioning,
If I lacked anything.

How gendered was Byzantine love? In George Herbert's beautiful poem 'Love', love seems to be cast in the male gender, and the term is boldly transferred to Christ, without explanation or defence. Something similar happened, as I shall argue, in an important sector of Byzantine literature, while conversely, the discourses of love commonly encountered in other societies, especially of course in modern ones,[2] are largely absent. This chapter will explore the implications of this absence, and suggest some of the problems and the possibilities inherent in any attempt to inquire into Byzantine gender and subjectivity.

In recent years feminist scholars have been much exercised by the question of gendered language. What does it mean to look for specifically male or female language? Is language itself gendered? Or does language become gendered in a given social context? And then (a different question), what might it mean for a scholar, and in our case a Byzantinist, to 'write as a woman'?[3]

Study of Byzantine gender poses both conceptual and methodological problems. First, there is the term 'Byzantine', which is used in a number of ways, depending on the relevant academic constituency. For most purposes this is not too serious, but it has serious implications for the present issue in view of the huge amount of recently published work on women and gender in late antiquity (fourth to seventh centuries).[4] In view of the central role of the

1

Church in society at large, the gender attitudes of medieval Byzantium, it may be plausibly argued, were themselves established in the early Christian, and especially the post-Constantinian periods. Thus, quite apart from other arguments as to terminology, it makes sense for us to take 'Byzantine gender' in a broad chronological sense, as Alexander Kazhdan does in an article on the attitudes to sex in Byzantine hagiography.[5] Here, therefore, the term 'Byzantine' will be used to designate both 'late antiquity' and the succeeding period. But there is still a problem, in that the evidence from late antiquity offers so exceptionally rich a scope for sophisticated interpretation; gender questions are difficult to separate in that context from related but strictly dissimilar questions about issues such as asceticism, self and individuality.[6] To carry these inquiries into the later period is a very different enterprise either from that of 'finding' Byzantine women, or from the essentially apologetic aim of demonstrating a sympathetic presentation of women in hagiographic and other texts.[7] But this is the material that we must use, for Byzantium is also a society without fiction as such (for the Greek novels pose their own rhetorical questions), and, overwhelmingly, without the women's writings, letters, diaries and so on that make a similar inquiry possible for more modern periods.

Byzantine writing is overwhelmingly men's writing. The odd exceptions (above all Anna Komnene's *Alexiad*) are just that; the many 'desert mothers' of early eastern spirituality left an enduring legacy in the long tradition of Byzantine women's monasteries, but until the foundation charters of the houses founded by aristocratic women in the eleventh and twelfth centuries, their voices have been drowned out by their male counterparts, and are little heard in the spiritual tradition of the Byzantine Church; neither the popularity of ascetic stories of repentant prostitutes nor the *Lives* of female saints do much to redress the balance.[8] Within the written tradition, a strongly misogynistic tone can often be found, embedded in the context of authoritarian prescriptions for the proper place for women, that is, on the outside, not intruding into male space.[9] Alongside the female monastic tradition, that of total exclusion of everything female from male orthodox monasteries continues in some instances to this day. Byzantium was a traditional society in which one would not expect women to have played an overtly active role in public life. The well-known strong empresses in Byzantine history can therefore be accommodated within the familiar model of the indirect influence of women in a male-oriented society, where only a few exceptional women are likely to achieve prominence, and then largely by means of their potential influence on men, or by virtue of occupying the special roles of the mother of a young emperor or the marriageable daughter or widow of a deceased one.[10] Yet at least in one period of Byzantine history the freedom of action of aristocratic women extended beyond this narrow circle.[11] And in a number of cases the actual behaviour of imperial Byzantine women such as Irene or Zoe indicates an apparently paradoxical determination and an ability to free themselves from the overt moral constraints laid on them by the prevailing male discourse.

There are therefore numerous contradictions inherent in issues of gender in Byzantium. Given the nature of much of the evidence, some aspects have received little study, among which one of them may be potentially most interesting, namely the subjectivity of Byzantine women. How did Byzantine women perceive their own role as females, and what conflicts did it present to them? As in other societies where a male discourse prevails, most women will have internalised its values for themselves, and even justified them to themselves with no sense of contradiction. In the case of Byzantium, the silence of women's voices adds an extra and serious level of difficulty. Perhaps we may look for some additions to the corpus: the female addressees in the correspondence of S. Theodore the Studite have recently come to the fore, for example.[12] But I wish to consider a different set of questions, and to ask how 'male' is the Byzantine language of love and gender, and if it is, what was the likely effect on society in general, and particularly on Byzantine women?

In this connection, it is worth considering our own subjectivity as scholars and writers. In writing about Simone de Beauvoir, and about the role that a training in psychoanalysis has played in her own formation as a feminist writer, Luce Irigaray comments: 'there are centuries of sociocultural values to be rethought, to be transformed. And that includes within oneself.'[13] In the same collection, she answers the question of whether she writes 'as a woman': 'I am a woman. I write with who I am. Why wouldn't that be valid, unless out of contempt for the value of women, or from a denial of a culture in which the sexual is a significant subjective and objective dimension?'[14] In the past, many of the Byzantinists who have written about Byzantine women (and especially about the most spectacular empresses and aristocratic women) have themselves been male scholars. This is now changing. Perhaps it is time therefore to look at the subjectivity of the scholar him/herself. We too are bound by our cultural prejudices, by the constraints of the surrounding discourse and by our own writing-practice. Women are well-represented among the present generation of Byzantinists; is that not relevant in itself?

A PERSONAL NOTE

When I was beginning research, the women's movement was beginning too; like many others at the time, however, I did not wake up to it for quite a while. Perhaps I am one of that generation of successful woman academics who consciously or subconsciously adopted male strategies. Of course I read Betty Friedan and Simone de Beauvoir, but I probably first encountered women's history as such only in 1967, in the early stages of the then highly controversial Women's Caucus of the American Philological Association. At that time and since, the politics of the women's movement in the United States and in Britain were very different. Moreover, I did feel, I admit, that women's history as such could only ever be part of the story; what I wanted to be was a historian, not a women's historian or a historian of women. Much later, I began to sense an expectation on the part of others that I should be doing something about women's studies. I think that in my case this was again probably because of later experiences in North America, and in particular of my awareness there of the strong pressures on senior academic women to act as role models for the younger or less senior women in their departments. But if young female academics feel under pressure, the ambiguities of the situation for those who have already reached senior positions may in fact be no less. Belonging to the female sex may be a distinct advantage in some cases, but quite the opposite in others. In the comportment of senior male academics towards their female colleagues, it is none other than a re-enactment of the age-old sexual pattern of advance and withdrawal. But in turn, after a generation's worth of teaching and writing since the early days of the women's movement, is it not possible to recognise the familiar female claim, not to think of oneself as a woman scholar as such, but simply as a scholar, for what it actually is – an internalisation of the surrounding (male) cultural values? Why did it take so long to reach this simple realisation?

One reason for the delay is suggested by the self-consciousness with which the female scholar is forced to act. Not least revealing are the ploys adopted by women scholars themselves when speaking in academic gatherings on issues of gender. The chosen strategy depends heavily on the nature of the intended audience; it can range from deliberately eschewing female adornment to the equally familiar tactic of adopting a highly seductive look while ostensibly talking in an apparently earnest manner about overtly sexual topics. The public dress codes of the modern academic woman can take many forms. In 1993, the *Guardian* newspaper contained a defence by Germaine Greer, an early feminist icon, now proudly post-menopausal, of the outfit in which she had chosen to appear in a recent television programme – 45cm shorts worn with sheer tights;[15] the occasion for her television appearance was the publication of a book in which she had praised the older woman's release from the necessity of cosmetic allurements. Conversely, the refusal of feminine allure may stand as a badge of cultural reversal; as Gillian Clark has pointed out, the first requirement of a woman ascetic was to make herself as non-sexual as possible by removing any external aid to female beauty.[16] The gaze of late antique and Byzantine males was all too prone to be seduced.

The age of the modern female writer is also significant in relation to the reception she can expect. In a short essay entitled 'How old are you?', the same Luce Irigaray comments: '"How old are you?" is a question that should hardly ever be put to a woman, for example, for risk of offending her. Because it would seem she's only loveable or desirable in her youth, or for other reasons, during her child-bearing years.'[17] Fortunately, passing that stage also conveys a certain freedom, including the freedom to indulge in self-analysis. I am now much more aware than formerly of the actual difficulties I have had as a woman writer. I am referring to the subjective conflict arising from cultural notions of gender and femaleness, or 'femininity', and success in the 'masculine' domain of creativity.

This is a well-known problem: in my generation, the successful woman in the creative sphere may typically have tried to ignore it, or to over-compensate, to excuse herself by being excessively apologetic, or to try to make up for a perceived inadequacy by being extra-caring or extra-efficient. The sense of that conflict was a strong theme in the analysis of Anaïs Nin by Dr Otto Rank in the 1930s, and in her later life. The first volume of Anaïs Nin's diaries, published in 1966, ends with a telling observation: 'Psychoanalysis did save me because it allowed the birth of the real me, a most dangerous and painful one for a woman, filled with dangers; for no one has ever loved an adventurous woman as they have loved adventurous men.'[18]

In an essay on Otto Rank she writes about the guilt that accompanies creative work (read 'scholarship'):

> Now in the woman this problem is far deeper, because the guilt which afflicts woman is deeper than man's. Man is expected to achieve. . . . But woman was trained to give first place to her personal commitments . . . when she reduced the hours of devotion and gave her energies to other interests, she felt a double guilt. She was made aware that she was failing in her personal responsibilities, and her other achievements were severely undermined by the culture.

Though she says 'It was only when I met Dr Rank that I realised I had my own work to do', Anaïs Nin believed instinctively in the prime importance of what she called her creative will, her own individual capacities, even though by the conventional views of her society this involved her in devoting herself to 'an egocentric work, an introspective and subjective work, a selfish work'.[19] But in her own life Nin also embodied the conception of woman's work which she claimed to have rejected, namely that woman's work *par excellence* lay in love and desire.

We now know that Nin's published journals tell only part of the story; the unexpurgated versions, published after her death, show that her subjectivity was itself a construct of her 'diaries' and of her writer's art, and her role as model for the woman-artist is therefore deeply ambivalent.[20] In that Anaïs Nin has played a substantial role in feminist literature, the recent publications, and her own deliberate choice not to tell the whole truth in her published diaries, diminish her substance, transform her into an exemplification of the dangerous power of representation, and the contradictions and dangers inherent in the construction of gender.

Nevertheless, if we go beyond the sensationalism of the 'revelations' of Anaïs Nin's florid sex life, whether in the unexpurgated versions of the diaries (or are those a construct too?) or in her remarkable erotic writings, those alert to texts and their problems will not find the ambiguity so very surprising. The problem of female subjectivity remains. Anaïs Nin's agenda is described by her earlier editor as consisting of 'self, femininity, neurosis, freedom, relationships, the confluence of art and life', an agenda for an early twentieth-century woman of a certain type and background, and one trapped within her own contradictory impulses towards 'love' and creativity. Byzantine women must also have had their agendas. The example of Anaïs Nin shows how our own psychology of gender as female thinkers, and especially as writers, is bound to influence in turn our study of gender in other societies. Finally, it underlines how important I think it is to try to explore not merely the construction and the operation, but also the subjectivity of gender.

BYZANTINE GENDER: STILL AN ISSUE?[21]

Not only is gender at Byzantium still an issue – the study of Byzantine gender has hardly begun. My own interest recently has been in discourse analysis – looking at the underlying rhetorical strategies of common literary and other representations which may be taken to reveal the inner concerns of a society. A familiar method in studying other periods, this approach also seems to offer new ways of reading Byzantine culture. It ought to be possible to look at the prevailing metaphors in Byzantine texts, to consider the use of particular linguistic terms across periods and genres, to analyse the sexual strategies of individual texts, and through these collective representations to learn more about the culture of Byzantium. Though much Byzantine literary study is still innocent of such approaches, the cognitive approach might perhaps illuminate several areas of Byzantine subjectivity, psychology and epistemology; ripe for study in this way are authoritarianism, attitudes to heresy, the construction of stereotypes, and all the 'plots' of Byzantine society round which subjective identity and gender identity were constructed. Although I shall be dealing here with texts, similar questions and approaches suggest themselves in relation to other forms of representation. Why, for instance, are there so many female saints depicted in Byzantine art, when their voices are so seldom heard? And what is the gender implication of the overwhelmingly large number of images of Virgin Mother and male Child in Byzantine art? The reality of the gap (real or supposed) between the prescriptive and the actual is a problem shared by students of text and image alike, nor indeed can text and image be separated in a full synthesis.

THE LANGUAGE OF LOVE

In returning to our main theme, we can begin by asking a deceptively simple question: what was the Byzantine language of love? For in this society, beginning with the early ascetic literature, eroticism as a field of discourse was effectively appropriated by the religious sphere. Until the twelfth century at least, this was a society without an erotic literature or erotic art in the usual sense; the passionate language of physical love was applied, instead, to spiritual relationships, and in particular to the relation between the ascetic and God, a procedure all the more paradoxical in that the ascetic discourse affected to deny sexuality and praise its very absence. The effects of this transference cannot but be important for studies of Byzantine gender. One such, I would argue, was that the very process of appropriation resulted in a heightened awareness of the very elements it ostensibly sought to control; the ascetic literature became a literature of eroticism. And since it was also a language of men, the implications for women of the spread of this discourse must have been very great.

The development of the ascetic discourse in the patristic, late antique or early Byzantine period (whichever term one prefers) has been well charted in recent literature. I have approached it myself with reference to the theme of virginity,[22] but other emphases lie open, including analysis of the word-clusters that appear in the texts around the motifs of temptation and lust. My own emphasis on the potential effects for society at large of the negative stereotyping of early Christian and Byzantine women which appears in these texts has been countered by a defence of patristic attitudes towards women on the grounds that even while adopting a conventionally misogynistic rhetoric, the Fathers still maintained the spiritual equality of women in the eyes of God.[23] Indeed, there is more ambivalence in this discourse than at first sight meets the eye, and it is not wholly negative or misogynistic. Furthermore, saving the text is essential at some level for contemporary Christianity. But this line of criticism denies the central place I give to vocabulary and thought-patterns by marginalising them, by adopting a rhetorical strategy in order to demote them to the denigrated category of 'rhetoric'. I would maintain on the contrary that they are so fundamental to the development of Christian and Byzantine thought that they should be privileged. Surely the constant assumption of a certain kind of gender language by a given society cannot fail to have broad implications for gender issues in that society?

Like the gender discourse and the ascetic discourse, the Byzantine language of love, and the rules for its application, were laid down by early Christian writers. The very term *eros* (desire, sexual love) was early appropriated by Christians and given a religious meaning. While *agape* may be more commonly used of Christian love, the terms are in fact often interchangeable.[24] But, in addition, *eros* acquired a special and privileged range of uses of its own within Christian writing. The question is, then, whether there is any relation between the denial of sex, the advocacy of virginity, and the presentation of woman as temptress, that are inscribed in the Byzantine sources, and the central importance accorded by the Church, or rather by Christian theologians and writers, to the concepts of 'love' and desire? If the concept of love is so universally presented in Byzantine discourse in spiritual terms, as a religious term, what does this mean for the actuality of gender relations in Byzantine society?

Alexander Kazhdan has made a brave attempt to find sympathetic Byzantine accounts of human love, but, it must be said, without much success.[25] Of course, it is well known that the Byzantine romances of the twelfth century and later do contain a strong love interest. Nevertheless, they represent a specific and separable literary strain from much of the rest of Byzantine literature, even though the elements of romantic fiction that they display can occasionally be glimpsed in Byzantine hagiography and ascetic literature (though even when they do appear in the latter context they reflect the influence of the tradition of the Greek novel on that genre too, and the uncertainties inherent in interpreting it as a guide to 'real life' in Byzantine society). Our present subject is mainly concerned with the formative stages of Byzantine gender consciousness; for with the romances, whose origins, like those of their earlier counterparts, are highly disputed, a particular literary past and new features of Byzantine society both come into play, and thus an audience differently attuned.[26] There is a case in general for separating the period from the twelfth century onwards from our present inquiry.[27] Another classical genre, that of the erotic epigram, also enjoyed a limited revival in Byzantine times, in the learned ninth-century compositions of Leo the Philosopher, and the activities of the compilers of what is now the Greek Anthology.[28] But leaving aside these élitist productions, together with the romances and more novelistic saints' lives, it remains the case that the modern discourse of sexuality and eroticism is largely absent, at any rate from earlier Byzantine literature; its very terminology has been transferred to the religious sphere.

In other types of writing from the eleventh to thirteenth centuries a more domestic sensibility can be detected; women are praised for conjugal and maternal virtues, in strong contrast with the ascetic virginity preferred in many earlier texts.[29] The subjects are, however, in the main the female members of the powerful families who now constituted the ruling élite, and through those marriage alliances that élite was created and perpetuated; the family and conjugal sentiments expressed in their formal literature – encomia, marriage and funerary orations and the like – therefore belong in a political as well as a social context.[30] They may have little to do with broader social attitudes to men and women.

It would be rash, therefore, to assume that the locus of affection was itself significantly different. Some saints' lives of around the ninth century do present a more domestic picture of male–female relations.[31] An emotional attitude of a different kind is also displayed in this period towards religious images, and Marie-France Auzépy has shown how at the ending of iconoclasm, love and intimacy – *aspasmos* and *pothos* – were in fact lavished upon them.[32] Icons were like intimate friends, objects of warm affection. Similarly, a ninth-century homilist, George of Nicomedia, writes of the emotion and passion of the Virgin, and invites passionate identification with her feelings as an appropriate response from the Byzantine believer.[33] The role of Byzantine women as mothers was recognised in law.[34] But the Byzantine body itself, whether male or female, was typically seen only as clothed and hidden, not a source of pride but something to be concealed.[35] In Byzantine art, 'the nude form that is customary in Greek and Roman art ... was employed in greatly reduced numbers, or else dressed'.[36] This does not imply indifference; rather, references to nakedness in hagiographic texts, as when Symeon the Fool attempted to enter the women's baths naked in order to demonstrate his *apatheia*, show a highly self-conscious erotic awareness. Thus just as any degree of emotional naturalism in Byzantine texts is hedged in by literary artfulness or political constraint, so the Byzantine psyche, I would argue, was subjected to heavy restrictions laid upon it by language use, and especially by the near-total reservation of 'human' erotic language for the religious sphere. In what follows I would like to explore the process whereby the latter transference came about during the early Byzantine period.

Among the most influential works in the formation of patristic and Byzantine spirituality were Origen's commentary and homilies on the Song of Songs, written in the 240s. It may seem surprising that what is actually an outpouring of erotic love should have become so central a text in Christian asceticism. It did so, of course, precisely because it lent itself so well to a series of allegorical interpretations whereby it could be made to refer to the Christian soul and its relation with God.[37] The Song is also one of the main texts that reinforced the use of bridal imagery in relation to Christ and the Church. It was largely Origen's exposition of this text (extant only in the partial Latin translations by Rufinus and Jerome) that did most to establish a lasting model of Christian spirituality based directly on the language of erotic love between men and women.

Origen's exegesis established the understanding of the Song in terms of ecclesiology – it was held to portray the role of the Church as Bride. But a parallel interpretation saw the bride in the Song as representing the individual soul, whose relation to God was thus defined as one of *eros*. In the prologue to the *Commentary*, Origen explicitly asks how the discourse of physical love and desire can be thought suitable in relation to the love of God – an argument that he must carry if he is to persuade his audience of the spiritual interpretation of the text. Having stated categorically in his opening sentence that the Song of Songs is an epithalamium for the mystic union of the soul, or the Church, with the Bridegroom, the Logos, he recalls the 'Greeks' (above all Plato in the *Symposium*), who have already demonstrated that it is indeed *eros* that leads the soul to union with God.[38] Nevertheless, Origen is somewhat concerned about the idea. He concedes that the term *agape* is often preferred to *eros* in the Scriptures so as not to mislead people or give them cause for temptation. But, he argues, the words *eros* and *erastes* are also used there, and concludes: 'you must take whatever Scripture says about charity (*agape*) as if it had been said with reference to passionate love (*eros*), taking no notice of the difference of terms, for the same meaning is conveyed by both'.[39]

The move is essential for Origen's project; however, it also inspires him to move on to a disquisition on love in practice, how, and whom, Christians ought to love in their own lives.[40] The argument takes the form of a syllogism arising from his observation that to feel desire (*eros*) is natural to human beings: while human beings desire many things throughout their lives, he says, the true object of *eros* is the good, which is also laudable, and the only laudable desire is that which is directed to God. Human love, he goes on to suggest, is good in so far as it is directed towards a good person, and this is the kind of love which functions as a metaphor for, or a preliminary to, the love of God. From certain kinds of human love one can reach divine love, but other kinds of *eros* are 'perverted'. We can see that this is a very qualified view of the goodness of human love. In the second homily, in commenting on Paul's injunction, 'Husbands, love your wives' (Eph. 5.25), Origen explains that 'even the love of husbands for their wives can be dishonourable';[41] the only truly honourable human love is love like that of Christ for the Church.

But if human *eros* must be reined in, on the model of religious love for God, Origen also implies that the love of God has all the attributes of human passion; thus 'erotic' language, like that used in the Song of Songs, is properly, or even only, applicable to religious experience. He therefore proceeds to explain phraseology such as 'Let him kiss me with the kisses of his mouth', and 'Thy breasts are better than wine' in purely religious terms.[42]

It would be difficult to exaggerate the subsequent influence of the Song of Songs, and specifically of Origen's interpretation.[43] It is strongly present, for example, in the works of Gregory of Nyssa, who also wrote a commentary on the Song.[44] Gregory's *Life of Moses* expresses the same ideas, and so, particularly, does his *Life of Macrina*, which ends with a strongly philosophical passage about the immortality of the soul; both works also draw on the imagery of Plato. In the *Life of Moses*, Gregory writes of the love (*eros*) that the soul feels for what is beautiful;[45] the soul feels ardent love and desire – which he explains in his commentary on the Song as an intense form of *agape* – and God is seen as the good and the beautiful. Moses seeing God, on top of a mountain, represents one who climbs the 'mountains of desire', to enjoy Beauty 'not in mirrors and re-flections', but face to face, in fact to see the archetype. Plato's *Symposium*, of course, is itself a dialogue about the nature of love, from carnal love, homosexual or heterosexual, to the spiritual desire for beauty and good.

In the *Life of Macrina*, Gregory's sister Macrina is given a role parallel to the woman philosopher Diotima in the *Symposium*, who can also point the way to this direct perception of the ultimate Good. She is the exemplification of the Christianised conception of the immortality of the soul that Gregory takes from other Platonic dialogues, and she represents the stages of the successful progression of the soul towards union with God, which, as we have seen, goes back to Origen. It is no less remarkable in her case than in the case of Diotima that this role is in fact given to a woman; each is presented by the male writer in question as having reached spiritual wisdom through transcending the limitations of their sex, and yet in a sense too, each is liberated by this to reach those very spiritual heights.[46]

Gregory too justifies his choice of vocabulary, and his use of such words as 'lover' and 'desire', by arguing that the passion of an ascetic for God is beyond human feelings, in fact is *apathes*. The classic ascetic virtue of *apatheia* turns logic on its head by claiming that passionlessness is reached through passion and desire. Similarly, 'true' virginity can be claimed to be not the rejection of sexuality, but a state liberated from and above sexuality, a state 'beyond gender'.[47] Not surprisingly, *porneia* ('lust') came to feature high on the list of temptations faced by the ascetic, and in the *Life of Antony*, a work deeply influenced by Origen, Antony's first temptation came to him in this form. The paradoxical corollary of such a view is that explicitly carnal language becomes licensed for use in religious contexts, as in Jerome's famous letter to Eustochium, where he imagines Christ as a lover looking for a crack in his beloved's window, or in Gregory Nazianzen's praise of his sister Gorgonia, a married lady whom he nevertheless represents as longing for Christ, her lover. Whether, as is claimed, such language, like other gendered language in Christian ascetic and mystical literature, is really simply allegorical and symbolic, merely standing for spiritual *eros*, seems to me to be a question that needs to be reopened.[48]

In the fifth century, similar terminology reappears in the vocabulary of desire and frenzy applied by Theodoret to the female ascetics whom he describes in the *Historia Religiosa*.[49] The holy women whom he describes long for their Bridegroom, are 'maddened' by yearning and desire, and see union with the Bridegroom as also representing the victory of the martyr or the athlete, their love as a 'firebrand' to be kindled by ascetic behaviour. To the collection of ascetic biographies is appended an epilogue on the subject of divine love, perhaps added to the second edition produced later by Theodoret himself, but in any case elaborating on the same kind of thinking. Its theme, according to its recent translator Richard Price, is that 'it is an ardent love of God which motivates the ascetics'.[50] Theodoret draws on Romans 8.35 ff., and the example of Peter in John 21.7 and elsewhere, texts used in a similar sense by John Chrysostom and Theodore of Mopsuestia, as well as on Genesis, the Song of Songs and the example of Moses. His usage alternates between *agape* and *eros*; as Price comments, there is no real distinction. 'It is impossible,' Theodoret says, 'for one who does not become fervently enamoured of God to succeed in philosophy.'[51] As St Paul was 'enamoured of beauty' and Peter motivated by 'desire', 'the new athletes of virtue', that is, the ascetics in the *Historia Religiosa*, whom Theodoret had met in his own diocese as bishop of

Cyrrhus, are 'intoxicated with yearning', 'wounded by the sweet darts of love, and, as limbs of the bride, exclaim with her, "We are wounded with love"'.[52]

How to interpret this absorption of erotic language into patristic, and later Byzantine, literature, and the possible consequences of that absorption? Other writers on spirituality in the early Byzantine period continued the trend, among them notably Pseudo-Dionysius the Areopagite and John Climacus, the author of the *Ladder of Divine Ascent*, who associates the idea of erotic love with the burning of fire – an image found also in Gregory's *Life of Moses*; this is not surprising, for Climacus was a monk of Sinai, and for him as for Gregory of Nyssa in his *Life of Moses*, the notion of mystical union, *theiosis*, is closely connected with the imagery of Moses and the burning bush. Climacus is quite explicit: this *eros*, the love of God, is like physical union: 'Lucky the man who loves and longs for God as a smitten lover does for his beloved.'[53] Again, Climacus adopts the language of physical desire for spiritual love, and compares the former adversely with the latter.[54] So carnal love must be transformed into spiritual love; if detached from its spiritual counterpart, it can lead to sin, uncleanness and even madness. While a positive interpretation can be placed on this conception of ascetic love, by arguing that it transcends gender altogether,[55] many would continue to feel that there is a *prima facie* contradiction in the use of such terminology for ascetics, whose ideal is presented as precisely the absence of passion, and yet who are at one and the same time 'inflamed with desire' for God. In the ascetic tradition, spiritual union with God embraces both *apatheia* and supreme desire, 'an abundance of *eros*'. The notion of the ascetic as being 'wounded' or 'pierced' by love, which was central to Origen (and was indeed a conventional *topos* in erotic literature), reappears in Climacus, and in many other ascetic treatises. In Syriac, Ephrem Syrus had written on love in the fourth century; he was followed especially by Isaac the Syrian in the seventh. Both of these are writers whose works regularly featured in translation in later Byzantine collections.

In such a context, 'desire' can be described as being literally divine. As such, the term is applied both to God's love and to man's love for God; Pseudo-Dionysius uses *eros* for the divine nature itself, also for divine beauty, and for God's love as binding subject and object together (as in the ideas of the *Symposium*). Similar language is taken up by the seventh-century writer Anastasius of Sinai and many others. According to John Rist, Pseudo-Dionysius 'was the first person to combine the Neoplatonic idea of God as *eros* with the notion of God's ecstasy'.[56] He was not the first, however, to equate *eros* and *agape*. Further, although he describes love as essentially 'ecstatic', and love has become for him something more than the Platonic neediness, his concept is still within the Platonic tradition, and love is given a powerful role in human and divine relations. In the monastic context too, the often-stated goal of *apatheia* does not mean a lack of all passion, but rather that all passion is reserved for God, in an abundance of *eros*; even prayer is a *sunousia* and *henosis* between the soul and God. Of course, in the end God was also seen as being above gender, as Gregory Nazianzen explicitly argues. It is wrong to imagine that God had gender: 'maybe you would consider God to be a male ... because He is called God and Father, and <suppose> that deity is feminine, from the gender of the word, and the Spirit neuter, because it has nothing to do with generation...'. But still, God could be described in terms of *eros*: 'the Father loved so much that He became as woman', and 'more affectionate than fathers, more caring than mothers, more erotic than bride and groom'.[57]

We have seen, first, the transference of the language of human love to the religious sphere, and second, the transformation of a technical philosophical language into a religious commonplace. But after all, why should one expect to find the expression of romantic or marital love and affection in a pre-modern and traditional society – are not such matters developments of the late medieval and modern sensibility? On this model, it is not its absence in earlier periods, but the appearance of this theme in the late Byzantine romances and in vernacular literature that needs to be explained.

Against these arguments I persist in supposing that the prevalence of such language use for so long, and its continuance into the post-Byzantine religious tradition of the orthodox east, cannot be without effect. It would be a mistake, however, to over-simplify. For instance, while such terminology implicitly (sometimes explicitly) relegates human sexual relations to second position at best, it may also license safe male/female contact, as it sometimes does in late antiquity.[58] Theodoret stresses the fact that men and women may participate together in the religious life: Domnina worshipped daily with both men and women,[59] and both men and women come to see her; in more general reference, the 'pious wrestling-schools', as he calls the monasteries, contain both men and women, 'meadows of virginity' not 'separated' by God 'into male and female, nor dividing philosophy into two natures'.

Moreover, ascetic desire applied to men just as much as to women. Indeed, Theodoret here cites Gal. 3.28, 'in Christ Jesus ... there is neither male nor female'. But there was some ambivalence, even conflict. No women were admitted to the presence of Symeon the Stylite or to Julian, the 'Old Man' of Osrhoene.[60] Scriptural citations, like the discourse itself, could be flexibly adapted to the subject. Surprisingly enough, Theodoret not only includes women among his ascetics, and praises them, but even objects to the view that virginity is superior to marriage.[61] Women could be praised for being like men, and this process of spiritual de-gendering taken as a metaphor for spiritual progress; but 'real' virginity transcended the bonds of flesh, and conferred a paradoxical freedom. It could be seen as a quality of the soul, not the gendered body.[62] Some voices explicitly championed the view that sexuality could be overcome to such an extent that men could take on womanly qualities as well as vice versa;[63] women could be models of sanctity for men, and women, too, were sometimes seen as having been made in the image of God. Mothers received a new attention in some patristic literature.[64] Finally, in late antiquity at least, other sorts of male/female friendships became a real possibility; if the terms for 'love' and 'desire' are taken into Christian writing, so are the terms for friendship.

Nor (and this is often overlooked) did the eastern tradition develop so extraordinarily minute and physical a discourse of denigration of female sexuality and sexual organs, such as is found in the western Augustinian and scholastic tradition;[65] there, the sheer difficulty of defending the doctrine of clerical celibacy played an important role in the evolution of a mass of theory as to the purpose of sexual relations and a whole technology of sexual rules, with a 'moral theology' that classified heterosexual activity (not to speak of homosexual relations) in terms of what was supposedly 'natural' and 'unnatural', and into venial and mortal sin. For Aquinas and many others since, the Aristotelian view of woman 'as a kind of flower pot for the male's semen' occupied canon lawyers and served to justify some bizarre arguments about the actual minutiae of sexual practice, in most of which the woman is held clearly to blame.[66] One effect was, paradoxically, that sexuality as such became a main topic of debate in the medieval west, where the details of female anatomy and the (often of course misunderstood) physiology of sex and reproduction were discussed at length by generations of male theorists. In the east, in contrast, while the issue of sexual continence, both generally and between husband and wife, is a topic in many saints' lives, the Augustinian fascination with the physiology of sex was lacking; excessive condemnation of the body was a sin against God's *oikonomia*, and a moderate asceticism could be commended.[67] Lacking as well the western tradition of penitentials, the east also failed to develop its sophisticated technology of sexual sins or its classifications of the minutiae of sexual practice. The Byzantines were more interested in defining the subtleties of heresy than in discussing female sexual organs and reproduction as such.[68] It is worth emphasising the difference, since after all both traditions had their roots in the same early Christian and late antique developments, and rested on very similar ascetic attitudes expressed by the fourth-century Fathers.[69] Church legislation against women also began very early; quite apart from Pauline and later restrictions on women,[70] by the fourth century, just when the transference of erotic language to the ascetic sphere was taking place, they were repeatedly forbidden to baptise, serve at the altar or sing in church choirs.[71] Anyone concerned with 'Byzantine' (or, for that matter, western medieval) sexuality or gender issues needs to be clearer than scholars usually are about what elements can legitimately be considered specifically eastern or western, and at what period. As for the later developments, the question of why the east and the west differed so markedly in relation to their discourse of sexuality and reproduction is not one that has been much explored. It surely deserves more attention from Byzantinists interested in the place of Byzantium in the history of sexuality.

CONCLUSION

Language is one of the first and most fundamental elements in the construction of sexual identity. If in a given society individuals are exposed to habitual language use that tends in a certain direction, which is licensed, by and large, for control by only one sex, and which is engaged in strategies of both deliberate denial and enforcement, the corresponding effects can easily be imagined. In this example of where linguistic use can take us, I have concentrated on only one aspect of the Byzantine language use bearing on issues of gender; I have suggested that the appropriation into the religious sphere of the language of erotic love is a primary factor to reckon with in assessments of Byzantine gender. A similar approach could

17

be taken on many other topics. How and in what contexts do Byzantine texts refer to children, to menstruation, to menopause, to ageing and to sexual intercourse? Surprisingly, perhaps, the linguistic usages surrounding the central cult of the Theotokos, the Mother of God, still demand attention in this connection. In the patristic period, it seems, the debates that reached a height at the time of the Council of Ephesus (AD 431) focused on Mary's virginity, and on the physical details of the miraculous birth of Christ.[72] Later, a softer image begins to show through, and it has recently been suggested that this is associated after the ending of iconoclasm with the increased use of the title Mother (*Meter*) of God rather than the more impersonal 'Theotokos' affirmed at the Council of Ephesus.[73] The suffering Virgin also appears in the lament tradition and in later homiletic and art.[74] But it would be important for the study of Byzantine gender if the full range of Byzantine linguistic usage in relation to the Virgin were brought into conjunction with the relevant iconography. Gender messages are not usually consistent, and those sent out by the image of the Mother of God are no exception in having both their positive and their negative sides.[75] Again, the configuration of language (and visual representation) differs between the east and the medieval and later west.[76]

There are, then, as yet many unexplored areas in the consideration of Byzantine gender. Byzantine love (outside the romances), Byzantine sexuality, and the relations between the sexes are topics not just regulated in the texts, but also neglected by Byzantinists. A history of Byzantine love, as of Byzantine sexuality or Byzantine gender, has yet to be written. Despite the usual complaint of lack of available evidence (though reading the available texts in different ways is the obvious first step), I hope that the appearance of this volume will encourage some to venture in these directions. And I think (dare I say?) that one's own experience 'as a woman' in a still-male society may just possibly have something to contribute.

NOTES

1 This is a revised version of the paper given in the original seminar, with thanks to that audience and to subsequent ones at Belfast, Birmingham and Princeton.

2 See, for instance, S. Kern, *The Culture of Love: Victorians to Moderns* (Cambridge, Mass., 1992), and G.J. Barker-Benfield, *The Culture of Sensibility: Sex and Society in Eighteenth-Century Britain* (Chicago, 1992). For an attempt to understand the 'inner world of private people

in the past' and for a theory of 'affective individualism', see Lawrence Stone, *Broken Lives: Separation and Divorce in England* (Oxford, 1993), the third volume of a trilogy about the history of divorce from the sixteenth to the eighteenth centuries.

3 See, for instance, Luce Irigaray, *Je, tu, nous*, Eng. trans. (London, 1993), 29–36, 'Women's discourse and men's discourse', and 51–9, 'Writing as a woman'; general introductions to the issue and to the possibility of an *écriture féminine*: Toril Moi, *Sexual Textual Politics: Feminist Literary Theory* (London, 1985); Susan Sellers, *Language and Sexual Difference. Feminist Writing in France* (London, 1991).

4 This tends to merge with the equally large or larger scholarly bibliography on women and gender roles in early Christianity. A welcome guide is now available: Gillian Clark, *Women in Late Antiquity. Pagan and Christian Lifestyles* (Oxford, 1993), and for further bibliography, see the introduction to Averil Cameron and Amélie Kuhrt, eds, *Images of Women in Antiquity*, rev. ed. (London, 1993); useful survey also in R.S. Kraemer, *Her Share of the Blessings* (New York and Oxford, 1992).

5 A. Kazhdan, 'Byzantine hagiography and sex in the fifth to twelfth centuries', *DOP* 44 (1990), 131–43. For the twelfth century as marking a transition at the upper chronological range, see further below.

6 See, for instance, the articles in *Discursive Formations, Ascetic Piety and the Interpretation of Early Christian Literature, Semeia* 57 and 58 (1992), and for a particularly interesting example of this genre, Elizabeth A. Castelli, 'Mortifying the body, curing the soul: beyond ascetic dualism in *The Life of Saint Syncletica*', *differences. A Journal of Feminist Studies* 4 (1992), 134–53; the *Life of Syncletica* is translated by Elizabeth Bryson Bongie, *The Life of Blessed Syncletica, by Pseudo-Athanasius* (Toronto, 1995).

7 For the former, see, for instance, J. Herrin, 'In search of Byzantine women: three avenues of approach', in Cameron and Kuhrt, eds, *Images of Women in Antiquity*, 167–89; for the latter, see, for instance, S. Ashbrook Harvey, 'Women in early Byzantine hagiography: reversing the story', in L.L. Coon, K.J. Haldane and E.W. Sommer, eds, *That Gentle Strength. Historical Perspectives on Women in Christianity* (Charlottesville, 1990), 36–57, and her *Asceticism and Society in Crisis: John of Ephesus' Lives of the Eastern Saints* (Berkeley and Los Angeles, 1990).

8 Early examples are represented in two useful source books: R.S. Kraemer, ed., *Maenads, Martyrs, Matrons, Monastics. A Sourcebook on Women's Religions in the Greco-Roman World* (Philadelphia, 1988), and V. Wimbush, ed., *Ascetic Behavior in Greco-Roman Antiquity: A Sourcebook* (Minneapolis, 1990). Repentant prostitutes (Pelagia, Mary of Egypt, Thaïs): see Benedicta Ward, *Harlots of the Desert* (Oxford, 1987), and see also S.P. Brock and S. Ashbrook Harvey, *Holy Women of the Syrian Orient* (Berkeley and Los Angeles, 1987).

9 See especially the monastic *typika* studied by Catia Galatariotou, of which that of Neophytos of Paphos is an extreme example: C. Galatariotou, 'Holy women and witches: aspects of Byzantine conceptions of gender', *BMGS* 9 (1984–5), 55–94; 'Byzantine *ktetorika*

typika: a comparative study', *Revue des Etudes Byzantines* 45 (1987), 77–138.

10 For gender issues in the visual depiction of empresses, see C. Barber, 'The imperial panels at San Vitale: a reconsideration', *BMGS* 14 (1990), 19–42; see also B. Hill, L. James and D. Smythe, 'Zoe: the rhythm method of imperial renewal', in P. Magdalino, ed., *New Constantines. The Rhythm of Imperial Renewal in Byzantium, Fourth to Thirteenth Centuries* (Aldershot, 1994), 215–30.

11 See S. Runciman, 'Women in Byzantine aristocratic society', in M. Angold, ed., *The Byzantine Aristocracy* (Oxford, 1984), 10–23, and see below.

12 See A.P. Kazhdan and A.-M. Talbot, 'Women and iconoclasm', *Byzantinische Zeitschrift* 84/5 (1991/2), 391–408.

13 Irigaray, *Je, tu, nous*, 11.

14 Ibid., 53.

15 *Guardian, Weekend*, Letters section, 31 July, 1993.

16 Gillian Clark, 'Women and asceticism in late antiquity: the refusal of status and gender', in V.L. Wimbush and R.Valantasis, eds, *Asceticism* (New York, 1995), 33–48, esp. 36–9; the contrast between the garments of spiritual marriage and those of the worldly bride was also a common *topos*, as in the fifth-century *Life of Syncletica*, attributed to Athanasius, trans. Bryson Bongie, chap. 92.

17 Ibid., 113.

18 *The Journals of Anaïs Nin, 1931–34* (London, 1966).

19 Anaïs Nin, 'On truth and reality', *In Favour of the Sensitive Man and Other Essays* (London, 1978), 57–65.

20 See Anaïs Nin, *Henry and June* (New York, 1986), and *Incest: From 'A Journal of Love'. The Unexpurgated Diary of Anaïs Nin, 1932–1934* (London, 1993).

21 The question formed the title of the original seminar in which this paper was delivered.

22 See Averil Cameron, 'Virginity as metaphor', in A. Cameron, ed., *History as Text* (London, 1989), 184–205; 'Early Christianity and the discourse of female desire', in L.J. Archer, S. Fischler and M. Wyke, eds, *Women in Ancient Societies. 'An Illusion of the Night'* (London, 1994), 152–68.

23 G. Gould, 'Women in the writings of the Fathers: language, belief and reality', in W.J. Sheils and D. Wood, eds, *Women and the Church, Studies in Church History* 27 (1990), 1–13. On the other hand see V. Wimbush, 'Ascetic behavior and color-ful language: stories about Ethiopian Moses', *Semeia* 58 (1992), 81–92, esp. 82.

24 Further below.

25 See the entry in the *ODB*, s.v. 'Love'.

26 See R. Beaton, *The Medieval Greek Romance* (Cambridge, 1989). Love in the Greek romances, on which much has been written already, would be the subject of a different chapter than this one.

27 For other changes in the perception of women in this period, see A.P. Kazhdan and A. Wharton Epstein, *Change in Byzantine Culture in the Eleventh and Twelfth Centuries* (Washington, DC, 1985), 99 ff. Kazhdan

also terminates his article on sex and Byzantine hagiography (above, n. 4) at this chronological point.

28 See Alan Cameron, *The Greek Anthology. From Meleager to Planudes* (Oxford, 1993), 333.
29 See the excellent discussion by Angeliki Laiou, *Mariage, l'amour et parenté à Byzance aux XIe–XIIIe siècles* (Paris, 1992).
30 See Paul Magdalino, *The Empire of Manuel I Komnenos, 1143–1180* (Cambridge, 1993), chap. 3; P. Cheynet, *Pouvoir et contestations à Byzance (963–1210)* (Paris, 1990), chap. 6.
31 As in the *Life of S. Philaretos*, for all its layers of romantic fantasy: see Marie-France Auzépy, 'De Philarète, de sa famille, et de certains monastères de Constantinople', in *Les saints et leurs sanctuaire: textes, images et monuments* (Paris, 1993), 117–35.
32 M.F. Auzépy, 'L'iconodoulie: défense de l'image ou de la dévotion à l'image?', in E. Boespflug and N. Lossky, eds, *Nicaea* II. *Douze siècles d'images religieuses* (Paris, 1987), 157–65.
33 See H. Maguire, *Art and Eloquence in Byzantium* (Princeton, 1981), 97 ff., 102.
34 J. Beaucamp, *Le statut de la femme à Byzance (4e–7e siècle)* I–II (Paris, 1990, 1992); J. Chrysostomides, 'Byzantine women', lecture delivered to the Lykion ton Hellenidon, 18 October 1993, Camberley, 1994.
35 See A. Kazhdan and G. Constable, *People and Power in Byzantium* (Washington, DC, 1982), 68.
36 *ODB*, s.v. 'Nude, The'.
37 See on this Verna Harrison, 'Allegory and eroticism in Gregory of Nyssa', *Semeia* 57 (1992), 113–30 (114: Gregory *allegorised* the expression of conjugal love which he found in the Song of Songs, because it was 'pastorally inapplicable in its literal sense'). But the desire felt by the ascetic is real: see 123 on the concept of desire in Gregory of Nyssa's interpretation of the Song of Songs, and 124: the 'essential work of the ascetic' is the redirection of energy away from bodily pleasure and towards God.
38 Origen, *Commentary on the Song of Songs*, prologue, 2, *PG* 13, 62–3.
39 Ibid., R.P. Lawson, tr., *Ancient Christian Writers* 26 (London, 1957), 34.
40 Ibid., 36.
41 *Homily on the Song of Songs* 2.1, *PG* 13, 47C.
42 Ibid., 1.1–3, *PG* 13, 37–41B.
43 For the whole complex of ideas, see A. Louth, *The Origins of the Christian Mystical Tradition* (Oxford, 1981), and Anthony Meredith, *The Cappadocians* (London, 1995), 78–84, with Patricia Cox, 'Pleasure of text, text of pleasure: Origen's commentary on the Song of Songs', *Journal of the American Academy of Religion* 54 (1986), 241–51.
44 See Verna Harrison, 'Receptacle imagery in St Gregory of Nyssa', *Studia Patristica* 22 (1989), 23–7; 'Male and female in Cappadocian theology', *Journal of Theological Studies* n.s. 41 (1990), 441–71.
45 Gregory of Nyssa, *The Life of Moses*, A.J. Malherbe and E. Ferguson, trs, Classics of Western Spirituality (New York, 1978), chap. 231: cf. Plato, *Symposion* 201d.
46 See D. Halperin, 'Why is Diotima a woman? Platonic Eros and the

configuration of gender', in D.M. Halperin, J.J. Winkler and F.I. Zeitlin, eds, *Before Sexuality. The Construction of Erotic Experience in the Ancient Greek World* (Princeton, 1990), 257–308. But while Gregory's choice in writing of his sister in this way may be telling for the recognition of women in late antiquity as spiritual beings, she, together with her mother and her female friends and household, is presented firmly within an ideology of sexual renunciation. For an interesting discussion of Gregory's perception of Macrina's physical body, see Patricia Cox Miller, 'Dreaming the body: an aesthetics of asceticism', in Wimbush and Valantasis, eds, *Asceticism*, 281–300.

47 At risk of citing Luce Irigaray again, one is struck by the fact that she makes a very similar claim, in arguing for women to reclaim a double identity as virgins and mothers: 'virginity, no more than female identity, isn't simply given at birth … becoming a virgin is synonymous with a woman's conquest of the spiritual' (*Je, tu, nous*, 117).

48 For the allegorical, see, for instance, V. Harrison, 'The allegorization of gender: Plato and Philo on spiritual childbearing', in Wimbush and Valantasis, eds, *Asceticism* (n. 41), 520–34, and above, n. 35.

49 Theodoret, *Historia Religiosa*, for instance at 29.6–7. Text ed. as *Histoire des moines de Syrie* by P. Canivet and A. Leroy-Molingen, 2 vols (Paris, 1977–9), and English translation by R.M. Price, *A History of the Monks of Syria* (Kalamazoo, 1985) at 184–5.

50 Price, *History of the Monks of Syria*, 206.

51 Ibid., 200.

52 Ibid., 203–4, cf. 194; see also P. Canivet, 'Le peri agaphes de Théodoret de Cyr postface de l'Histoire Philothée', *Studia Patristica* 7, TU 92 (Berlin, 1966), 143–58.

53 John Climacus, *The Ladder of Divine Ascent*, 30, C. Luibheid and N. Russell, trs (New York, 1982), 287.

54 J. Chryssavgis, 'The notion of "divine eros" in the Ladder of St John Climacus', *St Vladimir's Theological Quarterly* 29 (1985), 191–200, esp. 92.

55 See, for instance, J. Chryssagvis, 'Love and sexuality in the image of divine love', *Greek Orthodox Theological Review* 36 (1991), 341–52; P. Sherrard, *Christianity and Eros* (London, 1976). See also Harrison, 'Allegory and asceticism'; on the implications of the argument see G.G. Harpham, 'Old wine in new bottles: the contemporary prospects for the study of asceticism', *Semeia* 58 (1992), 134–48, esp. 143–5.

56 J. Rist, 'A note on Eros and Agape in Ps-Dionysius', *Vigiliae Christianae* 20 (1966), 235–43.

57 See K. Wesche, 'God beyond gender. Reflections on the patristic doctrine of God and feminist theology', *St Vladimir's Seminary Quarterly*, 30 (1986), 291–308.

58 On this see more generally C. Militello, 'Amicizia tra asceti et ascete', in U. Mattaioli, ed., *La donna nel pensiero cristiano antico* (Genoa, 1992), 279–304; Caroline White, *Christian Friendship in the Fourth Century* (Cambridge, 1992).

59 *Historia Religiosa*, 30.1, PG 82, 1492D.

60 Ibid., 26.21, 2.17.

61 *Compendium* 5.24, *PG* 83, 531C–538D.
62 C. Mazzucco, 'Matrimonio e verginità nei Padri tra IV e V secolo: prospettive femminile', in Mattaioli, *La donna nel pensiero cristiano antico*, 119–54, esp. 136, 140 f.
63 For instance, Palladius, *Lausiac History*, C. Butler, ed., 2 vols (Cambridge, 1898–1904) 34, 6.
64 See C. Anselmetto, 'Maternità e liberazione della donna', in Mattaioli, ed., *La donna nel pensiero cristiano antico*, 155–82.
65 A spine-chilling catalogue of this tradition, from antiquity to the present, can be found in U. Ranke-Heinemann, *Eunuchs for the Kingdom of Heaven. Women, Sexuality and the Catholic Church*, Eng. tr. (Harmondsworth, 1991).
66 See ibid., 160 ff.
67 See A. Ducellier, *L'église byzantine. Entre pouvoir et esprit (313–1204)* (Paris, 1990), 195 ff. For western hatred of the flesh, in contrast, see Ranke-Heinemann, *Eunuchs for the Kingdom of Heaven*, 103 ff.; menstruation as pollution, 21–5, 138–9.
68 Ducellier's book is indicative of this in the space it gives to heresy and the lack of specific discussion of sexual topics.
69 Thus J.E. Salisbury, *Church Fathers. Independent Virgins* (London, 1991), discusses virginity and attitudes to female sexuality in the early Church, including such eastern material as the *Lives* of Pelagia and Mary of Egypt, but does so from the perspective of a western medievalist, and includes a whole chapter on Augustine.
70 See, for instance, Kraemer, *Her Share of the Blessings*; R. Mortley, *Womanhood. The Feminine in Ancient Hellenism, Gnosticism, Christianity and Islam* (Sydney, 1981); Elizabeth A. Clark, *Women in the Early Church* (Wilmington, 1983) (sources).
71 Ranke-Heinemann, *Eunuchs for the Kingdom of Heaven*, 126 ff., 133–4.
72 See recently on the debate, some of which centred round the supposed state of Mary's hymen before and after the birth, D. Hunter, 'Resistance to the virginal ideal in late fourth-century Rome: the case of Jovinian', *Theological Studies* 48 (1987), 45–64; for the imagery that now developed in relation to the Theotokos, see N.P. Constas, 'Weaving the body of God: Proclus of Constantinople, the Theotokos and the loom of the flesh', *Journal of Early Christian Studies* 3 (1995), 169–94.
73 See Averil Cameron, *Christianity and the Rhetoric of Empire* (Berkeley and Los Angeles, 1991), chap. 6; and see I. Kalovrezou, 'Images of the mother: when the Virgin Mary became *Meter Theou*', *DOP* 44 (1990), 165–72.
74 Maguire, *Art and Eloquence*, 91–108; cf. M. Alexiou, *The Ritual Lament in Greek Tradition* (Cambridge, 1974); G. Holst-Warhaft, *Dangerous Voices. Women's Laments in Greek Literature* (London, 1992).
75 See J. Du Boulay, 'Women – images of their nature and destiny in rural Greece', in J. Dubisch, ed., *Gender and Power in Rural Greece* (Princeton, 1986), 139–68.
76 See briefly Ranke-Heinemann, *Eunuchs for the Kingdom of Heaven*, 340–8.

2

WOMEN AND ICONS, AND WOMEN IN ICONS

Robin Cormack

This chapter asks how gender might be understood as a factor in the interpretation of the production and meanings of Byzantine icons. It attempts to construct a methodology of reading texts and images which might elucidate both the role of women in the production of icons and also the choice of women for the subject matter of icons, particularly in the imagery of iconoclasm. This is a field influenced by 'feminist' scholarship, where one must work within rapidly developing frameworks; the situation in the Byzantine field offers no exception to this: previous commentaries are likely to reflect phases of feminist scholarship. In the case of women and icons, the field has been influenced by an empiricist period of feminist scholarship which emphasised the need to *find* women and give them a more visible role in history. In art history in general this significant phase of feminism involved looking beyond the recognition of Old Masters and looking for Old Mistresses – or explaining why old mistresses could not be found. The equivalent in Byzantine studies was the search for women artists or women patrons or women viewers, as an empirical and visible category. Their discovery might, it could be proposed, offer an insight into the values that enabled medieval women to live with dignity. The aim here is different. It is to focus on texts and icons as possible evidence for the nature of gender construction in the culture. It uses them, not as evidence for women, but as representations of women, no doubt mostly by men. In order to give a concise focus, the chapter responds to the issues set by one Byzantine icon recently acquired by the British Museum (see Plate 1). The prominent presence of women in the imagery of this icon cannot be understood in any straightforward way; but it offers clues to the complex issues of women's roles in Byzantium.[1]

The icon in the British Museum represents the annual commemoration of the ending of iconoclasm in 842; this *Triumph of Orthodoxy* is portrayed through portrait figures of victorious icon-ophiles accompanied by some of the icons that they have vindicated. The style of the icon points to a date of production around 1400, quite probably in Constantinople, although neither the precise date nor the precise provenance are crucial in the present discussion. More essential is the question of how to interpret it as a document connected with Byzantine iconoclasm. If the icon is a document about the portrayal of iconoclasm, then it, like texts about icono-clasm, should be seen as a profoundly ambivalent witness. The events of iconoclasm from 730 to 842 embodied the longest period in Byzantine history of sustained, bitter, political and ecclesiastical polemics. Whatever sparked off the actual war on religious images, it soon became a highly politicised struggle.[2] Both sides, whether fighting for or against icons, were involved in the presentation and packaging of their cases in order to encourage their supporters or to convert their opponents. Inevitably the texts and images that attempted to prove or disprove traditional acceptance of the Chris-tian use of icons are therefore not neutral historical records. They are wonderfully evocative documents.

Our perspective of iconoclasm, no less than did that of the Byzantines themselves, depends on such highly loaded documents. But we have the additional factors of viewing iconoclasm not only with hindsight and all the associations of the European Reformation and Enlightenment movements but also through the random sur-vivals of material, and chiefly through the eyes of the iconophile record (or their doctoring of the iconoclast materials). The gap between the events of the period and our perceptions is immense. Yet we do know that the materials we have must have expressed the desires of the iconophiles, or the anger and fears of the iconoclasts. They must be at the centre of any attempt to understand the 'rationality' of Byzantium, and of any exploration of the 'mystical' or 'magical' practices of the Middle Ages. Whether or not Peter Brown was right to cast 'the iconoclast controversy in the grip of a crisis of over-explanation', much still needs to be done to understand the 'distortions' of our evidence.[3] This is a different inquiry from the traditional questions of what iconoclasm was and why it happened at this particular moment in time, or how far we can recreate a 'sequence of events'. Rather than a source of 'facts', the documents of iconoclasm may be read as evidence of the discourses (both verbal and visual) of religious polemics. Read in this way, they do not tell us what happened; rather they tell us why it happened and what was at stake! No text, no picture about iconoclasm is what it seems at face value.

It became clear in Byzantium during iconoclasm that the resolution of the dispute over the legitimacy or otherwise of figurative images in Christianity depended on an agreed definition of orthodox belief. One side or the other would come to be judged as heretical. The issues were too important to be resolved in any other way than by the legal structure of a Church council.[4] Iconoclasm is therefore distinctively a period involved in the determination of heresy; and this means that our surviving materials must be totally imbued with the characteristics of such a period. Similarly, social patterns during iconoclasm are likely to match other historical periods of confrontational heresy. At the least we can expect iconoclasm to have promoted violent and chronic episodes of personal abuse and communal persecution, even if the name we give to the period may exaggerate the amount of actual destruction and play down the religious controversy over the legitimacy of Christian images.

The question that arises for art historians is how to apply such a historical pattern to visual analysis. What is at issue here is not the legitimacy of the theological arguments put forward, either to justify the use of icons as part of the tradition of Christianity, or on the other side to attack images as innovation and idolatry; and the art historian might in this context want to put to one side questions of the underlying political, social, cultural or even religious *causes* of the outbreak of iconoclasm at this historical moment. Instead it may be worth pursuing the implications of treating iconoclasm as a standard period of heresy in which we can predict that Byzantine society will have been plunged into the episodes of persecution that always accompany heresy: society must have been divided into groups who each perceived themselves at the centre, surrounded by the unacceptable marginality of heretics. In other words, there must have been definable *patterns* of polemics during the whole period of iconoclasm, which may have had long-term effects on the culture. The work of R.I. Moore has notably opened out the discussion of persecution in the medieval west and shadowed its art historical implications there; but since Moore treated the Byzantine record as a continuation of the repressive attitudes of the Roman Empire, and distinct from a more tolerant western European phase between late antiquity and the re-emergence of persecution in the eleventh century, he did not turn his attention to the east.[5]

The practices and effects of persecution should reveal themselves to the observer of Byzantine iconoclasm. For example, both during and after iconoclasm, certain groups are liable to be identified as the enemies of the norms of right-thinking society; we can expect to find both iconoclasts and iconophiles engaged in the activities of identifying and attacking individuals and groups as deviants in society. An implication of this model is that both sides may actually identify and attack the same deviants as 'the enemy', thereby complicating the picture. We have to untangle cases where both sides, while opposing each other, may actually produce similar polemics against the same groups – accusing the 'opposition', for example, of innovation, novelty and the perversion of proper tradition. Indeed it is part of my argument that the ambivalence of the targets and of the polemics of persecution during iconoclasm – a persecution that was both physical and mental, for we have iconophile and iconoclast martyrs and exiles – has not been fully recognised.

The potential targets of persecution in the Byzantine Middle Ages are not difficult to conjecture; we all know the commonest stereotypes of the other: Jews, Muslims, pagans, monks, hermits and women. It is only this last group, women, that I propose to examine as potential deviants, and the focus of anger, although the polemics over Jews and Muslims are equally revealing for the historian, and racism turns up in iconophile abuse against blacks (who as an additional complication happened to belong to Monophysite communities in this period!).[6] In focusing on women as deviants in this way, I shall be attempting to reverse what is increasingly being taken as established fact – namely that Byzantine women are the favoured champions of iconophile orthodoxy before, during, and after the fight over icons. I am suggesting that we have here a conspicuous case where an empirical, common-sense approach may over-simplify and distort the way in which this culture worked.[7]

This chapter re-examines the issues of women and icons through a new and evocative piece of visual evidence. The British Museum panel (39 × 31 cm) is a relatively small icon coloured in tempera and gold on gesso over cloth on wood (see Plate 1).[8] It represents the Restoration of Icons after iconoclasm, commemorated each year in the Orthodox Church as the Festival of Orthodoxy on the First Sunday in Lent (and probably instituted by Patriarch Methodios in 843). This painting is not from this foundation period, but dates on grounds of style from around 1400. It is a fine and delicate work of art, one of those successful Byzantine works of art that despite their small scale achieve a remarkable impression of monumentality. It originally included several inscriptions, though they are now badly rubbed (red letters on gold are generally quick to flake off). We can still see enough to be sure that naming the saints was a feature of the panel. The function of this panel may have been to act as the display icon for devotion and kissing in a church on the Sunday of Orthodoxy. Another feature of that day was the reading of the *Synodikon of Orthodoxy*, a long text that identified the orthodox and anathematised the heretics and was another pointer to the perception in Byzantium that iconoclasm was marked out as a violent period of deviance.[9] The restoration of 'Orthodoxy' in 843 meant that henceforth icons could be manufactured and venerated; the decision was confirmed not by a formal Church Ecumenical Council, in the way that the Council of Nicaea II in 787 marked the end of the first period of iconoclasm, but by the declarations written for the Sunday of Orthodoxy which re-established proper tradition.

The icon depicts the annual festival through portraits of iconophiles and representations of icons. The panel is divided horizontally into two registers, and the figures are set against a gold ground. The central representation at the top is one of the most renowned icons of Constantinople – the icon of the Virgin Mary *Hodigitria*, claimed to have been painted by the evangelist St Luke from life and so to represent her authentic appearance.[10] We know a great deal about this remarkable miracle-working icon of the Virgin and Child from other representations and texts.[11] By the fourteenth century it was kept in a special tabernacle in the Monastery of the Hodigitria in Constantinople, but taken out and carried publicly in procession every Tuesday. This miraculous icon is represented here on a red draped stand, with red curtains drawn back to reveal it.[12] This 'icon within an icon' is so much the central feature of our painting that at first sight its subject might have been taken as *The Icon of the Virgin Mary Hodigitria* rather than the *Triumph of Orthodoxy* or *The Restoration of the Icons*.[13] The felicitous notion that St Luke painted a portrait of the Virgin and Child seems first to be found in texts during the period of iconoclasm, and is just one indication of the inventiveness of the iconophiles.

The particular figures in the icon are no doubt selected for their special connection either with the struggle against iconoclasm or with the establishment of 'Orthodoxy'.[14] The text of the *Synodikon* included, in addition to the recitation of Orthodox doctrine, a section of salutations (*Euphemiai*) to individuals, living or dead. The prominent figures on the left in the upper register are the rulers at the time of the official ending of iconoclasm in 843: the regent empress Theodora together with her young son, the emperor Michael III. They wear the dress and insignia of their power and are clearly labelled with their titles. On the right is the Patriarch Methodios (in office 843–7) with three monks. In the register below, certain figures are made prominent by their position and by their triumphant act of displaying icons. In the centre the figures holding between them an icon of Christ are probably St Theophanes the Confessor and St Theodore the Studite. The name of St Theophanes is decipherable above the left figure.[15] To their right is a bishop, and four further figures, of which we can most confidently make out the names of the two on the extreme right: St Theophilaktos the Confessor and finally St Arsakios. Other fragmentary letters point to the inclusion between St Theodore the Studite and St Theophilaktos of the two monastic brothers who fought on behalf of the iconophile cause during iconoclasm, St Theodore and St Theophanes, the *Graptoi*.[16] On the left side are three more male saints, and on the extreme left is a martyr saint, portrayed as a nun. She too holds an icon of Christ (as Emmanuel?), its character as a panel painting made explicit by the clue of a little ring at the top. The nun is clearly identified by her inscription as St Theodosia (Plate 1).[17]

It might be reasonable at this stage to explain the particular choice of saints on this icon – including the more unusual figures in Byzantine art of St Theodosia and St Arsakios – as due to the special interests of the (unknown) patron or patrons of this commission. Perhaps, for example, these were their name saints. This line of interpretation is probably excluded by the fact that the special choice of saints is not unique to this particular icon; other representations of this subject also include St Theodosia.[18]

It seems therefore that we can assume a series of icons that regularly included the prominent figures of empress Theodora and St Theodosia. It is their inclusion in this scene and on this icon amongst all the theologians and monks to which this chapter draws attention.

The pride of position that highlights the empress Theodora records that it was her, rather than her infant son Michael, who personally legitimated the orthodoxy of the decision on icons in accord with the Patriarch Methodios. Yet despite the importance of the representation here of an empress, a woman in power, it might be argued that her presence here gives less an emphasis on woman

Plate 1 Icon of the *Triumph of Orthodoxy c.1400*
Source: Courtesy of the British Museum

than on imperial presence and consequent state legality of the triumph of icons. In this respect, the sole woman in the register below is therefore much more arresting, particularly as she is singled out as a person carrying an icon as well as a cross of martyrdom. The presence of St Theodosia and her possession of an icon is the more significant clue. It begins to look feasible to formulate an argument that this icon displays the importance of women in the promotion and use of icons in the Orthodox Church. Where else can you think of an image where women take such pride of place over men in Byzantium?

The British Museum icon would appear, then, to add new support to the view that icons are in some way the special concern of women. It might be said to be literally demonstrating the gendered role of women in the cult of icons. This is not the interpretation that will be maintained here. I shall be arguing, to the contrary, that we have a far from literal discourse here; only by treating this imagery as part of complex polemics of iconoclasm can we begin to see its evocations. For this reason there is a need to review critically the arguments that women in Byzantium did hold a special role in the promotion of icons, especially the case that is argued at length by Judith Herrin.[19] She initially saw, but dismissed, the conceptual trap in this subject: 'When I first read Byzantine accounts of female devotion to icons, I dismissed them as yet another example of the common slurs on womankind perpetrated by uniformly male writers; after closer inspection, I feel that this opinion should be revised.'[20] She accordingly went on to treat these male writings as reflections of empirical fact that could be taken to establish the crucial importance of women in the development of icons and triumph of iconophiles. Nevertheless, perhaps her first instincts were right!

The motive for asking about women as sponsors and consumers of art is obvious enough – there is the crude estimate after all that if half the population of medieval Byzantium consisted of women, then half the viewers of icons were women.[21] Women were certainly involved in the production of icons – quite frequently as patrons, as several donation inscriptions show, often referring to the patronage of widows. Women have often been supposed to participate in the manufacture of art too – silks and textile icons have been suggested as the products of women's labour, and it is not impossible that such a tapestry as the large sixth-century Virgin and Child with saints, now in the Cleveland Museum, was woven by women.[22] Any art history of the Middle Ages must therefore expect to consider the factor of women. The interest of Herrin's work is its radical claims: that women are the key factor in explaining the prevalence of icons in east Christian art. Her argument is that the whole Early Christian 'explosion' of art must be understood as a paradox, dependent on the role of women.[23] The scenario proposed is that once Constantine began to promote state Christianity, images were made for homes as well as churches; consequently women, despite their confinement to the private domain, found themselves privileged with access to imaged saints as intercessors – particularly to icons of the Virgin Mary. It was through their display in homes that icons promoted private, personal devotions – they became domestic cult objects. So it was women – homebound, restricted in their access to churches and frustrated in religious passion – who became the particular devotees of icons. Herrin concludes that icons, and especially icons of the Mother of God, were a suitable vehicle for the expression of female religiosity; with icons, women could make devotions privately at church or at home, at any time and independently of control by male priests: 'women were more probably iconophiles than iconoclasts'.

Such a skeletal summary cannot do justice to the detailed case put forward, but it should highlight the key issue for us. How far does the visual evidence work in support of such an interpretation? Herrin has two particularly notable works of art to enhance her case, both probably produced in the sixth century. The first example is the icon of the Virgin and saints in the collection of St Catherine's monastery on Mt Sinai.[24] Is this a plausible case of an icon that represents women's interests? There are certainly difficulties. One is the fact that we know nothing about any of the circumstances of the panel's production, except that at some unknown time it entered a male monastery.

The only way to connect the Sinai icon with women must therefore be from its own internal visual clues. How far does a formal analysis take us? The answer is that its evidence is at best ambivalent; and perhaps it is more indicative of male devotional practices – or at least male-based traditions. The question is how to analyse a painting that contains expressive sacred figures who belong spiritually to several hierarchical levels. The two figures who are portrayed as closest in status and visual accessibility to the viewer are the two male intercessionary saints, St Theodore and St George (unless this is St Demetrios). They are shown frontally, and the device of frontality is used also for their eyes; the visual effect of such eye contact is to link the gaze of the viewer with the saint viewed. The viewer is presented with reversing mirror, almost with a merging of, identities. Who is looking at whom?[25] Since it is the saints', and not the Virgin's, eyes who make this contact with the viewer, the visual logic is that the path of prayer in the icon passes from the viewer to the male saints through the Virgin to Heaven. The Virgin acts as a mediator who communicates *within* the sacred space of the icon between these interceding saints and the angels and God above. If the term 'patriarchal' means anything, this must be a case where it might seem applicable, for the values of the imagery are clearly intelligible within a male-oriented event. Had the artist wished the viewer to feel in direct and close contact with the Virgin, there were a number of compositional devices to employ that would have achieved this – most obviously the frontal gaze with all its evocations. Instead of this, however, all the compositional devices of the icon play down the effective prominence of the female figure. Mary is compositionally at the centre of the image, but she eludes the gaze of the viewer. Such considerations of the gaze do not, of course, allow us to determine the gender of the Byzantine viewing audience of this icon (which was no doubt a considerable one over the centuries); but they do demonstrate that to represent the Virgin Mary in an icon does not create a direct or simple platform of access to the Mother of God for the male or female viewer. The prominence of Mary in Christianity is demonstrated but not explained by her popularity in icons.[26]

The other key image that Herrin treats as an example of female art is the monumental sixth-century wall painting of Turtura in the catacomb of Commodilla in Rome. But in this case the painting includes its own textual documentation, and gives us some information about the details of the process of the production. The painting marks the tomb of Turtura, which was one of the latest burials, as it happens, to occur in the Roman catacombs.[27] A long verse in Latin inscribed directly below the painting records that this is a commemoration by her son on the death of his mother Turtura at the age of 60. He praises her chastity during 36 years of widowhood after the death of her husband Obas (she must have been widowed at the age of 24). It is her chastity that is emphasised: her name Turtura has given her the fidelity of a turtle, *turtur* (not a simile that has survived the test of time). He commemorates her function as both father and mother to her son.[28] The whole panel celebrates a solid 'patriarchal' view of the correct moral behaviour of women. The son proclaims *his* legitimacy and Christian family values. It is not remotely a 'feminist' painting.

The visual analysis of these two important images scarcely supports the idea of special female devotion or patronage. In this respect the situation seems comparable with the west where in the better documented Late Middle Ages the issue of male and female devotion to the Virgin has been characterised by Caroline Bynum as a time when 'there is no evidence that women were especially attracted to devotion to the Virgin or to married women saints – indeed there is some evidence that they were less attracted than men'.[29] Bynum argues that women were more attracted to meditate on the nature of Christ and men than on that of the Virgin, though she is careful to deny simple gender roles in the Middle Ages.[30]

The images discussed by Herrin are central productions of early Byzantine spirituality, and their visual evidence is certainly relevant to the issue of gender roles. But they offer an ambiguous and insufficient basis for Herrin's proposals. The visual evidence must lead us to query her whole case for a special connection between women and icons. It is not only the simple correlation between women's needs and the production of icons of the Virgin that is uncomfortable; so also is the proposed dichotomy of public and private circumstances. There is always the danger of an anachronistic extension of modern cultural notions of public and private to the Middle Ages.[31] These issues have recently been illuminated by a number of recent studies of religious practices in the home.[32] Perhaps it is true that icons in the domestic sphere were sometimes set up in 'bedrooms' (another cultural construction) or other rooms.[33] But one clear development in the Early Christian period, both in east and west, is that the liturgy was being widely celebrated at aristocratic homes in private oratories. Church officials opposed the practice, and their control over the celebration of the liturgy was to some extent reasserted in the period after iconoclasm by the expansion of private oratories in public churches. But the implication of oratories in private houses is that both the arrangements and the icons in them were likely still to have been in the control of male priests.[34] What is apparently true from a perusal of texts is that recorded cases of icons in the home appear equally in the domain of male and female devotions.

The case against Herrin's empirical construction of the role of women in the promotion of icons and the importance of private female devotions to icons seems to me substantial. One may accept that one of the factors leading to the period of iconoclasm in the eighth and ninth centuries was a reformist reaction to the over-production and abuse of icons; but this factor is not something that was created primarily by female power. The rise of icons and the increase in the cult of the Virgin is obviously something we want to explain; but a gender-specific explanation is too simple.

Yet this critical response to the suggested connection of women with icons brings us back again to the evidence of the British Museum panel, which at face value would seem to be a major new visual element in supporting the correlation of women and icons. Why otherwise does its imagery so conspicuously celebrate famous women iconophiles? Does it offer medieval support for seeing devotion to icons as a female rather than a male predilection? We shall therefore need to look at more of the primary medieval material and ask how to interpret it. This will bring us back also to the questions of the significance of heresy and persecution during iconoclasm and how to interpret the discourses of polemic. We must try to correlate all these trails before we can begin to understand the rhetoric of the British Museum icon.

There is no need here to bring together again all the primary texts that might be adduced to correlate women and icons, since reference to just a few key examples will show some structural patterns. When in the fourth century Eusebius wrote a letter, often interpreted as critical of image making, the recipient was Constantine's sister.[35] Tertullian attacked idolatry and material imagery in the context of the deceitful adornment of women.[36] As we get closer to iconoclasm, we appear to find more graphic correlations between women and icons: a 'grotesque' example is the sick woman who scraped off from her wall some of the fresco decoration of the two medical saints Cosmas and Damian, put the powder in water, and drank it as medicine.[37] We can also read that a group of women rioted in 726 when Leo III ordered the removal of the icon of Christ on the Chalke Gate, the main entrance to the Great Palace.[38] This incident has often been taken to mark the outbreak of iconoclasm. As for events during the periods of iconoclasm, there is the 'political' fact that both phases were officially ended by women: the empresses Irene and Theodora under whom icons were officially restored in 787 and 843 were both in power as regents for their sons.[39]

These few passages are enough to indicate the range of materials, though it must be obvious that they represent only a fraction of the examples of conduct connected with icons, relics and miracles by *both* men and women. No one has attempted to quantify the textual records in terms of gender; such an enterprise would be doomed anyway from the outset if we conceded that the texts are loaded and not an objective set of reports. Perhaps such stories as the sick woman and her *al fresco* medicine were not read as simple iconophile or iconoclast statements of fact; they may already have been manipulative and have caused a shiver to run down the Byzantine spine. Her conduct is anyway easy to match with the male equivalent: in 573 Gregory of Tours, shortly before his consecration as bishop, fell ill with dysentery and despaired of his life. His usual medicine of an infusion of dust from the tomb of St Martin fortunately did the trick.[40]

These passages also show that, although the period of iconoclasm brought the questions of the power of images to a head, the use of icons was a long-running issue in the disputes over the definition of an 'Orthodox' Christian world. Perhaps the clearest 'fact' among the ostensible championship of icons by women is the status and power of the empresses Irene in 787 and Theodora in 842. But how far can we deduce that the women were literally in control of events? There are alternative interpretations: one is to explore whether the façade of these widows as regents for their sons concealed a certain vacuum of power in the state, into which the court officials and Church stepped in alliance. There are also more specific questions when the sources are treated in detail. Can we be certain that the initiative in 842 was taken by Theodora, rather than by her co-regent Theoktistos? How true or how conventional is the kind of flattery of Theodora – 'manly nobility in feminine garb' – that appears in the *Life* of St Michael the Synkellos?[41] One possible response at this point is to argue that to pursue such details may be less important than to collect the expressed *perceptions* of the Byzantines. If the communal public view of events was that women were the cardinal promoters of icons, the notion that women played the pre-eminent role in icon worship might be maintained. Indeed so long as it was a 'myth' in which society believed (and which invigorated women), then the precise details may be left aside.

It does not, however, seem reasonable to leave the issue so much in the air. This is because the notion of a major gender-derived explanation for the prevalence of icons in Byzantium is too fundamental an interpretation of the society to be left open. Clearly the arguments for the promotion or banning of icons were not superficial issues about 'art'. They were fundamental questions about the nature of the sacred and the working of God's creation; it was an intensely religious and political decision, and both the secular and ecclesiastical authorities were implicated in the eventual outcome. In other words, the climate in which iconoclasm developed was intensely political and involved all the questions of how a Christian empire should properly function. Iconoclasm was inevitably to be viewed in its time as either the answer to problems faced by the Byzantine empire, or as a wrong turn for a Christian state. Ever since Constantine, unity and orthodoxy was the prime aim of official Byzantine state policy, well embodied in Justinian's *Novella*.[42] To achieve the 'general harmony' that Justinian desired, the emperor needed to control the Church and Christian belief. This involved the radical repression of religious dissidents, and the elimination or neutralisation of opposition: in a word, persecution. A well-tried technique of persecution was to define and polarise some opposition group outside the norms of society, although it might be as fictitious as modern constructions of the 'loony left'. On such a model of persecution carried out by iconoclasts against iconophiles, we would expect the construction of marginal groups conveniently to be tarred with heresy and to become scapegoats. Equally we would expect the iconophiles to employ the same techniques of polemic against their opponents. Unsurprisingly, attention was turned to representative groups of the 'other' for a Christian community: the Jews and Muslims. Since it is the iconophile evidence that we have most available, it is their version of the polemic that is easiest to view. The iconoclast emperors were classed as 'saracen-minded'; acts of iconoclasm are visually identified in the Khludov Psalter with the Jewish rejection of Christ and their behaviour during the Crucifixion; and we find that the champion of the iconophile side in the eighth century, John of Damascus, wrote a book on heresy in which Islam is characterised not as a rival religion, but as the 101st heresy of Christianity.

It is the perennial strategies of polemic, therefore, that may be embodied in Byzantine statements about women and icons, for here too is a traditionally marginal group in medieval society. The complication for an analysis of the surviving evidence along these lines is that it is difficult to find which of the two (or more) sides might have first implicated and exploited women as the unacceptable opposition. The story of rioting *women* at the Chalke Gate might be *iconoclast* polemic, but we first find it in *iconophile* sources from decades after the 'event'. Perhaps stories about women and icons coloured the perceptions of both sides, and in due course had to be absorbed somehow into later iconophile writing. Certainly the emphasised heroes of the iconophile side as represented in the art of the succeeding period are not women; they are the patriarchs and monks of the period, such as Nikephoros, Methodios and Theodore of Studion.

The post-iconoclast cultural history of the empress Theodora suggests further ambivalence and sub-texts rather than any straight-forward documentation of the literal role of an imperial woman. Her *Vita* is itself decidedly slanted towards the narration of events in the life of her husband Theophilos, the last iconoclast, and her loyalty to him after his death (before she lost power). Another text has the double-edged story of Theodora surprised in her bedroom by the court jester Denderis who denounced her as kissing icons, although we are led to believe that the story was discounted by Theophilos and that he accepted her version that it was no more than nostalgic play with dolls preserved from her childhood.[43] We can find pictorial images of Theodora that similarly act as more than narratives to be read at face value. Images of Theodora are comparatively rare in Orthodox art, and for that reason alone are likely when chosen to be the vehicles of some considered message. Although her inclusion in the Constantinopolitan pictorial church calendar of the illuminated 'Menologion' of Basil II (Vatican gr. 1613) may appear relatively straightforward to explain, if we go much later in time and to the sphere of the later Orthodox art of Russia, her appearances are much more evocative. One especially eloquent indication of the dramatic possibilities of her imagery is to be found in a recently discovered icon, sold at Sotheby's in 1991 and now in a private collection in London. This large and impressive Russian icon of the eighteenth century features Theodora, surrounded by a series of pictures of her 'life'.[44] While the production of such an image in Russia at that period may represent an affirmation of traditional Orthodox beliefs on icons in the face of the policy of the westernisation of Russia, or may have some other more political context, for the present discussion its significance lies particularly in its 'invention' of a set of events during Byzantine iconoclasm that inherently betray another ambivalent perception of the iconophile empress.[45] It is true that Theodora is conspicuously connected with icons – including the Mandylion of Edessa (which as a matter of fact only arrived in Constantinople in 944) – and used an icon to cure her sceptical iconoclast husband from an illness (although even this failed to cure his scepticism). Later on in the cycle, we see that Theophilos was rescued from Hell through the efforts of Theodora and we also see Theodora with her Orthodox son Michael parading the restoration of icons. It is clear that once again it is clear to see that we are in the presence of a visual affirmation of traditional male perceptions of the ideal woman as good mother and faithful wife rather than a gendered declaration of the 'female' devotion to icons of the iconophile empress Theodora.

If a method of interpreting the implications of representing women in icons has been adequately blocked out so far in this chapter, then we are ready now to focus on the figure of St Theodosia in the British Museum icon and ask how to understand her prominence in the icon, where she is one of the few figures displaying an icon – one that represents the figure of Christ.

Who is St Theodosia? There is in fact only one candidate with the distinguishing attributes of a martyr's cross and an icon: St Theodosia of Constantinople, whose first recorded notice is in the Menologion of Basil II (around 1000) where she appears on 18 July as a martyr of Constantinople during iconoclasm.[46] As a saint, she has received little attention in modern scholarship because of the *mythical* nature of her life. Her construction as a saint can be partially traced.[47] The Menologion notice is chronologically bizarre – she is described as living in the reign of Constantine V but killed under his father Leo III by a blow from a ram's horn. To understand her story, it is best to look at accounts of the first events of iconoclasm; it is in these accounts, as they evolve, that she makes her entrance into history. The key to St Theodosia lies in the details of the recorded destruction of the Chalke image of Christ under Leo III.

Among the recorded accounts that we have of the episodes at the Chalke Gate of the Great Palace, probably the earliest is in the *Vita Stephani iunioris* (written by the deacon Stephen in 806). In this version of the events (which the *Vita* dates to 730) we read of the involvement of 'pious women'. These women happened to get involved in the rioting and pulled down the ladder from which the emperor's agent was destroying the image; in retaliation for their act and at the request of the iconoclast patriarch Anastasios (730–54), the women were executed. In the *Chronographia* of Theophanes (written between 810 and 814), the text dates the events to the year 726 and mentions the crowd that attacked and killed the emperor's agents and was subsequently punished; this crowd is described not as women, but as citizens outstanding in nobility and culture. In the *First Letter of Pope Gregory II to Leo III*, an 'invented' document of the early ninth century, we return to the version that describes the involvement of zealous women who pulled down the ladder and killed the emperor's agent; these women were put to death by the soldiery.

These three versions all belong within the period of iconoclasm, though they were written down relatively late in that period and at several generations remove from the events that they purport to document. After 843, the accounts of the beginning of iconoclasm become more detailed (or more embroidered). For example, a *Passio* written soon after 869 tells about the discovery on 31 January 869 of the relics of the Orthodox who were involved in the fight at the Chalke Gate. The document tells the story of their martyrdom – and it is clear enough that the sources of information are the versions of the *Vita Stephani* and *Chronographia* of Theophanes: the text narrates that when the Chalke image was burnt on 19 January, the Orthodox came to the gate and killed the emperor's agent. One group consisted of ten saints and Maria the Patrician, a woman of imperial descent. The men were imprisoned and executed on 9 August. The intact bodies were found in 869 and included that of Maria.

Some of the details of this version of the Chalke Gate martyrs are altered in other writings of the tenth century and in the Menologion of Basil II. The aristocratic Maria who featured in the earlier version is now named Theodosia and is a nun. This is the St Theodosia of our icon, and it follows that the icon that she holds must be understood to be the Chalke icon of Christ that she tried to protect. Despite the flimsy, not to say bogus, historical basis from which St Theodosia of Constantinople emerged, she achieved increasing popularity in late Byzantium. Indeed when the Turks entered Constantinople on 29 May 1453, they met a crowd of the faithful going with candles to the church of St Theodosia. By this period St Theodosia of Constantinople had been merged with St Theodosia of Tyre, and had taken over her festival day of 29 May. The pilgrim Antony of Novgorod also records the cult of the relics of St Theodosia (kept in a silver casket and carried in procession in 1200 to cure the sick).[48] Her relics were even more famous for their healing abilities after 1261.[49]

The saint who appears on the British Museum panel as a champion of icons was then an invented fictitious woman. In fact as we go through all these texts about the destruction of the Chalke icon and the involvement of differently defined trouble-makers, it seems clear that another radical interpretation needs to be considered: that this icon of Christ never existed either, and iconoclasm did not begin with this episode at all. All the evidence is compatible with the interpretation that the idea of an icon of Christ over the imperial doorway in 726 or 730 was an iconophile myth invented around 800 when a new icon was put there by Irene (perhaps in her sole reign of 797–802) and a false pedigree of tradition was invented, in order to forestall any backlash attack on iconophiles as innovators (and hence heretics).[50] This became an amazingly powerful myth – both in the primary and secondary writings, although it is significantly not mentioned, for example, in the reports of the 787 Council of Nicaea.[51] The power of polemics is the best way to understand both the 'propaganda' that iconoclasm began with the incidents at the Chalke Gate and that women as a group were implicated in the defence of icons.

The invention of 'evidence' by all sides during iconoclasm is indeed phenomenal. They were at this game all the time and knew it: indeed at the Council of Nicaea in 787, you were not allowed to quote texts to support your case, unless you brought along the whole manuscript and could point to your text in context; the iconoclasts in 754, so it was said, had brought along only quotations (*pittakia*) which they had either invented or doctored.[52] But the iconophiles were just as guilty in the invention of an extraordinary quantity of documents during the period – imperial letters (e.g. Leo III to Muslims), references to icons that never existed (St Luke's icon of the Virgin and Child which features in the British Museum panel), Church councils that never existed and so on.[53] No text from the period of iconoclasm can be handled as an objective piece of writing to be taken at face value; such texts and pictorial evidence were designed to have a function in a period of a polemic. Arguments about whether St Theodosia existed or not are quite fruitless; equally fruitless is the literal use of her story to prove that it was women who were the chief iconophile opponents of iconoclasm.

It is often noted that the accounts that we have of Byzantine iconoclasm are written by the winners, not the losers. But their interpretation involves far more considerations than this alone. Another issue is the sources of the accounts of the events at the Chalke Gate, since the texts are not written by eyewitnesses. How far would a knowledge of their sources (and of the character of their sources) influence their interpretation? In any case the *Life* of St Stephen the Younger is in a special category of saints' lives, highly rhetorical and polemical, a brilliant piece of literary discourse which sets out to character-assassinate the leading figures of the iconoclast movement. Similarly the *Chronographia* of Theophanes is less a list of chronological events than it might appear: its telegraphic sections, written in the years immediately before the second outbreak of iconoclasm, seek to blacken the characters of the iconoclast emperors through various constructed images. A problem that faced the writers of these texts was how to gloss the initial failure of the iconophiles; how to convey in the best light the right and proper conduct of the dissent and opposition of the iconophiles at the outbreak of iconoclasm, but at the same time how to exonerate their failure. One strategy was surely to identify this as a struggle between unevenly matched social groups. In the account of Theophanes, the iconophiles comprise the nobility and the intelligent who find themselves opposed in Leo III with an emperor who is both upstart and stupid and with a patriarch without scruples. The image is of the traditional aristocracy destroyed by new radicals. In the *Life* of Stephen the Younger, the opposing groups are the brutal soldiery and pious defenceless women (who naturally must lose). This is the fictional discourse of the unfair opposition between the strong and the weak. Indeed there may be a further sub-text connected with the inclusion of women here. Are not women potential Amazons, enemies of established society? Was it therefore iconoclast sources that first spoke of a crowd of screaming women at the Chalke Gate, opposing law and order?

The accounts of the superiority of the iconoclasts at the Chalke Gate reflect conventional discourses of opposition and dissent. We cannot from their words draw the sure conclusion that iconoclasts were stupid; or that women were particular promoters of icons. Such texts are themselves interpretation, not fact.[54] So, of course, is our icon. But there is more to say about the particular metamorphosis of the character of opposition at the Chalke Gate. From the initial stories of a crowd of right-thinking men or pious women, a crowd that failed to stop iconoclasm, both texts and icon have developed the identification of one outstanding female martyr saint. She herself in time evolves from 'Maria the patrician' into 'Theodosia the nun', and this metamorphosis must again represent a dynamic of Byzantine perceptions.[55] It is perhaps relevant in finding an explanation that a dominant key figure among Byzantine iconophiles at the time of the emergence of Maria the Patrician was the aristocrat and intellectual Photios. Her transformation around 1000 into Theodosia the nun again takes place against a shifting cultural climate in

Constantinople, when we can detect a predominance of stated monastic values.

This chapter set out to examine the possibilities of interpretations of specific gender roles in the production, viewing and choice of imagery of Byzantine icons. The panel in the British Museum was taken as the starting point, since at face value it might offer a visual document of the importance of women in the promotion of icons; it offered a site where all these issues seemed to intersect. But in the event the icon has offered less a depiction of women's attitudes than a frame through which to seek the Byzantine techniques of presentation of iconoclasm. Women are visible because they had a part to play in the discourses of heresy and persecution.[56]

In the Byzantine state, heresy was a serious problem for the emperor, who saw it as a threat to imperial unity. All dissidents must be converted or eliminated. They needed to be judged by society as 'the enemy'; they had to be undermined by some strategy. Among all the potential strategies, subverting opposition into some unacceptable grouping was an obvious one. Hence the subversive value of infiltrating the female element into the perception of the opposition, of implying some feminine and unacceptable component.[57] It may be no coincidence, therefore, that Eusebius likewise bolsters his argument against the use of images by insidiously connecting the desire for them with a woman. Women were the natural victims when a group was needed who must be losers. For the iconoclasts, women could be identified as the opposition – as iconophiles – because they were 'outsiders' and made to be scapegoats. Paradoxically, iconophile writers might elusively accept the idea that women were the champions of icons; it would then exonerate them for the decades of being on the losing side. One needs to be circumspect in assessing the idea of Kazhdan that 'in the words of deacon Ignatios, the author of Tarasios's biography, during iconoclasm feminine weakness turned out to be more steadfast than masculine strength'.[58]

All this adds up to the conclusion that the supposed special importance of women in the promotion of icons is a chimera. What we see in the British Museum icon and read in these texts is to be interpreted as shadowing something much closer to a traditional model of male oppressive strategies. The gender equation in the production and viewing of icons is as much in need of investigation as ever. But in looking for frameworks to explain the rise and popularity of devotional icons as well as the violence of the iconoclast ban, the preferable model is one in which icons are seen as *necessary* as a symbolic expression of a Christian world view rather than any simple and mechanistic connection of women and icons.

NOTES

1 See Catia Galatariotou, 'Byzantine women's monastic communities: the evidence of the typika', *JÖB* 38 (1988), 263–90, for an important treatment of the issues. Also see L. Brubaker, 'Image, audience and place: interaction and reproduction', in L. Brubaker and R. Ousterhout, eds, *The Sacred Image, East and West* (Urbana and Chicago, 1995), 204–20, esp. 206 ff.

2 M. Barasch, *Icon. Studies in the History of an Idea* (New York, 1992), maps philosophical and religious thinking on images that preceded Byzantine iconoclasm.

3 Peter Brown, 'A Dark Age crisis: aspects of the iconoclastic controversy', *English Historical Review* 88 (1973), 1–34; reprinted in P. Brown, *Society and the Holy in Late Antiquity* (London, 1982), 251–301.

4 Iconoclasm was foreshadowed by a similar situation when the Quinisext Council addressed some key questions of artistic representative practices (canon 73 banning crosses on floors, thus repeating earlier council decisions; canon 82 proclaiming a high-profile decision about representing Christ as a person, not as a lamb, which apparently precipitated an increase in images of Christ – as on the coins of Justinian II; and canon 100 excommunicating all corrupting images). These discussions formed a precedent (if not a catalyst) for the elevation of decisions about imagery to this ecclesiastical level. See H. Ohme, *Das Concilium Quinisextum und seine Bishofsliste. Studien zum Konstantinopeler Konzil von 692* (Berlin, 1990).

5 See R.I. Moore, *The Origins of European Dissent* (Oxford, 1977 and 1985) and *The Formation of a Persecuting Society* (Oxford, 1987). This is not the place to ask how far the 'Dark Age' period represented changing methods of persecution – there are many different ways of suppressing opposition. For Byzantium, see P.J. Alexander, 'Religious persecution and resistance in the Byzantine empire of the eighth and ninth centuries: methods and justifications', *Speculum* 52 (1977), 238–64; reprinted in P.J. Alexander, *Religious and Political History and Thought in the Byzantine Empire* (Variorum, 1978); and for Islam see J. Bray, 'The Mohammetan and Idolatry', *Studies in Church History* 21 (1984), 89–98. For anti-semitism and questions of heresy in the seventh century, see J.F. Haldon, *Byzantium in the Seventh Century* (Cambridge, 1990), esp. 337 ff.

6 K. Corrigan, *Visual Polemics in the Ninth-Century Psalters* (Cambridge, 1992), uses anti-Jewish and anti-Muslim texts to identify the precise imagery used in the visual polemics of the Khludov and other marginal Psalters.

7 Similarly P. Brown, *Power and Persuasion in Late Antiquity. Towards a Christian Empire* (Wisconsin, 1992), makes the point that 'our' view of

the fourth century has been distorted by the fifth-century Christian rhetoric of triumph.

8 The British Museum icon came to light at Sotheby's at a sale on 15 February 1984; the provenance was a private collection in Sweden (see the catalogue *Russian Pictures, Icons*, lot no. 156). It was subsequently exhibited at Bernheimer Fine Art in 1987: see Y. Petsopoulos, *East Christian Art* (London, 1987), 49–50. It was acquired by the British Museum in 1988 (inventory no. M&LA 1988, 4–11,1). For other discussions of the icon, see U. Abel, *Ikonen – bilden av det heliga* (Hedemora, 1988), 32–3; R. Cormack, 'The Triumph of Orthodoxy', *National Art Collections Fund Review* 1989 (London, 1989), 93–4; and N.P. Ševčenko in 'Icons in the liturgy', *DOP* 45 (1991), 45–57, esp. 48.

9 J. Gouillard, 'Le synodikon de l'orthodoxie: édition et commentaire', *Travaux et Mémoires* 2 (1967), 1–316.

10 This icon of the Virgin Mary has the usual sigla for Mother of God.

11 See G.P. Majeska, *Russian Travelers to Constantinople in the Fourteenth and Fifteenth Centuries* (Washington, DC, 1984), esp. 363–6, for references to texts; for images, see M. Acheimastou-Potamianou, 'The interpretation of a wall-painting in Vlacherna Monastery near Arta' (in Greek), *Deltion tis Christianikis Archaiologikis Etairias* 13 (1985–6), 301–6, and Ševčenko, 'Icons in the liturgy', 45–57.

12 The large panel of the *Hodigitria* is held up by two winged figures with red hats, not apparently angels. N.P. Ševčenko saw these as members of the brotherhood who maintained the cult, suggesting that their wings were a device to elevate both them and the festival to a 'heavenly' or 'liturgical' level so that 'the image celebrates simultaneously the historical event, its inner meaning, and its eternal reenactment'. Dionysius of Fourna speaks of two 'deacons' with 'shoes woven of gold' holding the *Hodigitria*; see P. Hetherington, *The Painter's Manual of Dionysius of Fourna* (London, 1974), 64.

13 There are traces of a title on the icon to the right of the representation of the Virgin Hodigitria; the letters that can be made out (..IA..) most likely represent ORTHODOXIA.

14 The eighteenth-century compilation of Dionysius codifies the subject as 'the Restoration of the Holy Images'; see Hetherington, *The Painter's Manual*, 64–5.

15 The name of the right figure began with TH.

16 For the sources and discussion of the *Graptoi*, see M.B. Cunningham, ed. and tr., *The Life of Michael the Synkellos* (Belfast, 1991).

17 The identifications of the figures given here differ in some cases from the original Sotheby's catalogue entry of 1984 and the entry by Petsopoulos of 1987. The inscriptions are considerably rubbed, and some are more certain than others. For example, in the upper register, the name and title of emperor Michael III is easily legible; beside the empress Theodora, we can read THEODO(ra) and PISTE (faithful in Christ). Beside the figure of Patriarch Methodios wearing a sakkos, ME(ethodios) is readable. In the lower register with eleven figures, the extreme left saint is clearly inscribed THEODOSIA. The next three inscriptions cannot be read. The fifth figure from the left (Theophanes) has the letters

(Theo)PHAN(es) and his companion TH(eodoros). The next few inscriptions are very rubbed, and it is not entirely clear to which figures they apply. The seventh figure, the bishop, may have the letters (Th)EO(dore) and the eighth may have THEOPH(anes); the tenth and eleventh figures have THEOPHILAK(tos) and ARSAKIOS. Petsopoulos read the last three figures as Theodore, Theophilos and Thessakios.

18 Two other later icons of this subject are published. One panel (43.5 × 37.5 cm) is in the collection of the Church of St George of the Greeks in Venice; see M. Chatzidakis, *Icônes de Sainte-Georges des Grecs* (Venice, 1962), no. 63, 96. It is signed by the Corfiote painter Emmanuel Tzanfournaris (c.1570–5; died after 1631), and is titled *Orthodoxy* (*Orthodoxia*). Chatzidakis recorded the various inscriptions that allow identification of most of the participants: Theodora and Michael III; Methodios; Theophylactos of Nicomedia; Michael of Synnada; Euthymios of Sardis; and Emilianos of Cyrica. In the register below Chatzidakis identifies the figures as the 'confessors': Theophanes and Theodore the Studite in the centre with an icon. On the left: Theodosia (with an icon); Ioannikios; Stephanos the Higoumenos; Thomas; and Peter. On the right: Makarios of Pelekete; Stephen the Younger (with an icon of the Virgin); Joseph; John Katharon; Arsenios; Andrew. The other icon (50 × 40.5 cm) in the Benaki Museum, Athens, is entitled *The Restoration (Anastelosis) of the Icons*; see A. Xyngopoulos, *The Collection of Helen A. Stathatos* (in Greek) (Athens, 1951), cat. 6, 8–10. This has the signature of the same artist as the icon in Venice. This is the largest of the three icons, and the most complex; there are more figures including several women and singers (with 'authentic' coloured costumes), for which see N.K. Moran, *Singers in Late Byzantine and Slavonic Painting* (Leiden, 1986), fig. 87, 136, 149. Some hold candles or inscriptions that anathematise iconoclasts. Xyngopoulos assumes that the figure of the nun with the icon of Christ Emmanuel on the left side of the lower register is St Kassia. Our parallels would, of course, suggest that she is St Theodosia, but the suggestion is no doubt based on the notice by Dionysius of Fourna, who mentions this saint and not Theodosia; see Hetherington, *The Painter's Manual*, 65. In the 'Restoration of the holy images', Dionysios enumerates Methodios, deacons holding the Hodigitria icon, Theodora and Michael, and other figures including John, Arsacios, Isaiah and Kassia. St Kassia would, of course, have been an appropriate choice: she was a hymnographer in the first half of the ninth century who supposedly competed in a bride show for the emperor Theophilos with Theodora, and who was assumed to be on the iconophile side. (Since writing, this icon has been restored and restudied by A. Drandaki).

The subject also appears in the wall-paintings of 1525 by Theophanes the Cretan in the catholikon of the Laura monastery on Athos and at Stavroniketa on Athos. In the Athonite examples (for the Laura, see G. Millet, *Monuments de l'Athos* [Paris, 1927], plate 131, 2; and also M. Chatzidakis, *The Cretan Painter Theophanes* [Athos, 1986], pls 122–3) the scene (*Anastelosis ton sebaston kai hagion eikonon*) is altered by the placing of the Hodigitria icon and the imperial figures and Methodios below and the other figures in the register above. Tassos Papacostas has pointed out to me that the *Triumph of Orthodoxy* appears in the sixteenth century in wall paintings at the catholicon of the monastery of St Neophytos near Paphos around 1500 (the cycle includes Church councils) and at St Sozomenos at Galata in 1513. The list can be further increased from wall paintings in the Balkans.

19 See J. Herrin, 'Women and the faith in icons in Early Christianity', in R. Samuel and G. Stedman Jones, eds, *Culture, Ideology and Politics* (London, 1982), 56–83; its thesis is repeated in her book *The Formation of Christendom* (Oxford, 1987), esp. 307 ff. and 331–2. She has considered the issues in other papers, in particular 'In search of Byzantine women: three avenues of approach', in A. Cameron and A. Kuhrt, eds, *Images of Women in Antiquity* (Beckenham, 1983, and reprinted, London, 1993), 167–89. Her most recent study is found in '"Femina Byzantina": the Council in Trullo on Women', *DOP* 46 (1992), 97–105. On Herrin, see also A. Cameron, *Christianity and the Rhetoric of Empire* (Berkeley and Oxford, 1991), esp. 202–3; and E. Kuryluk, *Veronica and her Cloth* (Oxford, 1991). For a different study of 'women's place' with reference to a later period, see L. Garland, 'The life and ideology of Byzantine women: a further note on conventions of behaviour and social reality as reflected in 11th and 12th century historical sources', *B* 58 (1988), 361–93.

20 Herrin, 'Women and the faith in icons', 68.

21 Jeffrey Hamburger, 'The visual and the visionary: the image in late medieval devotions', *Viator*, 20 (1989), 161–82, has important observations on women as an audience for art in the late medieval west.

22 For a study of the period that revolves around the Cleveland tapestry, but which does not even mention the issue of women, see J. Pelikan, *Imago Dei. The Byzantine Apologia for Icons* (New Haven and London, 1990). Of course the famous case of the Bayeux Tapestry needs to be taken as a methodological caution, for there is no straightforward evidence for its traditional attribution to women; see Rozsika Parker, *The Subversive Stitch: Embroidery and the Making of the Feminine* (London, 1984). A wider question raised by the notion of women as artists is what is to be defined as 'art'; see within the frame of Islamic art, R. Hillenbrand, 'The major minor arts of Islam', *Art History* 1 (1989), 109–15.

23 Sister Charles Murray, 'Art and the Early Church', *Journal of Theological Studies*, N.S. 28 (1977), 303–45, remains an important but controversial treatment of the Early Christian period which plays down the dichotomy seen by Herrin between the Old Testament prohibition of images and their encouragement within the pagan commemoration of the dead.

24 K. Weitzmann, *The Monastery of Saint Catherine at Mount Sinai. The Icons I* (Princeton, 1976), cat. 3, 18–21. Also on this icon, Robin Cormack, 'Reading Icons', *Valör. Konstvetenskapliga Studier* 4 (1991), 1–28.

25 For an important analysis of how the frontal gaze influences the meanings of such a picture, see R.G. Osborne, 'Death revisited; death revised. The death of the artist in archaic and classical Greece', *Art History* 11 (1988), 1–16.

26 See M.P. Carroll, *The Cult of the Virgin Mary* (Princeton, 1992).

27 See J. Osborne, 'The Roman Catacombs in the Middle Ages', *Proceedings of the British School at Rome* 53 (1985), 278–328.

28 For a transcription of the text, see B. Bagatti, *Il Cimitero di Commodilla o dei Martiri Felice ed Adautto* (Vatican, 1936), esp. 42:

> Suscipe nunc lacrimas mater natique suprestis,
> quas fundet gemitus; laudibus ecce tuis,
> Post mortem patris servasti casta mariti
> sex triginta annis. sic viduata fidem
> Officium nato patris matrisque gerebas
> hic reqiexcit in pace Turtura.
> In subolis faciem. vir tibi vixit Obas
> Turtura nomen abis set turtur vera fuisti
> cui coniux monens non fuit alter amor
> Unica materia est quo sumit femina laudem
> quod te coniugio. exibuisse doces
> que bisit PLM annus LX.

29 C.W. Bynum, *Jesus as Mother. Studies in the Spirituality of the High Middle Ages* (California, 1982), 140–1.

30 J.D. Breckenridge, *The Numismatic Iconography of Justinian II* (New York, 1959), esp. 64, discusses the new development of the discourse of Pope John VII (705–7) as 'servant of the Mother of God', and in tenth-century Byzantium the representation of Leo Sakellarios in his Bible in the Vatican Library (Reginensis gr. 1) offers a striking example of the representation of male devotion to the Virgin. There are notable other examples of devotion to the Virgin from the early Byzantine period, such as the (lost) mosaic panel in St Demetrios at Thessaloniki which is roughly contemporary with the Mt Sinai icon of the Virgin and saints. It shows a prominent male donor presented to the Virgin by St Demetrios, whereas the woman in the composition, presumably his wife, is relegated far off to the right at the very margin of the panel; see R. Cormack, 'The Church of Saint Demetrios: the watercolours and drawings of W.S. George', reprinted in R. Cormack, *The Byzantine Eye* (Variorum, 1989), study II, fig. 32.

31 See L. Imray and A. Middleton, 'Public and private: marking the boundaries', in E. Gamarnikow, D. Morgan, J. Purvis and D. Taylorson, eds, *The Public and the Private* (London, 1983), 12–27; S. Ardener, ed., *Women and Space. Ground Rules and Social Maps* (London, 1981), esp. L. Sciama, 'The problem of privacy in Mediterranean Society', 89–111. For a feminist consideration of the intersection of the dichotomies of political/social and public/private, see J.B. Elshtain, *Public Man, Private Woman* (Princeton, 1981).

32 See T. Mathews, '"Private" liturgy in Byzantine architecture: toward a re-appraisal', *Cahiers Archéologiques* 30 (1982), 125–38; N. Teteriatnikov, 'Upper-storey chapels in churches of the Christian East', *DOP*, 42 (1988), 65–72, esp. 71; J.P. Thomas, *Private Religious Foundations in the Byzantine Empire* (Washington, DC, 1987); J. Haldon, *Byzantium in the Seventh Century* (Cambridge, 1990).

33 See A. Wallace-Hadrill, 'The social structure of the Roman house', *Proceedings of the British School at Rome* 56 (1988), 43–97.

34 See N. Gendle, 'The role of the Byzantine saint in the development of the icon cult', in S. Hackel, ed., *The Byzantine Saint* (London, 1981), 181–6.

35 Eusebius, *Letter to Constantia*, PG 20, 1545 ff; see C. Mango, *The Art of the Byzantine Empire 312–1453* (Englewood Cliffs, 1972), 16–18.

36 D. Freedberg, *The Power of Images* (Chicago, 1989) esp. 397 ff. Tertullian, *De cultu feminarum*, I, 8, *PL* 1, 1312–13. One question here is how far this was already a repetition of a classical *topos*.

37 L. Deubner, *Kosmas und Damian* (Leipzig and Berlin, 1907), 137 ff., lines 17 ff. see E. Kitzinger, 'The cult of images in the age before iconoclasm', 107 n. 89 and 147–8, esp. n. 273, on the question of the date of the story, whether before or during iconoclasm. This article is reprinted from *DOP* 8 (1954), 83–150, in W.E. Kleinbauer, *The Art of Byzantium and the Medieval West: Selected Studies by E. Kitzinger* (Bloomington, 1976).

38 The sources do, of course, offer several cases of female iconophiles – such as the mother of St Stephen the Younger and the mother of St Theodore of Stoudios, and also the wife of the jailor of St Stephen the Younger and his fellow iconophiles in prison who both fed them and even showed them icons which she kept locked up in a chest (one a Virgin and Child, the others represented Peter and Paul). But the sources likewise offer instances of male iconophilism.

39 The well-known reports that the empresses Irene and Theodora kept icons in their rooms happen to date some time after iconoclasm (George Kedrenus, *Synopsis historion*, I. Bekker, ed., 2 vols [Bonn, 1838–9], I 901A, and Theophanes Continuatus, I. Bekker, ed. [Bonn, 1838], 105A).

40 Gregory of Tours, *History of the Franks*, L. Thorpe, ed. (Harmondsworth, 1974), 13, n. 67, referring to *Vita Sancti Martini*, II, I.

41 See Cunningham, *Life of Michael the Synkellos*, chap. 25, 101 and 162, n. 171; the editor sees this as a *topos*.

42 J. Meyendorff, *Imperial Unity and Church Divisions. The Church 450–680* (New York, 1989), esp. 209–10. See M. Maas, *John Lydus and the Roman Past* (London, 1992), esp. chap. 5, on Justinian's manipulations of pagans as the opposition.

43 The primary source is Theophanes Continuatus, 105.

44 See *Russian Pictures, Icons and Works of Art* (Sotheby's, London), sale catalogue for 28 November 1991, lot 559, 110–11. The scheme of the icon is to show St Theodora in the centre, surrounded by twelve scenes of her life.

45 In discussion at Princeton, Simon Franklin pointed to the possible political significance of such a reference to royal women in eighteenth-century Russian; and Russian colleagues pointed to the existence of a cycle of St Theodora in the Moscow Kremlin.

46 For St Theodosia of *Constantinople*, see Menologion text in *PG* 117, 548–9; cf. H. Delehaye, *Synaxarion ecclesiae Constantinopolitanae* (Brussels, 1992), 828–9. For laudations of St Theodosia, see *BHG* 1773(2).

The only other candidate is St Theodosia of Tyre, martyred in Caesarea on Easter Sunday, 307, but she has no particular connections with icons.

47 See Cyril Mango, *The Brazen House. A Study of the Vestibule of the Imperial Palace of Constantinople* (Copenhagen, 1959), esp. 117 ff., for a sceptical treatment of the legend of St Theodosia.

48 Antony of Novgorod, see B. de Khitrowo, *Itinéraires russes en Orient* (Geneva, 1889), 103 (translated from Loparev, 26).

49 For collected information on the cult and Church of St Theodosia, see Majeska, *Russian Travelers to Constantinople*, 346–51. From the early thirteenth century a series of icons of St Theodosia was produced at the monastery of St Catherine on Sinai, where she obviously had a special significance – explained by Doula Mouriki as 'due to her important contribution in the safeguarding of icons'; see Mouriki, 'Icons from the twelfth to fifteenth centuries', in K.A. Manafis, ed., *Sinai. The Treasures of the Monastery of Saint Catherine* (Athens, 1990), 111 and fig. 39.

50 That the episode of the Chalke icon's existence on the Gate and its destruction under Leo III is a fiction, see the full treatment by Marie-France Auzépy, 'La destruction de l'icône du Christ de la Chalcé par Leo III: propogande ou réalité?', *B* 60 (1990), 445–92, who concludes that the story of an icon as well as the story of its destruction was invented around 800.

An obvious parallel to the Chalke icon 'myth' is the iconophile claim that the pre-iconoclast apse of Hagia Sophia had contained a figurative image which was destroyed by the iconoclasts; the claim is found in iconophile writings and displayed in the famous epigram around the Virgin and Child of 867 (see C. Mango and E.J.W. Hawkins, 'The Apse mosaics of St Sophia at Istanbul', *DOP* 19 [1965], 113–51). Interestingly the public inscription written above the Chalke icon of empress Eirene (according to the *Scriptor incertus de Leone*, I. Bekker, ed. [Bonn, 1842], 355) has been described as a 'garbled version' of the Hagia Sophia epigram (see S.G. Mercati, 'Sulle iscrizioni di Santa Sofia', *Bessarione* 26 [1922], esp. 204–5, and Mango, *The Brazen House*, 121): '[The image] which Leo the emperor had formerly cast down, Eirene has re-erected here.' Mango and others accept this text as a source contemporary with the events; the only dissident seems to be Lydia Tomic, 'Fragment of a historical work of the 9th century' (in Serbo-Croat), *Zbornik radova Vizantoloskog Instituta* 1 (1952), 78–85, who, on the basis of the references to Bulgaria, dates the text after 864. One answer to this argument is that these references may be a later accretion. The epigram may, however, be evidence that supports her later dating. D. Stein, *Der Beginn des byzantinischen Bilderstreit und seine Entwicklung bis in der 40er Jahre des 8 Jahrunderts* (Munich, 1980), had already hinted that the story of the destruction of the Chalke icon could be a literary *topos* (modelled on the *Vita Symeonis Stylites*, for example, in which a soldier destroys an image of the saint; see P. van den Ven, ed., *La vie ancienne de S. Symeon Stylite le jeune* [Brussels, 1962], 140).

51 Mango, *The Brazen House*, esp. 108 ff., discusses the Chalke image; and he devotes Appendix 1, 170–4, to a detailed treatment of the controversy over the dating of the destruction of the image to 726 or 730. He points

out (111) that the *Parastaseis* text has a missing folio which means that the description of the Chalke Gate in this version is incomplete; the lacuna is filled by Preger from the later *Patria* which speaks of an image of Christ on the Gate below the statues of Maurice and his wife and children. Mango points out that if the *Parastaseis* was written during iconoclasm, it could not have included this passage. A. Cameron and J. Herrin, eds, *Constantinople in the Early Eighth Century: The Parastaseis Syntomoi Chronikai* (Leiden, 1984), 174–5, 'tend to think' that the *Patria* does represent the original text of the *Parastaseis*. But much is resolved if one accepts that the Chalke Christ icon did not exist until the reign of Eirene. The *Patria* passage would then become one further document compiled after the early ninth century.

52 See C. Mango, 'The availability of books in the Byzantine Empire, AD 750–850', in *Byzantine Books and Bookmen* (Washington, DC, 1975), esp. 30–1, reprinted in C. Mango, *Byzantium and its Image* (London, 1984), study VII; and cf. D.J. Sahas, *Icon and Logos: Sources in Eighth-Century iconoclasm* (Toronto, 1986), 39. Also for the texts, see H. Hennephof, *Textus Byzantinos ad Iconomachiam pertinentes* (Leiden, 1969).

53 A. Jeffery, 'Ghevond's text of the correspondence between 'Umar II and Leo III', *Harvard Theological Review* 37 (1944), 269–332; see esp. 322 for a statement on icons. 'Umar II was caliph 717–720, and Leo emperor 717–741. We only know the text from the Armenian history of Ghevond (perhaps to be dated to around 900), and from a Latin version in *PG* 107, 315–24, attributed to Leo VI; together, they imply a Greek basis. See also R. Cormack, *Writing in Gold* (London, 1985), 261–2.

54 During discussion of a version of this chapter which I gave at Princeton in January 1993, the point was made against my reasoning that when ninth-century writers recorded information, they *knew* the facts, because they were as intelligent as us; they were not stupid. Their accounts should, then, be treated as a correct record of these facts. It will be clear that I do not accept this criticism, just as I would not accept at face value many contemporary reports about women – like, for example, the suggestion that Nancy Reagan was more influential over the President's formulation of foreign policy than were his advisers.

55 Yet another transformation would seem to have occurred by the time of Dionysios of Fourna (c.1670–c.1745–6) who lists St Kassia: see above, n. 16.

56 Similarly, the seventh homily of Photios on the unveiling of the image of the Virgin in Hagia Sophia in 867, while celebrating the victory of the iconophiles, conspicuously devotes much of the text to the acceptance into the Church of a group of repentant heretics. See C. Mango, *The Homilies of Photios* (Cambridge, Mass., 1958), 290 ff.

57 As a parallel see C. Edwards, *The Politics of Immorality in Ancient Rome* (Cambridge, 1993), on the manipulations of the notions of male and female in imperial Rome.

58 A.P. Kazhdan, 'Byzantine hagiography and sex in the fifth to twelfth centuries', *DOP* 44 (1990), 131–43, esp. 132: see *BHG* 1698.28–9.

3

MEMORIES OF HELENA: PATTERNS IN IMPERIAL FEMALE MATRONAGE IN THE FOURTH AND FIFTH CENTURIES[1]

Leslie Brubaker

The augusta Helena was an important symbol in Byzantium. More thoroughly and perhaps even more quickly than her son Constantine, the empirical Helena became subsumed into a network of quasi-legendary material. By 395, about 65 years after her death, Helena was credited with the discovery of the true cross in Jerusalem; soon, monuments in the Holy Land commissioned by others were reattributed to her; and in subsequent centuries various authors inserted Helena as a major participant in legends about the life of her son.[2] But while changes in the symbolic importance that Byzantine imperial ideology accorded to her son have been amply studied,[3] Helena has remained confined within the meta-narratives of Constantine and the true cross: the ways in which memories of Helena were constructed in the late antique and Byzantine worlds have been largely ignored.

The tendency of historians to privilege male actors and to focus on written communication plays into the neglect of Helena as metaphor. It was primarily aristocratic and imperial women in the fourth and fifth centuries who reconstructed a Helena with particular symbolic functions that built upon, but went beyond, her relationship to Constantine and purported discovery of the true cross. These women left few written records aside from inscriptions that might help us decipher their memories of Helena.[4] Instead, they associated themselves with Helena through commissioned monuments; they participated in a reconstruction of Helena based on visual rather than written stories. How and why this is so are the subjects of this chapter.

Late antique and, especially, Byzantine women have only lately become a focus of serious study, and these studies have been, almost inevitably, based on texts, particularly on law codes but also hagiography and theological writings.[5] As has often been noted, the attitudes and assumptions enshrined in these texts are unavoidably male:[6] beyond the fact that they were voiced by a culture that saw the male viewpoint as normative, virtually all of the texts were originally written by men;[7] as important, but less frequently remarked, the texts that have come down to us were preserved because they espoused ideas acceptable to the later men who had them copied. Narrative text was an élite male genre, and while discourse can form and reflect social attitudes that may impact upon or respond to women as well as men,[8] even texts that purport to be about women ultimately reveal at least as much, often more, about men, and male rhetorical strategies, as about women.[9] Elite females did, however, share one form of public communication with their male counterparts: aristocratic women and men alike commissioned images and monuments.

Statues and monuments were a form of public communication considered appropriate for wealthy women from at least the time of the Roman republic.[10] Like works commissioned by men, these monuments communicated status and promoted specific concepts. In the Augustan period, for example, Livia's 'magnificent' shrine to Concordia (7 BC) championed marriage, motherhood and traditional family values; the empress's claim to be associated with the virtues of marital concord was so successful that 150 years later, on the Egyptian fringes of the empire, weddings were performed in front of her statue.[11] Monuments commissioned by Roman women could provide a fairly overt form of public discourse in ways that women's words did (or could) not, though it was not necessarily a 'female' discourse in any subversive sense. This pattern continued into the late Roman and early Byzantine periods, when both aristocratic and imperial women commissioned images of lineage to structure their public discourse-through-monuments.

Perhaps the most overt visual evocations of family by a late Roman imperial woman were commissioned by Aelia Galla Placidia (c. 388–450), daughter of Theodosius I and his second wife Galla.[12] Sometime after moving to Ravenna in 425, Galla Placidia commissioned a church dedicated to St John the Evangelist. As commemorated by inscription – 'to the holy and most blessed apostle John the evangelist, Galla Placidia Augusta, with her son Placidus Valentinianus Augustus and her daughter Iusta Grata Honoria Augusta, fulfil a vow concerning [their] liberation from the danger of the sea' – the church repaid St John for saving the three from disaster at sea.[13] There were indeed mosaics detailing this rescue, but as described by Rossi in the sixteenth century the decoration at S. Giovanni Evangelista evidently had a second agenda as well:

> there are images of Constantine, Valentinian, Gratian and others who belong to the imperial house. To them referred the inscription *Galla Placidia fulfilled her vow for herself and for all of these*. The following portraits were on the arch of the apse, five on the right side with the following inscriptions: *Divus Constantinus, Divus Theodosius, Divus Arcadius, Divus Honorius, Theodosius Nepos*; on the left wall: *Divus Valentinianus, Divus Gratianus, Divus Constantinus, Gratianus Nepos, Ioannes Nepos*.[14]

The apse, in short, was lined with images of the augusti, east and west, from the time of Constantine, who were somehow related to Galla Placidia (see Figure 1) – Arcadius and Honorius (her half-brothers), Theodosius (her father), Valentinian I (her grandfather),[15] Gratian (her half-uncle) and Constantine himself (Gratian's grandfather-in-law, hence distantly related to Galla Placidia) – along with Galla Placidia's deceased brothers Gratian and John, her deceased son Theodosius, and probably her deceased husband Constantius III.[16] Galla Placidia also stressed her ties with the ruling emperor in the east, Theodosius II (her half-nephew), by having him depicted with his wife Eudokia and their children Arcadius and Licinia Eudoxia (who had been betrothed to Galla Placidia's son Valentinian III in 424, at age 2) elsewhere in the church.[17] The mosaics commemorated the rescue of the augusta, her son, and her daughter, but the Theodosian family portrait and the legend expressing her vow 'for all of these' – in other words for the honour of her extended family – also celebrated Galla Placidia's imperial kinship ties, while the apse portraits linked her immediate family fortune to her strong dynastic lineage, with its claimed roots in the Constantinian house.[18]

Galla Placidia also signalled her interest in familial ties, and her active participation in the imperial network, through involvement in the refurbishing of monuments built by her forebears. In 384,

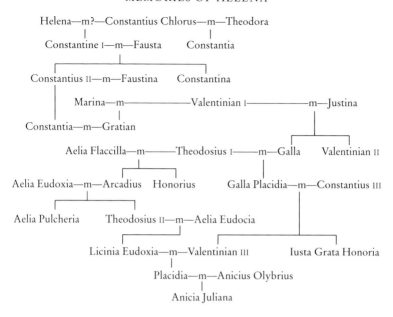

Figure 1 The relationship between female members of the Constantinian, Theodosian and Valentinian houses

Theodosius I commissioned a large basilica on the site of St Paul's tomb in Rome (S. Paolo fuori le mura), and his work was completed by Honorius. Both were commemorated in inscription: *Theodosius coepit perfecit Honorius* [. . .]. Repairs in the 440s, after S. Paolo had been damaged in a storm, were apparently undertaken by Galla Placidia in conjunction with Pope Leo I. Her own inscription reads: 'the pious mind of Placidia rejoices that the whole beauty of her father's work is resplendent through the zeal of the pontiff Leo'.[19] Whatever Galla Placidia's contribution was, it is the association with her father that she stressed in the mosaic inscription.

The use of decorative programmes to celebrate family was not invented by Galla Placidia – *vide* Livia's shrine to Concordia, though here the emphasis was admittedly somewhat different – nor was it restricted to female commissions.[20] Like Galla Placidia's implicit genealogies at S. Giovanni and S. Paolo fuori le mura, the real or metaphorical lineage chains traced by, or in honour of, illustrious men are virtually always extended *through* men. Late antique and early Byzantine women did not, however, perpetuate family ties only through the male line.[21] Related women sometimes contributed to the same church: in 439, for example, Eudocia (wife of Theodosius II) brought relics of St Stephen – and also, apparently, Sts Lawrence and Agnes – from Jerusalem to Constantinople, where they were placed in the church of St Lawrence, a building completed 14 years later by Eudokia's sister-in-law Pulcheria.[22] More strikingly, on occasion several generations of women began and continued work on the same building. As recorded in a dedicatory inscription registered in the *Greek Anthology*, Licinia Eudoxia founded a church dedicated to St Euphemia (in the Olybrios district of Constantinople); Licinia Eudoxia's daughter Placidia embellished the church; and Placidia's daughter, Anicia Juliana, in turn completed it.[23] These three generations of women contributed to the same church over a considerable period of time: Licinia Eudoxia presumably commissioned the church in the 440s or early 450s;[24] Placidia's contributions must have been made between 461 and 472;[25] and Anicia Juliana completed the building before her death in 527/8.[26] Toward the end of her life, between 524 and 527, Anicia Juliana also rebuilt the church of St Polyeuktos, a foundation that had been established by another of her female ancestors, this time her great-grandmother Aelia Eudokia.[27] Once again, the female family line is stressed and commemorated in inscription:[28]

> The Empress Eudokia . . . was the first to build a temple to the divinely inspired Polyeuktos; but she did not make it as fine or as large as this . . . because she had a divine premonition that her family and descendants would have the knowledge and resources to provide grander embellishment. From this stock Juliana, bright light of blessed parents, sharing their royal blood in the fourth generation, did not disappoint the hopes of the empress, who was mother of its finest children, but raised this building from its small original to its present size and form.[29]

Chronologically, these particular matronage chains carried on from Licinia Eudoxia and Aelia Eudokia by Placidia and Anicia Juliana overlap, repeat and reinforce a series of commissions that evoked a more distant, and sometimes purely metaphorical, female ancestor, the empress Helena. The Helena who was memorialised in late antique and early Byzantine élite female commissions may or may not have much to do with any actual person; the Helena who was important to this group of women depends on memories preserved through stories and, especially, objects that recreated her in the following centuries. Memories of Helena embalmed in objects are unstudied, and it is these memories that interest me here; the following sketch is, then, focused less on empirical data about Helena than on what later generations believed about her activities and commissions.

Helena was born around 250, apparently in Bithynia. Later sources are vague about her parents' background; we may perhaps conclude that her family was not aristocratic. Whether or not she was ever married to Constantius Chlorus, Constantine's father, Constantius married someone else after Constantine's birth, and Helena did not come to Rome until after Constantius's death in 306.[30]

Shortly thereafter, during the second decade of the fourth century, Helena – who, Eusebius tells us, had 'authority over the imperial treasury'[31] – acquired a large tract of land in Rome, the *fundus Laurentus*.[32] Here either she or Constantine (or both together) built the cemetery church of Sts Marcellinus and Peter, a basilica with an adjoining mausoleum where Helena was apparently eventually interred.[33] While the intricacies of the commission are lost to us, Helena's connection with the complex is, and was, clear. It was built on land that Helena owned and personally maintained: her palace was there, and her repairs of at least one building – the *thermae Helenae* – were recorded in a public inscription; she donated gifts to the church – one, a massive gold cross, jointly with her son – and was buried in the mausoleum.[34] Perhaps by the fifth century, the area acquired a new name, *Subaugusta*, that referred to her.[35] The continuing association of Helena with the site is attested by a (probably) sixth-century graffito, incised into the walls of the basilica by a Greek pilgrim, which invokes her specifically as a saint; by the seventh-century *Notitia Ecclesiarum Urbis Romae*, which calls the church *ecclesia Helenae*; and by the eighth- and ninth-century records in the *Liber pontificalis* which refer to the site as *basilica beate Elene*.[36]

In 324, Helena, along with Constantine's wife Fausta, was named augusta.[37] She appeared on coins so identified, a fact that Eusebius, followed by the mid-fifth-century historian Sozomen, found significant enough to mention.[38] The coins, which were widely minted, normally show a bust of Helena on the obverse with the title FL[avia] HELENA AUGUSTA and, on the reverse, a standing female figure with the legend 'security of the republic' (SECURITAS REIPUBLICE [sic]);

rarely, the standing female holds a child.[39] It is unlikely that the coins reflect Helena's initiative; rather, as is clear from the inscription – with its message that the security of the empire depended on Helena and, implicitly, her son[40] – they perpetuate the integration of women into Roman state ideology as images of dynastic strength and state stability.[41] While the coins conveyed no message from Helena, they none the less ensured that an image of, and about, an idealised Helena was disseminated throughout the empire.

Helena is, and was, most often remembered in connection with her pilgrimage to Jerusalem in 326, when she was credited with the discovery of the true cross.[42] This is almost certainly a later invention: though relics of the cross are mentioned earlier, and the cross may even have been unearthed in Constantine's time, Helena's participation is first noted only in 395.[43] Her commissions in the Holy Land, however, are already recorded by Eusebius, who attributed the Church of the Nativity in Bethlehem and the Church on the Mount of Olives in Jerusalem (the Eleona basilica) to Helena's initiatives.[44] Here, too, Helena's role expanded: the pilgrim Egeria, who was in the Holy Land between 381 and 384, associated the decoration of the Holy Sepulchre with Helena;[45] and by 403, Rufinus credited her with the whole church, an attribution repeated in the revised Greek edition of his work prepared in the 430s by Sokrates, and by most subsequent authors.[46]

Back in Rome, and probably between Helena's return from the Holy Land in 326 and her death in 329, a large chapel was constructed in the Sessorian Palace, which stood on Helena's lands near the Peter and Marcellinus church.[47] The *Liber pontificalis* claims that the chapel housed a relic of the true cross from its inception, and certainly by the second quarter of the fifth century it was referred to as the Jerusalem Church (*ecclesia* or *basilica Hierusalem*), or, sometimes, as Helena's basilica (*basilica Heleniana*), reflecting the belief that the relic was brought to Rome by her;[48] certainly in the sixth century, and possibly already in the fifth, the station service for Good Friday was celebrated here.[49] It is unclear at what point the chapel acquired the name Sta Croce in Gerusalemme.

Helena was also remembered in Constantine's new capital, Constantinople. According to a seventh-century source, Constantine named the courtyard by the Senate the Augustaion 'because he had set up ... a monument of his mother, lady Helena Augusta, on a porphyry column' there.[50] There were, in fact, statues and other likenesses of Helena throughout that city; some were preserved at least until the eighth century and catalogued in the *Parastaseis Syntomoi Chronikai*.[51] In most of these, Helena was coupled with Constantine, and the pair were often shown with the cross.[52]

When Helena died, around 330,[53] she was already associated with monuments in Rome, Bethlehem and Jerusalem, and memorialised on coins – and perhaps in the Augustaion at Constantinople – as a state symbol.[54] In contrast, few monuments connected with the women of the Constantinian house whose lives overlapped Helena's are now recognised; while it would be valuable to know how Helena's female relatives responded to her initiatives – and whether or not they participated in the creation of Helena-as-metaphor – evidence of their commissions is slight.[55]

Fausta, Constantine's wife from 307 until 326, when she was murdered and placed under *damnatio memoriae*, was named augusta along with Helena in 324.[56] Coins struck in her honour resemble Helena's, though Fausta is usually celebrated as the 'safety and hope' rather than the 'security' of the republic.[57] The *damnatio memoriae*, however, erased her from public consciousness as an agent of Constantinian state solidarity; that her role was absorbed by Helena is suggested by a statue, standing on an inscribed base, erected by the people of Surrentum (Sorrento): originally honouring Fausta, after 326 the words FAUSTA and UXORI were rubbed out, and replaced by the words HELENA and MATRI.[58]

Fausta's daughter Constantina was luckier: she survived until 354 and has been immortalised by what is now called Sta Costanza, in Rome.[59] This small, centrally planned building, apparently conceived from the outset as Constantina's mausoleum, was built alongside a cemetery basilica dedicated to Sant'Agnese on Constantina's estate on the Via Nomentana, probably between 337 and 351.[60] The combination closely recalls the complex at Sts Marcellinus and Peter – both were built on imperial estates, both combined a cemetery basilica with a centrally planned mausoleum with interior niches, and both mausolea had double-apsed vestibules – and it seems likely that Helena's granddaughter was emulating her example. As observed by Eugene Kleinbauer, the most notable difference between the two sites is that Helena's mausoleum is 'single-shell' while Sta Costanza is 'double-shell'; he suggests that Constantina's builder may have been inspired by the rotunda at the Holy Sepulchre.[61] If so, Constantina was not only hoping to benefit from the sanctity of her architectural model; she was also commemorating her family's connection with the sites of the Holy Land, and may even have been associating herself with Helena's pilgrimage.[62]

Helena's great-granddaughter (and Constantina's niece) Constantia married Gratian, the son of Valentinian I and his first wife Marina, in 374.[63] Valentinian began a new dynastic line which was continued by the children of his second wife Justina,[64] but, as Galla Placidia's commissions have already demonstrated, the link with the Constantinian house established by the marriage of Gratian and Constantia was not forgotten by following generations.

In 379, Theodosius I was named augustus; in 383, his (first) wife Aelia Flavia Flaccilla was elevated to the rank of augusta.[65] Her change in status was widely known: it was recorded in histories and commemorated by the issue of a new series of coins that were minted until her death in 387.[66] Flaccilla was the first woman to be named augusta since Helena and Fausta in 324, and the designation was not universally popular: in the eastern half of the empire, the imperial women who followed Flaccilla retained the designation augusta, but the reintroduction of the title was apparently resented in the west and is not found on coins minted there until c.425, over 40 years later.[67] In this atmosphere the reintroduction of the title is unlikely to have been incidental; as Kenneth Holum has already noted, 'Flaccilla's new rank must have impressed contemporaries as a dramatic innovation and as reversion to prestigious Constantinian practice'.[68]

Theodosius had founded a new dynasty; it was only after Flaccilla's death that he established lineage ties with the old Constantinian house through his second marriage, to Galla, daughter of Valentinian I and Justina (see Figure 1). One reason for his restoration of the title, and for its numismatic commemoration, was, however, evidently the same as Constantine's had been fifty-five years earlier: Flaccilla, named augusta in the same year as her son, Arcadius, was designated augustus, was portrayed as an embodiment of dynastic stability.[69] As important, the reintroduction of the title augusta was a deliberate evocation of the past, with Helena almost certainly the intended point of reference.[70] By the time the designation augusta was accepted in the west, the implied association between this rank and its first Christian holder, Helena, had become sufficiently overt in the east that, between 420 and 422, coins commemorating the augusta Aelia Pulcheria depicted a victory-figure holding a jewelled cross, in reference to the gemmed cross sent at this time to Jerusalem to commemorate the true cross found by Helena.[71]

Coins were not, so far as we know, designed by the women they commemorated. But imperial women themselves also drew parallels with Helena, and they did this in a different way: by replicating her types of architectural commissions and by replicating her acts.

There are a surprising number of examples. We have, for example, records of more female imperial commissions in Syro-Palestine. The earliest of these – after Helena's of course – was by Aelia Eudoxia (wife of Arcadius and daughter-in-law of Flaccilla). She sent a plan, marble, columns and money to Gaza in 402, to build a church 'shaped like a cross' that was in the end called, after her, the Eudoxiana.[72] Like Helena, too, her statue was erected in the Augustaion; its base still exists, and sits in the grounds of Hagia Sophia.[73]

About a quarter of a century later – sometime after her return to Ravenna from Constantinople in 424/5 – Galla Placidia commissioned Sta Croce and the adjacent chapel of S. Lorenzo in Ravenna.[74] The chapel survives; though the augusta was ultimately buried in Rome, it was probably originally intended as her mausoleum, the designation by which it is now familiarly known.[75] Sta Croce has largely perished,[76] but its dedication is an obvious reference to the true cross discovered by Helena; we may also see in the complex, composed of a basilican church with an attached centrally planned mausoleum, a reference to Helena's complex at Sts Marcellinus and Peter.

That Galla Placidia was consciously associating herself with Helena is rendered abundantly clear by her embellishment of Helena's chapel, Sta Croce in Gerusalemme, in the Sessorian Palace in Rome. Sometime before 438, Galla Placidia funded mosaics, in the name of herself and her two living children, in the chapel; though these are now lost, the inscription was recorded: 'May the kings of the earth and all peoples, leaders, and all judges of earth praise the name of the Lord. Valentinian, Placidia, and Honoria, augusti, have paid their vow to the Holy Church Hierusalem.'[77] Whatever the mosaics depicted, the inscription documents the deliberate association of Galla Placidia, and her children, with a building of Helena's. Like her mosaics at S. Giovanni in Ravenna, these linked Galla Placidia and her family with the Constantinian house; but unlike the Ravenna mosaics, those at Sta Croce in Gerusalemme appealed to Helena.

At about the same time, in 438, Aelia Eudokia (wife of Theodosius II and daughter-in-law of Eudoxia) herself followed Helena's footsteps to Jerusalem, where she stayed with Melania the Younger in the monastery on the Mount of Olives, up the hill from Helena's church, the Eleona, and attended the dedication of a shrine to St Stephen, whose relics had been discovered in 415.[78] Eudokia was the first augusta to travel to Palestine on pilgrimage since Helena; though the association was not expressed by contemporary chroniclers, it is almost unthinkable that the connection was lost on Eudokia and her entourage.[79] In any event, after her return to Constantinople in 439, bearing relics, like Helena before her was by then believed to have done,[80] Eudokia had an image painted in a now-unknown church that apparently showed her praying at Christ's tomb in Jerusalem; depending on its location, such an image would have conveyed a more or less public visual link with Helena.[81] Though no other early augusta travelled to Jerusalem, the physical emulation of Helena evinced by Eudokia's pilgrimage is perhaps not entirely isolated: Sozomen's account of Aelia Pulcheria's excavations around the shrine of St Thyrsos, where she unearthed relics of the 40 martyrs of Sebaste sometime between 434 and 446, suggests to suspicious modern minds that Pulcheria staged the discovery in such a way as to parallel Helena's invention of the true cross.[82]

The implicit affiliations between imperial women and Helena suggested by this chain of commissions and acts was, in 451, finally and officially recognised by men: Aelia Pulcheria was acclaimed the 'New Helena' by the Council at Chalcedon.[83] Henceforth, the verbal association of imperial women with Helena would continue intermittently throughout the remainder of the Byzantine period.

At about the same time that Helena-as-symbol entered the male rhetorical vocabulary, however, women stopped evoking her memory through monuments: there are few 'Helena commissions' after the mid-fifth century. This is not because aristocratic women stopped funding buildings, and it is not because matronage chains ceased to be important: the Anicia Juliana inscriptions document both well into the sixth century.[84] But Helena ceased to be the primary legitimising figure invoked by imperial women; increasingly from 431, when the Council of Ephesus declared in favour of the Theotokos, her place seems to have been taken by the Virgin Mary.[85]

The matrix of values that Helena came to represent – upholder of traditional Roman social codes, mother of the Constantinian house, commissioner of public buildings, and representative of élite female piety – gave validity to late Roman women within a female structure that was based on continuity rather than disruption: Helena provided a model for women who had little alternative but to act from within acceptable social roles. From the time of her death until the middle of the fifth century, memories of Helena were evoked to buttress family continuity and dynastic stability, on the one hand, and the appropriation of sanctity by élite women, on the other. While the former was a concern inherited from imperial Rome, the latter was a new issue and it did not remain Helena's sole preserve for long.

Evocation of Helena in the imperial promotion of family and stability had several sides: it furthered the long-standing ideological reading of women as exemplifications of the honour of men;[86] it supported an equally venerable commitment to family; and it advanced specific lineage claims.[87] The first and last of these have been demonstrated especially in the coins of Helena and her female successors, and in Galla Placidia's various commissions. The implication of Helena in the late Roman and early Byzantine celebration of the idea of family is obvious from her role as Constantine's mother, but it is worth remarking that while the idea of Helena as mother tied into certain early Christian patterns, it conflicted with the ascetic life style championed by other women with sufficient means to be independent of family and husband.

Discussions of both issues, the tightly bound categories of women and family, and the emerging interest in asceticism and virginity, are numerous. It has been observed that most expressions of women's religiosity written by males in late antiquity confined women within traditional societal roles: women were to marry, and if they did not marry men, they married Christ.[88] Similarly, nearly all of the 'good' women who appear in the lives of male saints are firmly entrenched in a family structure; they appear as wives, occasionally daughters, and most frequently as mothers.[89] The rhetorical strategies of these texts express male concerns, and the binding of women to family was not, of course, a purely Christian phenomenon – it was encouraged by the legal system and had its roots in imperial Roman tradition – but the relationship between the ways in which women were portrayed in religious texts and the ways in which most real women could express religion seems, in this instance, to be worth signalling. This continuity has been chronicled with great sophistication by Caroline Bynum, who has noted that some of the most familiar patterns of male religiosity, reversal and inversion, did not appear as possibilities in many women's lives.[90] They were certainly not possibilities in Helena's life, nor in the lives of any but one of the augustae who followed her, whose status depended on becoming, like Helena, mothers. Among the augustae considered here, only the porphyrogenita Aelia Pulcheria escaped this circle, and it was she, of course, who practised virginity – in this context, an inversion role – and advocated a different image of the mother: the virgin mother, the Theotokos.[91]

Helena also had supplied the model for élite female appropriation of sanctity. Her mausoleum, next to the relic church of Sts Marcellinus and Peter, allowed her to be proximate to the saints yet separate from the often anonymous graves that covered the floor and grounds of the basilica; this spatial organisation, in which sanctity by association and exclusivity coexist, evidently appealed to later imperial women: Constantina and Galla Placidia borrowed the formula.[92] Helena's association with the sites and the most holy relic of Christianity was also absorbed, most overtly by Eudokia and Galla Placidia. In the fifth century, however, imperial women were increasingly buried in the dynastic mausolea in Rome and Constantinople,[93] and Helena's discovery of the true cross had barely achieved common currency when a new, and more radical, model of female sanctity was authorised by the Council of Ephesus.

The 'Helena commissions' were a relatively short-lived phenomenon, in large part because they promoted a particular fusion of old Roman traditions with new Christian ideals that was soon superseded. The Helena created to accommodate this fusion was not exclusively the property of women; but only aristocratic women communicated their memories of Helena through mimesis and through monuments: men could appropriate Helena, but they could not and did not imitate her actions or her commissions. The women who have been the subjects of this study relied on Helena in their construction of a past in ways defined by gender, though with the resources defined by class: the monuments evoking Helena – and the overlapping monuments evoking family – constructed part of their public personae. The commissions that insistently hark back to Helena, or to female family relationships, assume, however, a public memory prompted by spatial relationships, images and inscriptions: one, that is, that has relatively little affinity with the types of knowledge preserved by the writers of books. The monuments, or some of them, remain; but the public memory addressed by the women considered here has disappeared.

NOTES

1 This chapter was delivered as 'Gendered memories: imperial Byzantine matronage in the 4th to 6th centuries' to the Byzantine Seminar *Gender in Byzantium: Still an Issue?* at the Institute of Classical Studies, London (2 June 1992). I thank the organisers, Charles Barber and Liz James, and members of the seminar for an unusually enlightening discussion after the talk; I am grateful to Mary Skinner and Chris Wickham for additional comments. During the preparation of the paper, I held a Senior Research Fellowship awarded by the Getty Grant Foundation, and it is a pleasure to thank that Foundation as well. My final acknowledgement is to a group of students who nearly a decade ago asked to know more about Byzantine empresses: Charles Diehl did not suffice, and this is the result.

2 Though a brief account of the development of the true cross narrative and Helena's reported building activity appeared in E.D. Hunt, *Holy Land Pilgrimage in the Later Roman Empire AD 312–460* (Oxford, 1982), 28–49, the first systematic study of Helena and the legends that later accrued around her was published only in 1989: J.W. Drijvers, *Helena Augusta: Waarheid en Legende* (Groningen); this appeared, slightly revised, in English as *Helena Augusta: The Mother of Constantine the Great and the Legend of Her Finding of the True Cross* (Leiden, 1992). As Drijvers incorporates virtually all earlier bibliography and contemporary sources, I have, whenever possible, simply cited *Helena* in the following notes. On Helena and the *vitae* of Constantine, see F. Winkelmann, 'Das hagiographische Bild Konstantins I. in mittel-byzantinischer Zeit', in V. Vavřinek, ed., *Beiträge zur byzantinischen Geschichte im 9.-11. Jahrhundert* (Prague, 1978), 179–203, and A. Kazhdan, 'Constantin imaginaire. Byzantine legends of the ninth century about Constantine the Great', *B* 57 (1987), 196–250.

3 In addition to the articles cited in the preceding note, see P. Magdalino, ed., *New Constantines: The Rhythm of Imperial Renewal in Byzantium, 4th–13th Centuries* (Aldershot, 1994).

4 This was not due to inability to read or write. For comments on literacy among a circle of women closely related to those whom we shall be discussing, see P. Brown, *The Body and Society: Men, Women and Sexual Renunciation in Early Christianity* (New York, 1988), 369–70. More generally, see M. Mullett, 'Writing in Early Medieval Byzantium', in R. McKitterick, ed., *The Uses of Literacy in Early Mediaeval Europe* (Cambridge, 1990), 156–85, esp. 156–7 and ns 3–4; A. Weyl Carr, 'Women and monasticism in Byzantium', *Byzantinische Forschungen* 9 (1985), 1–15, esp. 8–9.

5 For late antique legislation about women, see esp. J. Beaucamp, *Le Statut de la femme à Byzance (4e–7e siècle) I: Le droit impérial* (Paris, 1990); H. Saradi-Mendelovici, 'A contribution to the study of the Byzantine notarial formulas: The *Infirmitas Sexus* of women and the *Sc. Velleianum*', *Byzantinische Zeitschrift* 83 (1990), 72–90; J. Herrin, '"Femina Byzantina": The council of Trullo on women', *DOP* 46 (1992), 97–105; G. Clark, *Women in Late Antiquity: Pagan and Christian Lifestyles* (Oxford, 1993), 6–62. For hagiography, see J. Seiber, *Early*

Byzantine Urban Saints (Oxford, 1977), 26–37; S.A. Harvey, 'Women in Early Byzantine hagiography: reversing the story', in L. Coon, K. Haldane and E. Summers, eds, *'That Gentle Strength': Historical Perspectives on Women and Christianity* (Charlottesville, 1990), 36–59. For theological texts, see Averil Cameron, 'Virginity as metaphor: women and the rhetoric of early Christianity', in Averil Cameron, ed., *History as Text: The Writing of Ancient History* (London, 1989), 184–205, and the references in notes 8 and 9 below.

6 For instance, J. Herrin, 'In search of Byzantine women: three avenues of approach', in Averil Cameron and A. Kuhrt, eds, *Images of Women in Antiquity* (London, 1983), 167–89, esp. 168. To paraphrase Caroline Bynum, the texts on which we must rely and many of the scholars who have used them look *at* women, they do not look *with* them: 'Women's stories, women's symbols: a critique of Victor Turner's theory of liminality', in R.L. Moore and F.E. Reynolds, eds, *Anthropology and the Study of Religion* (Chicago, 1984), 105–25, esp. 109, 117.

7 On an apparent exception (from c.203) and the problems it immediately caused – and continued to cause – for male editors, see B.D. Shaw, 'The passion of Perpetua', *Past and Present* 139 (1993), 3–45. From the ninth century on, an increasing number of texts written by women have been preserved: see esp. A.E. Laiou, 'Observations on the life and ideology of Byzantine women', *Byzantinische Forschungen* 9 (1985), 59–102.

8 See, for instance, S. Elm, 'Evagrius Ponticus' *Sententiae ad Virginem*', *DOP* 45 (1991), 97–120; Bynum, 'Women's stories'; Clark, *Women in Late Antiquity*, 2; Averil Cameron, 'Early Christianity and the discourse of female desire', in L.J. Archer, S. Fischler and M. Wyke, eds, *Women in Ancient Societies. An Illusion of the Night* (Houndsmills, 1994), 152–68, esp. 153, 165.

9 See esp. K. Cooper, 'Insinuations of womanly influence: an aspect of the Christianization of the Roman aristocracy', *Journal of Roman Studies* 82 (1992), 150–64. This is not, of course, a phenomenon restricted to Christian authors: for the Julio-Claudian period, see S. Fischler, 'Social stereotypes and historical analysis: the case of the imperial women at Rome', in Archer, Fischler and Wyke, eds, *Women in Ancient Societies*, 115–33. The fundamental discussion about the rhetorical strategies of hagiography remains E. Patlagean, 'Ancient Byzantine hagiography and social history', in S. Wilson, ed., *Saints and their Cults: Studies in Religious Sociology, Folklore and History* (Cambridge, 1983), 101–21 (orig. published in French in 1968).

10 See, for instance, R. van Bremen, 'Women and wealth', in Cameron and Kuhrt, eds, *Images of Women in Antiquity*, 223–42.

11 M.B. Flory, '*Sic exempla parantur*: Livia's shrine to Concordia and the Porticus Liviae', *Historia* 33 (1984), 309–30, esp. 319. On public activities of Roman women, see also S. Dixon, 'A family business: women's role in patronage and politics at Rome 80–44 B.C.', *Classica et Mediaevalia* 34 (1983), 91–112; on the political implications of Concordia in the Roman world, B. Levick, 'Concordia at Rome', in R.A.G. Carson and C.M. Kraay, eds, *Scripta Nummaria Romana. Essays presented to Humphrey Sutherland* (London, 1978), 217–33.

12 *PLRE* 2 (1980), 888–9; S.I. Oost, *Galla Placidia Augusta, A Biographical Essay* (Chicago, 1968).

13 *Sancto ac beatissimo apostolo Iohanni euangelistae Galla Placidia augusta cum filio suo Placido Valentiniano augusto et filia sua Iusta Grata Honoria augusta liverationis periculum* [sic] *maris votum solvent*: recorded by Agnellus, *Liber pontificalis ecclesiae Ravennatis* 42, ed. O. Holder-Egger, in *Monumenta Germaniae Historica, Scriptores rerum langobardicarum et italicarum sace. VI–IX* (Hanover, 1878), 307. Galla Placidia's son Valentinian (III) was born in 419 and made augustus in 425; her daughter Honoria was probably born 417/18 but it is unclear when she received the title augusta (the date suggested in *PLRE* 2, 568, is based on another inscription recorded from this church, which must, however, be incorrect: see note 17 below). A similar inscription was recorded in the sixteenth century by Rossi (see following note). On the church, see also Oost, *Galla Placidia*, 273–5; R. Krautheimer, *Early Christian and Byzantine Architecture*, 4th ed., rev. by R. Krautheimer and S. Ćurčić (London, 1986), 184–5, both with earlier bibliography. For another imperial ex-voto church, see note 72 below.

14 G. Rossi, *Historiarum Ravennatum libri decem* (Venice, 1572), 85–6; C. Davis-Weyer, tr., *Early Medieval Art 300–1150* (Englewood Cliffs, 1971), 16–17. The mosaics are lost; Rossi's is the only complete description.

15 Davis-Weyer, *Early Medieval Art*, 16 n. 21, suggests that *Divus Valentinianus* refers to Valentinian II, Galla Placidia's uncle, who ruled as emperor of the west from 375 until 392. The arrangement of the portraits in the apse is hierarchical, and Valentinian's location – foremost of the left-arch portraits, and thus pendant to Constantine the Great on the right arch – seems to me better to suit Galla Placidia's grandfather, who was more important in terms of family line (and in terms of court politics) than her uncle.

16 Assuming, along with all other commentators, that the second *Divus Constantinus* is a misreading for Constantius. For the identification as Constantius III (Galla Placidia's second husband, who died in 421), see Davis-Weyer, *Early Medieval Art*, 16 n. 23; Constantius II (Gratian's father-in-law, and son of Constantine) is less likely given the figure's location after Gratian himself.

17 Only Rossi (see note 14 above) records the inscription: 'Close to the choir bench at the right in the outermost position were: *Dominus Theodosius and Domina Eudokia*; at the left: *Dominus Arcadius and Domina Eudoxia Augusta*.' On this basis, the church and its inscriptions have sometimes been dated after 439, the year in which Licinia Eudoxia was named augusta after her marriage to Valentinian III in 437 (see *PLRE* 2, 130, 568, for the repercussions). But surely there has been a transcription error: Licinia Eudoxia is the only figure given the imperial title (though Theodosius was named augustus in 402, and Eudokia named augusta in 423), and had the mosaic been set after Licinia Eudoxia's marriage in 437, she would not have been shown with her parental family but with her husband, Galla Placidia's son.

18 She also stressed the family's Constantinian base in a letter to

Theodosius II discussed by Oost, *Galla Placidia*, 289.

19 See Oost, *Galla Placidia*, 269–70; Krautheimer, *Early Christian and Byzantine Architecture*, 87–9. For discussion of late fourth-century interest in Paul, see J.M. Huskinson, *Concordia Apostolorum: Christian Propaganda at Rome in the Fourth and Fifth Centuries, a Study in Early Christian Iconography and Iconology* (Oxford, 1982), esp. 35–6 on S. Paolo fuori le mura.

20 See, for instance, the essays in Magdalino, *New Constantines*.

21 In addition to the chains of matronage noted below, the female members of a family were apparently sometimes presented in a group portrait: e.g. according to the *Parastaseis*, a statue of Aelia Eudoxia (wife of Arcadius) with her daughter Pulcheria 'and two other daughters' – presumably Arcadia and Marina – stood in Constantinople. Averil Cameron and J. Herrin, eds, *Constantinople in the Early Eighth Century: The Parastaseis Syntomoi Chronikai* (Leiden, 1984), 92–3.

22 See J. Wortley, 'The Trier Ivory reconsidered', *Greek, Roman, and Byzantine Studies* 21 (1980), 384–5; Alan Cameron, 'The empress and the poet: paganism and politics at the court of Theodosios II', *Yale Classical Studies* 27 (1982), 278.

23 *Anthologia Palatina* I, 12; W.R. Paton, tr., *The Greek Anthology*, Loeb Classical Library (Cambridge, Mass., and London, 1916); P. Waltz ed., (Paris, 1928), I, 18. See also C. Mango and I. Ševčenko, 'Remains of the Church of St Polyeuktos at Constantinople', *DOP* 15 (1961), 244; R. Janin, *La géographie de l'église byzantine III: Les églises et les monastères* (Paris, 1969), 124–6.

24 Licinia Eudoxia (422–*c*.462) married Valentinian III in 437 and was made augusta in 439; after Valentinian's death in 455 she was away from Constantinople until 461: *PLRE* 2, 410–12. Valentinian is not mentioned in the inscription.

25 Placidia's 'blessed [but unnamed] husband' is mentioned in the *Anthology* inscription, and these are the years when she was in Constantinople and married to Anicius Olybrius: see *PLRE* 2, 796–8 (Olybrius), 887 (Placidia).

26 See *PLRE* 2, 635–6.

27 See Mango and Ševčenko, 'St Polyeuktos', 243–4; M. Harrison, *A Temple for Byzantium. The Discovery and Excavation of Anicia Juliana's Palace-church in Istanbul* (London, 1989), 33.

28 It is worth stressing that Anicia Juliana could have traced her lineage back to Theodosios (and hence, ultimately, to Constantine) through either the male or female sides of her heritage (see Figure 1), and that all of the women involved in the St Euphemia and St Polyeuktos projects had illustrious husbands: the female line was commemorated for reasons other than familial status. It is unlikely that shifts in Anicia Juliana's family power base made references to the male line less pressing, for the inscription also records an image of Constantine. Harrison, *Temple*, 36–40, makes much of Anicia Juliana's need to respond to the rise of Justin I; for other speculations, see G. Fowden, 'Constantine, Silvester and the Church of S. Polyeuctus in Constantinople', *Journal of Roman Archaeology* 7 (1994), 274–84; and C. Milner, 'The image of the rightful

ruler: Anicia Juliana's Constantine mosaic in the church of Hagios Polyeuktos', in Magdalino, *New Constantines*, 73–81.

29 *Anthologia Palatina* I, 10, lines 1–10; Harrison, tr., *Temple*, 33.

30 *PLRE* 1 (1971), 410–11, is not entirely accurate; see instead Drijvers, *Helena*, 9–19. We do not know whether Helena was born, or later became, Christian. On the conversion of Roman women to Christianity, see P. Brown, 'Aspects of the Christianization of the Roman aristocracy', *Journal of Roman Studies* 51 (1961), 1–11; repr. in Brown, *The Age of Saint Augustine* (New York, 1971), 161–82; with the more cautious remarks in A. Yarbrough, 'Christianization in the fourth century: the example of Roman women', *Church History* 45 (1976), 149–65; M.R. Salzmann, 'Aristocratic women: Conductors of Christianity in the fourth century', *Helios* 16/2 (1989), 207–20; and esp. Cooper, 'Insinuations'.

31 *Vita Constantini* III.47: *PG* 20.1107–8. So too Eusebius's continuator, Sozomen: *Ecclesiastical History* II.2 (ed. J. Bidez and G.C. Hansen [Berlin, 1960], 51).

32 See Drijvers, *Helena*, 30–3.

33 Ibid., 31–3, 74–5, on the evidence of the *Liber pontificalis*, argues that Constantine alone was responsible for this complex; F.W. Deichmann and A. Tschira, 'Das Mausoleum der Kaiserin Helena und die Basilika der heiligen Marcellinus und Petrus an der Via Labinicana vor Rom', *Jahrbuch des deutschen archäologischen Instituts* 72 (1957), 44–110, esp. 76–7, note Helena's gifts to the building and suggest that she was involved with the construction. The votive gifts that Constantine presented to the church are recorded in the *Liber pontificalis* as 'both for the love of his mother and to honour the saints', and the most recent commentator on the text concluded that 'Constantine was far less interested in the martyrs than in honouring his mother's memory' (*The Book of the Pontiffs (Liber Pontificalis)*, tr. R. Davis [Liverpool, 1989], xxv; *pace* Drijvers, *Helena*, 74–5 n. 10). Whatever Helena's measure of responsibility for the complex, her association with it is clear, and her involvement at some level would not have been exceptional at the time (see note 10 above). The building complex, too, is unexceptional in context: family mausolea were a commonplace of aristocratic Rome, and cemetery churches on non-public land were the norm under Constantine (see R. Krautheimer, *Three Christian Capitals. Topography & Politics* [Berkeley, 1983], 6–40); the linkage of mausoleum and church finds a roughly contemporary general analogue in the Church of the Holy Sepulchre in Jerusalem and the slightly later Holy Apostles complex in Constantinople. The mausoleum itself finds imperial analogues at Split and, apparently, in Constantinople: see C. Mango, 'Constantine's mausoleum and the translation of relics', *Byzantinische Zeitschrift* 83 (1990), 51–62.

34 See Drijvers, *Helena*, 31–3, 45–8; on Helena's burial, perhaps in a porphyry sarcophagus that may have been originally intended for Constantine, see ibid., 74–5, with note 33 above.

35 Deichmann and Tschira, 'Das Mausoleum', 68, 77–8.

36 All are noted by Drijvers, *Helena*, 31 n. 34, 53 n. 46, 75 n. 15.

37 Elevation to the rank of augusta had been quite common for imperial women in the Roman empire from the time of Livia (the first augusta,

who, Tacitus tells us, was willed her husband's name in feminine form). After Helena and Fausta, the title was dropped until 383. In Byzantium thereafter, it was normally given to imperial wives only after they had borne a child, or to imperial women 'born in the purple' (e.g. Pulcheria): see D. Missiou, 'Über die institutionelle Rolle der byzantinischen Kaiserin', *JÖB* 32/2 (1982), 489–98.

38 For the coins, see Drijvers, *Helena*, 41–4; Eusebius, *Vita Constantini* III.47 (*PG* 20.1107–8); Sozomen, *Ecclesiastical History* II.2 (ed. Bidez and Hansen, 51). Fausta's appearance on coins was noted by neither Eusebius nor Sozomen.

39 Discussion and references in Drijvers, *Helena*, 42, 44–5 n. 26, and I. Kalavrezou, 'Images of the mother: when the Virgin Mary became *Meter Theou*', *DOP* 44 (1990), 165–72, esp. 166. Both note that the legends on Fausta's coins commemorate safety and hope (SALUS ET SPEC REIPUBLICAE). The use of women to convey such sentiments follows imperial Roman practice: see Flory, '*Sic exempta parantur*'; Fischler, 'Social stereotypes'; and Cooper, 'Insinuations'.

40 Similarly, after Constantine's death in 337, when the sons of his father's second (?) wife, Theodora, contested the claims of Constantine's own sons to the throne, a posthumous coin of Helena was minted with the legend PAX PUBLICA: see Drijvers, *Helena*, 43–4.

41 See Fischler, 'Social stereotypes', esp. 129.

42 Kenneth Holum has argued that her journey is not only significant as an early pilgrimage, but was also the first time that an imperial woman had ever travelled without an emperor or troops on what was essentially an imperial progress to the provinces: 'Hadrian and St Helena: imperial travel and the origins of Christian Holy Land pilgrimage', in R. Ousterhout, ed., *The Blessings of Pilgrimage* (Urbana, 1990), 67–81, esp. 75–6.

43 In Ambrose's funeral oration for Theodosius: Drijvers, *Helena*, 95; on the development and diffusion of the legend, ibid., 79–180 (83–90 on the possibility that the cross was found during the reign of Constantine). For additional discussion of Ambrose's motivations, see E.T. Brett, 'Early Constantine legends: a study in propaganda', *Byzantine Studies/ Etudes byzantines* 10/1 (1983), 62–6, and F.E. Consolino, 'Il significato del *Inventio Crucis* nel *de obitu Theodosii*', *Annali della facoltà di lettere e filosofia* 5 (1984), 161–80.

44 *Vita Constantini* III.41, 43 (*PG* 20.1101–6). Drijvers, discounting Eusebius, attributes both to Constantine, though he admits that Helena might have 'inspected the progress' and 'endowed them with suitable gifts': *Helena*, 63–4. Drijvers rightly notes that the Bordeaux pilgrim (333) attributed all of the Palestine churches to Constantine; his argument that 'The foundation of churches must be seen as part of the policy of the Christianizing of the empire. This policy was initiated and executed by Constantine, which makes him solely responsible for the actual foundation of the Christian churches' (64) is less compelling: whether or not Constantine actively pursued a policy of Christianisation, and whether or not the foundation of churches was part of some such strategy (for counterindications in Rome, see Krautheimer, *Three*

Christian Capitals, 7–40), the conflation of policy with its execution on the ground is unsound. E.J. Yarnold, 'Who planned the churches at the Christian Holy Places in the Holy Land?', *Studia Patristica* 18 (1985), 105–9, suggests on tenuous grounds that Constantine had even less to do with the Holy Land sites than Eusebius suggests.

45 *Itinerarium Egeriae* 25, 9: eds A. Franceschini and R. Weber, Corpus Christianorum, series Latina 175 (Turnhout, 1965), 71. The relevant phrase reads 'quam Constantinus sub presentia matris suae'.

46 Rufinus of Aquileia's *Church History* is itself a condensed (though modified) version of Eusebius, augmented by two books covering the intervening years 324–95, which may follow a (lost) adaptation by Gelasios of Caesarea: *ODB* 3, 1815–16. He attributes the Holy Sepulchre to Helena in book 10.7–8: see Drijvers, *Helena*, 79–80. Sokrates, *Ecclesiastical History*, I.17 (*PG* 67.119–20).

47 R. Krautheimer, *Rome, Profile of a City, 312–1308* (Princeton, 1980), 24; Krautheimer, *Three Christian Capitals*, 23; Krautheimer, *Early Christian and Byzantine Architecture*, 50; C. Petri, *Roma christiana. Recherches sur l'église de Rome, son organisation, sa politique, son idéologie de Miltiades à Sixte III (311–440)* I (Rome, 1976), 14–17.

48 Drijvers, *Helena*, 33–4, who questions the assertion in the *Liber pontificalis*; Krautheimer (*Three Christian Capitals*, 129 n. 16), however, sees 'no reason to doubt the tradition of Helena's having brought to her Roman palace the relic of the cross from her pilgrimage to the Holy Land'. On the names of the chapel, see Drijvers, *Helena*, 34 n. 43; Krautheimer, *Three Christian Capitals*, 156 n. 22; Petri, *Roma christiana*, 15.

49 Krautheimer, *Rome*, 58; Krautheimer, *Three Christian Capitals*, 118–19.

50 *Chronicon Paschale* 328: ed. L. Dindorf (Bonn, 1832), 529; trs, M. and M. Whitby, *Chronicon Paschale 284–628 AD* (Liverpool, 1989), 16. On the Augustaion, see also *ODB* 1, 232.

51 Statues of Constantine and Helena in the forum were visible to the authors; a porphyry statue of Helena, with bronze statues of Constantine and Fausta, is 'preserved up to the present day': Cameron and Herrin, *Parastaseis*, 78–9, 118–21; cf. note 58 below. It is unclear whether other images of Helena were still *in situ*: see ibid., 70–3 (three statues of Helena – one porphyry, one silver, one ivory – among those removed by Justinian from Hagia Sophia and distributed about the city; 'those who know the foregoing will find a good number of them if they go round the city and look for them'), 134–5 (statues of Constantine, Helena, and Constantine's sons, enthroned, at the Philadelphion: the statues of the sons, at least, seem to have survived until the fifteenth century [see ibid., 247]). Others are even more tenuous: ibid., 94–5 (statues of Constantine and Helena, with a cross, on the roof of the Milion), 126–7 ('likenesses' of Constantine and Helena holding a cross, in the Forum Bovis), 128–9 (representations of Constantine and Helena, with Christ and the Virgin, in the Church of the Theotokos at Kontaria).

52 For extant statues that have been identified as Helena, see Drijvers, *Helena*, 189–94.

53 Ibid., 73–6.

54 In addition, one or, following Sozomen, two cities were re-named Helenopolis by Constantine: Ibid., 9–10.

55 Ceiling paintings showing four women, three men, and a number of putti in a grid were found during excavations under the cathedral at Trier in a large structure tentatively identified as the imperial compound; these, dated to around 320 on archaeological evidence, have been sometimes interpreted as portraying Helena and Fausta together with Constantia (Constantine's half-sister) and Helena (wife of Constantine's son Crispus): the literature is summarised in Drijvers, *Helena*, 24–30. Were this interpretation accepted, the paintings would document the projection of female solidarity within the Constantinian house through the public display of images; unfortunately, the identifications are tenuous at best, and have not been accepted in most recent scholarship. The famous letter that Eusebius supposedly sent to Constantia denying her request for a portrait of Christ is also extremely problematic, and probably an eighth-century forgery; I shall therefore not consider it here: see C. Murray, *Rebirth and Afterlife: A Study in the Transmutation of Some Pagan Imagery in Early Christian Funerary Art* (Oxford, 1981), 25–30.

56 *PLRE* 1, 326–7; with the sensible commentary in *Zosimus, New History*, Byzantina Australiensia 2, tr. R.T. Ridley (Sydney, 1982), 152 n. 26, 156 n. 63.

57 See note 39 above.

58 See Drijvers, *Helena*, 49. This casts considerable doubt on the accuracy of the *Parastaseis* identification of two statues as Fausta: Cameron and Herrin, *Parastaseis*, 64–5, 118–21.

59 *PLRE* 1, 222.

60 On the cemetery basilica of Sant'Agnese, see Krautheimer, *Early Christian and Byzantine Architecture*, 52–4; and F. Tolotti, 'Le basiliche cimiteriali con deambulatorio del suburbio romano: Questione ancora aperta', *Römische Mitteilungen* 89 (1982), 153–211, esp. 164. On Sta Costanza, see H. Stern, 'Les mosaiques de l'église de Sainte-Costance à Rome', *DOP* 12 (1958), 159–218, esp. 159–66; and Krautheimer, *Rome*, 25–6. D.J. Stanley, 'New discoveries at Santa Costanza', *DOP* 48 (1994), 257–61, has confirmed the existence of a building beneath Sta Costanza, which is physically bonded with the substructure of Sta Agnese; his assertion that this structure 'was undoubtedly still in use when Constantina died' (260) is not, however, substantiated by the material presented in this preliminary report. If fuller publication or excavation demonstrates that Sta Costanza post-dates the mid-fourth century, we will have valuable evidence of later emulation of Helena in Rome.

61 W.E. Kleinbauer, 'The double-shell tetraconch building at Perge in Pamphylia and the origin of the architectural genus', *DOP* 41 (1987), 277–93, esp. 290.

62 Though not about Sta Costanza, see the pertinent remarks in R. Ousterhout, 'Loca Sancta and the architectural response to pilgrimage', in Ousterhout, *Blessings of Pilgrimage*, 108–24.

63 Constantia, the daughter of Constantina's brother, Constantius II, and his wife Faustina: *PLRE* 1, 221.

64 Justina is probably best known for her battles with St Ambrose in Milan: *PLRE* 1, 488–9. She may have been buried in the chapel of Sant'Aquilino attached to San Lorenzo in Milan, a centrally planned structure with alternating rectangular and curved interior niches and a double-apsed vestibule that Dale Kinney has linked with Helena's mausoleum in Rome: D. Kinney, '"Capella Reginae": S. Aquilino in Milan', *Marsyas* 15 (1970/2), 13–35, esp. 31–5. See also Krautheimer, *Three Christian Capitals*, 150–1 n. 40, and note 33 above.

65 *PLRE* 1, 341–2.

66 Discussion in K. Holum, *Theodosian Empresses. Women and Imperial Dominion in Late Antiquity* (Berkeley, 1982), 32–4, though his suggestion that Flaccilla's coin portraits were more 'imperial' than Helena's is true only to the same extent that Theodosius's coin portraits were more 'imperial' than Constantine's: i.e. both Helena and Constantine wear diadems; both Flaccilla and Theodosius are more elaborately decorated.

67 Discussion in Holum, ibid., 127–30.

68 Ibid., 31.

69 See notes 37 and 66 above.

70 See Holum, *Theodosian Empresses*, 30–1. Theodosius seems to have made other attempts to link himself with the Constantinian house: e.g. M.J. Johnson, 'On the burial places of the Theodosian dynasty', *B* 61 (1991), 330–9, esp. 330–1, notes that although Theodosius died in Milan, his body was carried to Constantinople to be interred in the mausoleum of Constantine.

71 Fausta, whether or not she was Christian, was for obvious reasons forgotten in this equation. On Pulcheria's coinage, see Holum, *Theodosian Empresses*, 109–10; on the cross sent to Jerusalem, see K.J. Holum, 'Pulcheria's crusade AD 421–22 and the ideology of imperial victory', *Greek, Roman and Byzantine Studies* 18 (1977), 153–72.

72 Like Galla Placidia's S. Giovanni Evangelista in Ravenna, this was an ex-voto church, funded in gratitude for the birth of the future Theodosius II. See Mark the Deacon, *Life of Porphyry*, chaps 42–4 (vow), 75–92: ed. Teubner (1895), 37–9, 61–74; tr. G.F. Hill (Oxford, 1913), 52–4, 85–102; citation from chap 75 (ed. Teubner, 62; tr. Hill, 86). The church was perhaps modelled after the Church of the Holy Apostles in Constantinople: Krautheimer, *Early Christian and Byzantine Architecture*, 112, 158. Cf. Holum, *Theodosian Empresses*, 56.

73 C. Mango, 'The Byzantine inscriptions of Constantinople: a bibliographic survey', *American Journal of Archaeology* 55 (1951), 63; C. Mango, *The Brazen House* (Copenhagen, 1959), 56, 59. It was this statue that occasioned the final rift between Eudoxia and John Chrysostom: see Holum, *Theodosian Empresses*, 76–7.

74 Oost, *Galla Placidia*, 275–7.

75 On the chapel, see Krautheimer, *Early Christian and Byzantine Architecture*, 181–2; G. Mackie, 'New light on the so-called St Lawrence panel at the mausoleum of Galla Placidia in Ravenna', *Gesta* 29 (1990), 54–60; G. Mackie, 'The mausoleum of Galla Placidia: a possible occupant', *B* 65 (1995), 396–404. On Galla Placidia's burial in Rome, see Johnson, 'Burial places', 336–8.

76 See Krautheimer, *Early Christian and Byzantine Architecture*, 181–2 and 481 n. 35.
77 See Krautheimer, *Three Christian Capitals*, 156 n. 22; Oost, *Galla Placidia*, 270–1. On Valentinian and Honoria, see note 13 above.
78 Eudokia and Melania had met when the latter visited Constantinople in 436/7: see Hunt, *Holy Land Pilgrimage*, 221–3, 229–32.
79 It has not been lost on modern scholars, who have variously called Eudokia 'a true second Helena' (Wortley, 'Trier ivory', 384) or 'a latter-day Helena' (Holum, *Theodosian Empresses*, 188). In the seventh century, the two augustae were sufficiently affiliated that one source attributed the discovery of the true cross to Eudokia: see H.A. Drake, 'A Coptic version of the discovery of the Holy Sepulchre', *Greek, Roman and Byzantine Studies* 20 (1979), 381–92.
80 See p. 58 above.
81 Discussion in Holum, *Theodosian Empresses*, 187–8. It should be noted, however, that the epigram recording this image is not very explicit: *Anthologia Palatina* I, 105: ed. Waltz I, 40–1.
82 Compare Sozomen, *Ecclesiastical History* II.1 and IX.2 (eds Bidez and Hansen, 47–50, 392–4). Cf. Holum, *Theodosian Empresses*, 137. H.F.H. Zomer, 'The so-called women's gallery in the medieval church: an import from Byzantium', in A. Davids, ed., *The Empress Theophano. Byzantium and the West at the Turn of the First Millennium* (Cambridge, 1995), 290–306, credits Pulcheria with the introduction of galleries in imperial Constantinopolitan churches, in direct emulation of the galleried basilicas in Jerusalem then attributed to Helena; unfortunately, the evidence is very weak.
83 See Holum, *Theodosian Empresses*, 216.
84 The case of Anicia Juliana also indicates that inability to trace family lineage back to Helena did not create this situation: Anicia Juliana could have done so but, so far as we know, did not.
85 See, for instance, J. Herrin, 'Public and private forms of religious commitment among Byzantine women', in Archer, Fischler and Wyke, eds, *Women in Ancient Societies*, 181–203, esp. 196–7; and V. Limberis, *Divine Heiress. The Virgin Mary and the Creation of Christian Constantinople* (London, 1994), though her use of the textual and visual sources is sometimes uncritical.
86 See esp. Cooper, 'Insinuations', and Fischler, 'Social stereotypes'.
87 The latter was no longer possible for members of the imperial family after the death of Anastasius I in 518, when the increasingly tenuous links with the Constantinian house were finally severed with the elevation of Justin I to the throne, though Anicia Juliana may have played on it (see note 28 above). Later affiliations with both Constantine and Helena (e.g. Justin II and Sophia: see Averil Cameron, 'The empress Sophia', *B* 45 [1975], 5–21) were metaphorical rather than genealogical.
88 Elm, 'Evagrius Ponticus' *Sententiae ad Virginem*', 97–120; see also Herrin, 'Femina Byzantina', 100–1.
89 J. Grosdidier de Matons, 'La femme dans l'empire byzantin', in P. Grimal, ed., *Histoire mondiale de la femme* III (Paris, 1967), 11–43, esp. 19, 34–9. See also J. Gouillard, 'La femme de qualité dans les lettres de Théodore Stoudite', *JÖB* 32/2 (1982), 445–52, esp. 449–50; C.

Galatariotou, 'Holy women and witches: aspects of Byzantine conceptions of gender', *BMGS* 9 (1984/5), 55–94, esp. 78–83.

90 Bynum, 'Women's stories', demonstrated that, in most inversion stories, the protagonist is released from a dominant position into a liminal/spiritual one; hence, for men, inversion as a female implied spiritual release. While we do not have sufficient documentation from the late antique or Early Byzantine periods to test all aspects of Bynum's model (but see the preliminary remarks in Harvey, 'Women in Early Byzantine hagiography', 45), the liminal position women could occupy for men in the early years of Christianity is clear, as Peter Brown has shown: e.g. *Body and Society*, 153–4. At this time, too, male authors imposed a similar pattern on women. The identification of ascetic or holy women as 'honorary men' has been amply discussed (e.g. Harvey, 'Women in Early Byzantine hagiography', 40–1, 48; Cameron, 'Virginity as metaphor', 191–2); and so has fascination with female saints who dressed as males (E. Patlagean, 'L'histoire de la femme déguisée en moine et l'évolution de la sainteté féminine à Byzance', *Studi Medievali*, ser. 3, 17 [1976], 597–623; repr. in Patlagean, *Structure Sociale, Famille, Chrétienté à Byzance* [London, 1981], XI, remains the classic account). Because inversion reinforced the existing social order, status reversal only fully makes sense to the dominant group; hence, when we find women transposed temporarily into men in late antique or Early Byzantine texts, I would suggest that the male author is not only expressing ideas about female moral or physical weakness: beyond this topos, shaping female lives around male patterns absorbs women's experience into men's. Imposing a pattern that worked for male protagonists onto female ones forces a male construction of religious experience on females: individual women are recast as men when male authors, limited by their own frame of reference, wish to express female transcendency.

91 On inversion, see the preceding note. On Pulcheria, see Holum, *Theodosian Empresses*, 93–6, *passim*; Limberis, *Divine Heiress*, 47–61; and esp. K. Cooper, 'Contesting the nativity: virgins, matrons, and Pulcheria's *Imitatio Mariae*' (forthcoming). The emphasis on female asceticism and virginity peaked in the late fourth and early fifth centuries: see esp. Cameron, 'Virginity as metaphor', and Cameron, 'Discourse of female desire'. Though the period between the sixth and eleventh centuries has been understudied, the importance of family was apparently preserved throughout the Byzantine period, while the roles of female asceticism and virginity atrophied but did not disappear entirely: see A.E. Laiou, 'The role of women in Byzantine society', *JÖB* 31/1 (1981), 233–60, esp. 233–41; Laiou, 'Observations', esp. 65–8, 72–8, 101; Herrin, 'Forms of religious commitments', esp. 195–6.

92 As also, perhaps, Justina: see note 64 above.

93 See Johnson, 'Burial places'; Mango, 'Constantine's mausoleum'.

4

IMPERIAL WOMEN AND THE IDEOLOGY OF WOMANHOOD IN THE ELEVENTH AND TWELFTH CENTURIES

Barbara Hill

When searching for powerful imperial women in the Byzantine empire, an obvious place to look is the eleventh and twelfth centuries, where the evidence for imperial women is fruitful and provocative in a variety of ways; here it is most likely that powerful women will be found if they are there to be found. Having located visible women, it is more difficult to explain how their power holding was viewed and allowed in a society that seemed to require of women that they be silent and in submission to a man.

One recent explanation for the power of these imperial women is that they escaped from the restrictive ideology of their society, using it as a cloak behind which they exercised power in a fashion defined as masculine, without affecting their femininity.[1] The conclusions reached by Lynda Garland are that imperial women in the eleventh and twelfth centuries 'could be in their own right the obvious and unchallenged embodiments of Byzantine imperialism'[2] and that empresses 'were free to make their own choice of lovers and husbands, married, unmarried or widowed'.[3] These conclusions seem to me to be overstated and the basic premise of escape from ideology theoretically inadequate; the evidence that these women were self-consciously rejecting the ideology of their society and manipulating it deliberately is missing.[4] People do escape their ideology, like feminists in every age and every country, but they usually leave some evidence of it behind them to explain their awakening consciousness.

The problem with Garland's approach is that she takes too simple a view of ideology. The article offers no theoretical discussion of ideology and its complicated relation to reality: the author has no choice but to postulate an escape from restrictive ideology, since the women who appear are obviously not silent or submissive.[5] Yet, if this explanation is rejected, how are the ambiguous remarks of Psellos, the approval meted out to Eudokia Makrembolitissa by Skylitzes, the riot of the citizenry at the exile of Zoe, the transportation of Theodora from nun to empress and the long rule of Anna Dalassene to be understood?

This chapter will argue a contrary explanation for the visibly powerful behaviour of imperial women in these two centuries. Rather than the women escaping their ideology, it was ideology that conferred the power that they exercised. This argument stems from an understanding that there may be more than one ideology operating in any given society at one and the same time, as I will argue below. The dominant ideology, which appears with greatest vibrancy in the writings of the Church fathers and religious ascetics, demanded that women be modest and powerless in accordance with their inferior status.[6] The ideology of the court, however, made little mention of submission, concentrating on beauty and piety.[7] The eleventh century is more complicated to unravel than the twelfth because the main characters of the first half, Zoe and Theodora, slotted into two ideologies that were normally exclusive: woman and absolute ruler. This produced confusion and ambiguity for the historians of the time. The years after the deaths of these two demonstrate the simpler operation of one ideology. This is the ideology of the widowed mother, lauded by all sections of the population as a figure to be admired and obeyed.[8] By investigating how these several ideologies worked in society and by examining each woman separately to avoid distortion, this chapter will produce a theoretically viable explanation of the power of the women of the eleventh and twelfth centuries.

First, it is necessary to be completely clear which imperial women are in question. The imperial women of these two centuries can be divided up into two categories. One category is small and consists of Zoe and Theodora, the daughters of Constantine VIII. These women were sovereign empresses who ruled in their own right, and the ideology that granted them their power was that of hereditary and dynastic right to rule through blood.[9] The second category is much bigger and encompasses all the other imperial women who were relatives of the emperor, who obtained their power because of their relationship with him. The women who count are Eudokia Makrem-bolitissa, Maria of Alania, Anna Dalassene, Irene Doukaina, Anna Komnene, Maria of Antioch and Euphrosyne Doukaina.[10] The evidence for other wives of emperors, Catherine, Irene Piroska, Bertha-Irene of Sulzbach, Anna and Maria,[11] suggests that they acted only as one would expect from a cursory glance at the ideology of Byzantium. In other words, hardly anything is known about them.

No theory can explain why some of these women were more interested in public affairs than others; only unobtainable knowledge about their characters could do that. It should be noted that none of the women who were interested in public affairs escaped criticism entirely, but it is possible to explain why some women were criticised more savagely than others. The women who gained most approval for their wielding of power were those who were widowed mothers acting for their children. The ideology of the widowed mother allowed the woman to confront the world in her children's interests. If this included running an empire, then it was her responsibility as a mother and her actions were justified by the needs of the role. It must be made clear that a confusion of these two categories of imperial women will result in a distorted view of what these women were allowed to do and of the ideology that motivated and justified them.

Ideology as an historical tool of analysis presents certain challenges. It is essential to grasp the difficulties attendant on any attempt to relate ideology and reality and extract historical truth out of the resulting equation.[12] It is widely recognised that ideology is not a reflection of reality or vice versa. Aspects of ideology that appear to be restrictive may confer power on women, and ideologies that look as if they should free women to be what they want, like the western twentieth-century variety, may cause more problems than they solve for a woman's self-identity.[13] It is also recognised that strident proclaimers of ideology may be building sandbags rather than demonstrating how pervasive and secure an ideology is. For the purposes of my argument, the most useful way of understanding the working of ideology is to view it as a dictator of roles. There are roles for different jobs in society, like doctor or teacher, but more importantly there are gender roles, into which individuals are expected to fit.[14] When they do not, they incur criticism. Society teaches the role to the individual, thereby perpetuating itself. Innovation can take place in a role without severe criticism, so long as the innovative behaviour is not so radical that it splits the role apart.[15]

As long as one individual is expected to fill only one role, the society is undisturbed. However, any society can have more than one ideology circulating at the same time, and frequently does.[16] When one individual finds themselves filling two roles at the same time, particularly when those roles are contradictory, like woman and absolute ruler, society becomes uneasy and unsure of the role of that person, and what opinion it should hold of them. This was the situation at the beginning of the eleventh century in Byzantium and the explanation for the very erratic, yet existent, support given to imperial women in power.

INHERITANCE BY BLOOD

Byzantium did not function as a self-conscious hereditary society, yet at the end of the Macedonian dynasty the historians of the time insisted that the Macedonian princesses Zoe and Theodora ruled by right of the blood that flowed in their veins. Their involvement in government is undeniable: Psellos revealed by his criticism of Michael V's treatment of Zoe that she had access to all government buildings, and Theodora was clearly an absolute ruler.[17] Far from escaping from ideological restraints, however, Zoe and Theodora were justified in the power that both of them exercised by the ideology of inheritance. All support that they received from the historians and the courtiers of the day, although ambiguous and far from consistent, resulted from their blood relationship to Constantine VIII and Basil II.

However, as women, they had another role, which was to be in the background, concerned about women's affairs only. Zoe incurred most criticism from the eleventh century, and receives most credit from the twentieth, when she too overtly fulfilled one of the functions of the heir to the throne: looking for a mate. The problems caused by the convergence of these two roles in these two women appear in the accounts of the historians who wrote about them. Psellos, who has left behind the most detailed account of these years, was an uneasy supporter of Zoe and Theodora, because although he admitted their right to rule as the daughters of Constantine VIII, he felt instinctively that it was fitting that a man be at the head of the empire. Zoe's role, for most of her life, was to be a legitimiser of emperors, and with this role Byzantine historians were at ease, because legitimising emperors was a female function that had been exercised by many empresses in the past.[18]

Neither Psellos nor Skylitzes saw any problem in the reign of Romanos Argyros as an emperor legitimised by his marriage to Zoe. Neither of them felt that Zoe should be in sole command herself. Skylitzes had reservations about the legality of the marriage which he solved to his own satisfaction, but they did not include doubts about where power should reside.[19]

Psellos accepted the right of Michael IV to rule as the husband of Zoe, as did Skylitzes, and both measured out a certain amount of approval on Michael's character and reign, although both had something to say about his route to power. Psellos was more interested in the gossip of the love affair between Zoe and Michael and represented Zoe's passion as true love while Michael was merely using Zoe as a channel to power.[20] Skylitzes was disgusted by Zoe's conduct, accused her openly of adultery, and recounted the scandalous rumour that Romanos was drowned in his bath by Michael's men after being poisoned slowly by Zoe.[21] But despite their separate reservations about Michael's accession, they felt that he had the right to rule and that Zoe had fulfilled her role by legitimising him. Psellos was disquieted by Michael's enclosure of Zoe and his ban on her access to the state rooms and the treasury, because it was her blood that was imperial, which granted to Michael his power, and therefore Michael should not have treated the real possessor of power in a manner inconsistent with her dignity and rights.[22]

This disquiet became acute in both historians during the reign of Michael V Kalaphates when his treatment of Zoe propelled them both from viewing Zoe primarily as a woman to a view of her as the blood heir of Basil II. It was at this time that they both started to designate her as the heir to the throne, as its legitimate ruler, descended from a long line of emperors. Both stated that when Michael IV died, power was Zoe's by inheritance.[23] In Psellos's account, John the Orphanotrophos recognised Zoe's claim to power and acted on it to elevate his nephew, Michael V. Unfortunately for the family, Michael did not recognise the source from which his power flowed and attempted to exile Zoe from the palace. The accounts of this attempt and the reactions it provoked in the city are recounted in detail not only by Psellos and Skylitzes, but also by Attaleiates. Their witness is identical: the people, after an initial acceptance of Michael, no sooner realised what he had done to their empress than they turned on him, looting and rioting, in defence of the one whom they recognised as the legitimate ruler. Michael's ingratitude was condemned in no uncertain terms and his fate held up as divine punishment[24] and a warning to ingrates forever.[25]

When Michael V committed his outrage towards Zoe, her right to rule was emphasised. This right brought Zoe and Theodora to a position of sole rule which was approved by its observers. Both Psellos and Skylitzes commented on the good nature of the government that was set up by the two sisters, in which corruption was rooted out, posts no longer for sale and justice was administered with equity.[26] The two sisters carried out all the business of government just as previous emperors had done, hearing embassies, giving orders; Psellos presented a favourable picture of it.[27] Nevertheless, both Psellos and Skylitzes were happier with Constantine Monomachos at the helm, although they both admitted the right of the two sisters to rule. Psellos showed his unease more clearly by opining that the two sisters had not the temperament to rule a state, confusing the matters of the women's quarters with weighty affairs of state.[28] What was needed was a man to guide and to govern. Zoe took the initiative by sending Theodora once more into exile and finally choosing Constantine Monomachos to be her new husband and the new emperor.

Skylitzes, whose Zoe is a more energetic person in any case,[29] placed the initiative for picking an emperor solely on Zoe's shoulders, a Zoe who was unwilling that Theodora should have any voice in government. He did remark that it was the opinion of all that an emperor should be chosen, but this reason was not the overriding one for Skylitzes that it was for Psellos. That Zoe slid into the background again after the accession of Monomachos was perfectly acceptable to them. Zoe was the heir of the empire by virtue of her imperial birth, and both Psellos and Skylitzes considered that she had certain rights and a particular role to fulfil, but this role did not consist of sole rule unless her rights had been outrageously violated, as in the case of Michael V.[30]

When the time came for Theodora to rule, both Psellos and Skylitzes regarded her as the legitimate inheritor of the empire. Psellos remarked that the empire was her natural inheritance, and Skylitzes stated that she succeeded by inheritance to the empire of her forefathers.[31] Psellos recorded the surprise of everyone that she refused to marry, although he could understand why: he commented that she had seen the consequences of raising a man to power in Zoe's lifetime and was in no hurry to experience the same herself.[32] This observation reveals that Psellos was astute enough to perceive the contradictions inherent in filling two roles at once. His own attitude was ambiguous, for while he had to admit that the state was well run and in good order, he also declared that it was felt to be improper that the head of the state was a woman rather than a man, or at least that was what the people seemed to think.[33] Psellos's opinion of Theodora's servant and helper, Leo, was coloured by his own eclipse after the death of Monomachos and should not be taken as a true representation of Leo's abilities, or of Theodora's talent in picking advisers. Attaleiates, with no reason to hate Leo, judged him as full of good sense and not lacking in experience, with the result that the government was good and pleasing to God.[34] Theodora's worst fault was that she made no provision for the succession, a trend in Macedonian emperors.[35]

Zoe and Theodora were in a unique position, the last of a long and respected line. They succeeded to the throne because it was not impossible that a woman could rule in Byzantium. Their involvement in the functions of government cannot be postulated for the other imperial women of these two centuries, because their justification for their position was more than any other imperial woman could claim. The failure of Anna Komnene's attempt to be her father's heir demonstrates the difference in justification between the daughter of the first emperor of a dynasty and the daughters of the seventh. While there was a man with the same blood to rule, a woman would never be chosen, despite her priority of birth. The last remaining shoots of an old and magnificent tree had a chance that no other woman in Byzantium could have. Zoe and Theodora were in that enviable position and ruled in their own right, despite the difficulties their reign caused for the men around them, who regarded them as women as well as legal heirs. The ideology of womanhood under which these men laboured resulted in their confusion over whether Zoe and Theodora were good rulers or weak women; without the ideology of inheritance by blood neither of them would have had the chance to try. One ideology was gendered and restrictive but there was another one that could be mobilised to justify a woman in power in her own right: the ungendered ideology of blood inheritance.

THE IDEOLOGY OF THE WIDOWED MOTHER

The expectation of Byzantine authors that the ideal mother should be a skilled *intrigueuse* has been noted in passing by modern scholars,[36] but what this means for the mother's role has not been addressed. From the middle of the eleventh century to the end of the twelfth, a number of women are visible in the sources whose prominence is best explained as one ideology in triumph, that of the power of the widowed mother. These women, Eudokia Makrembolitissa, Maria of Alania, Anna Dalassene, Irene Doukaina, Maria of Antioch and Euphrosyne Doukaina, did exercise power in a very visible way during the eleventh and twelfth centuries. All of them appear in the sources, several of them in control of the empire, performing essential and public functions. However, if they are compared carefully, it becomes clear that the majority of them were exercising the prerogatives enshrined in the ideology of the widowed mother. The two exceptions, Irene Doukaina and Euphrosyne Doukaina, wives rather than mothers, prove the rule. Although even the mothers were not unchallenged by the men of their time, the criticism directed against them was less consistent and much more ambiguous than that which has survived concerning Irene Doukaina and Euphrosyne Doukaina, which is almost universally negative. This is because the women acting as mothers were not considered to be betraying their femininity, while powerful wives were.

By the eleventh century, the role of mother was the most powerful ideological role for women. From the fourth to the seventh centuries, the denial of sexuality through perpetual virginity, by whatever means, was the route to power by choice. As this changed, the dominant ideology came to represent the married life of the family as the locus of sanctity for women.[37] Both options, virginity and motherhood, are forms of social control of women's sexuality;[38] in this context there is little point in attempting to decide whether Byzantium became more or less repressive as far as women were concerned. However, it is important to know where the dominant ideology considered virtue to be found, since fulfilling the ideals of ideology is one form of power.[39]

The law, both reflecting and encoding the ideology, considered the mother to be the most proper person to have guardianship of minors after the death of a father. The widow became the head of the family, fulfilling the duties which that position entailed, managing the property, and providing for the education, the marriage and the dowries of her children. The children were under the legal obligation to render their mother respect and were forbidden to usurp her position.[40] The ideal life pattern for a twelfth-century man was given expression by Prodromos in political verses written to celebrate the

IMPERIAL WOMEN

birth of the son of the sebastokratorissa Irene. The boy will first of all excel at games, then at hunting, then in battle, a worthy wife will be found for him, he will father children, reach an old age and serve his mother until the end of his life.[41] The importance of the mother could hardly be more clearly emphasised. In Laiou's words, Byzantine ideology 'made motherhood the greatest and most glorious function of a woman'.[42]

While the operation of such an ideology tied women to the family and to their reproductive abilities,[43] and could therefore be criticised as both oppressive and patriarchal, it opened great vistas of influence to the woman who fulfilled the ideal, as all these visible imperial women did. The ideal role that mothers were expected to fill included the moral duty to prepare the children for life, whatever that involved. In the case of imperial mothers, this moral duty raised the mother high in the public sphere and legitimised a certain amount of authority. It is therefore erroneous to postulate a split between ideology and reality to explain the role of these women, because the ideology legitimised the power that they exercised.

The lofty moral high ground that motherhood occupied during these two centuries is amply expressed by the sources. Theophylact of Ohrid proclaimed in his speech to Constantine and Maria of Alania that motherhood was pleasing to God and the salvation of mothers, and brought his praise of Anna Dalassene to a climax by applauding her successful motherhood with a quotation from Psalm 112 referring to the mother gladdened by children as 'blessed'.[44] A twelfth-century view was supplied by George Tornikes, who stressed that children were more important for a wife than a husband, for they strengthened the indissoluble link between man and wife and restored the attachment to its former level.[45]

The production of children, to extend the family to grandchildren and great-grandchildren, was the means by which Anna Dalassene surpassed and eclipsed the achievements of other women. Not only the production of the raw material, but the socialisation of it into the stuff of civilisation was the duty of the mother. Maria of Alania was reminded that a mother must guard her children's temperance, and Anna Dalassene was praised because of the growth and unity of the different branches of her family which were nourished by her. Preparing children for the world meant providing proper tutors for them to stretch and develop their minds as well as training them in temperance.[46] Anna Dalassene made provision for the education of her younger sons as well as instituting a temperate and prudent atmosphere in the imperial palaces; her family was a living example of how life should be lived and an inducement to virtue to those who surrounded them.[47] Mothers were likewise expected to cater for the religious growth and maintenance of their children: Anna Dalassene provided three spiritual fathers for Alexios Komnenos.[48] The duties of providing tutors and spiritual fathers for children required knowledge on the part of the mother concerning suitable people for these posts. In other words, she had to know the intelligentsia, both religious and secular, and be in a position to establish contact with them.

The role of care for children was one in which women could act on their own initiative and be praised for it. Innovation can take place inside an accepted role as long as the innovative behaviour is not perceived as inappropriate for the role.[49] This was demonstrated by the behaviour and fate of Irene the Athenian, who was mother of and regent for Constantine VI during his long minority. Exploiting the powerful position of mother to an under-age emperor, legitimised by the dominant ideology as a proper role for women, she managed to retain full power after her son reached his majority. That action generated an unease that her regency had not, although her reputation as a mother to the Church overshadowed her role as child-blinder to later generations. Her period of sole rule was short in comparison to her regency, because blinding the child for whom the mother's energies are supposed to be acting is not appropriate behaviour.

On the other hand, disloyalty to a husband can be justified under the rubric of acting in a child's interests, without exposing the mother to criticism. Anna Komnene explained the treachery of Maria of Alania towards Nikephoros Botaneiates as loyalty to her son Constantine.[50] Significantly, all the women for whom detailed information is given in the sources up to the eleventh century are mothers acting as regents for their sons, a phenomenon that highlights the point at issue: authority is vested in the mother acting for her children.[51]

A detailed consideration of the women who were visible reveals a recurrent pattern of invisibility as a wife followed by approved exercise of authority as a mother. Eudokia Makrembolitissa did not have any important function as the wife of Constantine Doukas. It was only when she was left as regent for their sons after his death that she appears in the sources as an energetic and capable woman. Eudokia ran the empire and made the decision to elevate another emperor, Romanos Diogenes, to the throne. Her role as regent and legitimiser of the next emperor is described by Psellos, Attaleiates and Skylitzes Continuatus. Maria of Alania had no visibility as a wife of Michael Doukas, only meriting the praise from Psellos that she practised the virtue of silence. She came into her own as a mother, bargaining with the Caesar John and facilitating a change in regime. Anna Dalassene, mother of Alexios I Komnenos, is presented almost without exception as a mother by Anna Komnene and Zonaras. Anna was probably the ultimate Byzantine mother, in the right place at the right time, the confidante of her sons, the one who shared and shaped their plans. Maria of Antioch was regent for her son after Manuel Komnenos's death, though as a wife she had no importance.

The potential of the role that widowed empresses who were mothers of sons could exploit was demonstrated by Eudokia Makrembolitissa and Maria of Antioch. They had some sexual freedom to choose husbands and lovers, but in their case the expectations of those who surrounded them were so geared towards a remarriage that real freedom of choice was in staying unwed. The chroniclers of Eudokia's reign were favourable towards her as regent and complimentary about her abilities, but they diverged in opinion once the question of a re-marriage appeared.[52] All were uneasy about the breaking of the oath taken to Constantine Doukas, although all of them excused it on the political grounds of a foreign invasion which required a man's hand. Psellos admired Eudokia whole-heartedly as long as she relied on his advice. He intimated his reservations over the elevation of Romanos, but threw in the sop of the need to divert danger to the empire. His opinions, as always, were coloured by his own prospects for survival, which he divulged perhaps unintentionally in his reaction to Eudokia's news, which was astonishment and a concern for what would become of him.[53] He did not mention the physical beauty of Romanos Diogenes, and combated the opinion, expressed by Attaleiates and implied by Skylitzes Continuatus, that the empress had fallen in love and was ruled by her heart rather than her head.[54] Romanos's accession spelled the end of Eudokia's rule of the empire, in which time she had attended to all affairs of government herself.[55] None of the historians objected to her relegation into the background by the man she had elevated. As in the case of Zoe and her husbands, sole rule by a woman was not to be preferred to rule by a man. Psellos averred that Eudokia's relegation was her own fault, for it was her error of judgement that saved Romanos when he was under sentence of death, and a more serious one that made her think that she could control him once she had raised him to the position of emperor.[56] Eudokia had to plot very carefully and use her cunning to accomplish the move from mother to wife without toppling herself from her position. The Patriarch was manoeuvred into agreement by the lure of a crown by marriage for his nephew,[57] upon whom he doted, the Caesar John was sent off to his estates, and the sons of Constantine and Eudokia were not told of the change in their status until the deed was complete.[58]

The chroniclers, who were ready to approve of Eudokia's abilities while she remained the mother of the emperor, begin to criticise her once she exchanged her single state for a wedded one. Her personal safety was far from guaranteed when her husband Diogenes was defeated and taken captive at Mantzikert. Eudokia was removed from the palace by a consortium of the Caesar John and his sons and those of the Senate whom they had subverted to their side.[59] The Caesar threatened Eudokia with violence, and given the number of shouting soldiers in the palace it was not hard to imagine what he meant.[60] Eudokia had removed herself from the privileged and safe position of chaste mother. That ideological position would have protected her from physical violence and justified her continuing rule.

Maria of Antioch, also a mother of an under-age son, demonstrated even more graphically the danger inherent in relinquishing the ideology of the chaste mother. Maria tried to avoid the inevitable consequence of elevating a man to the throne by taking lovers instead. Her choice of Alexios the protosebastos was censured in the strongest terms by Choniates, who was of the opinion that he was the reason for the ruin of the empire.[61] No doubt Maria's choice was generally unpopular, not because of the impropriety involved, but because it represented a drawing of power lines.[62] Manuel I Komnenos's daughter, also called Maria, could find a ready source of support for her rebellion in the disaffected men who had not had the good fortune to be chosen to fill Manuel's place in all but name.[63] Had the protosebastos Alexios been able to marry the empress and succeed to the throne itself, he would have survived longer. In the end both the empress and her lover, and the crowned emperor, suffered at the hands of a successor who was able to assert that he had a legitimate claim. Andronikos Komnenos was able to point to Maria's behaviour as proof that she was unsuitable as a mother. Having turned public support against her in this fashion, he was able to have her disposed of with impunity. Taking lovers to fill the gap left by the death of the emperor was not a route that resulted in success for the empress. Too attractive in both physical and power terms, Maria became a bone to be fought over by a number of dogs. Her strategy for dealing with her situation was unwise, for it removed from her the most potent protection she had: her high status as a mother. Her right to rule as regent was not in question, but in the eyes of her world she had no right to behave as she chose. Remaining single was the most powerful option, but Maria did not have the strength of character to act it out. In any case, it was almost impossible given the pressures for male rule.

The way to deal with changing emperors while staying alive was demonstrated by Maria of Alania. Although never a regent, she was the mother of an under-age emperor, and held the right of transfer of succession in her hands. After the abdication of Michael VII, and the accession of Nikephoros Botaneiates, Maria had a certain amount of bargaining power, which she used to ensure her return to the throne as a consort. Botaneiates was already emperor, having entered a deserted Constantinople, but that he recognised the value of establishing a link with a previous dynasty to bolster his legitimacy is shown by his immediate marriage negotiations with the family of Eudokia Makrembolitissa, Maria of Alania and various senators' daughters.[64] The story of the marriage of Botaneiates and Maria is always told as that of the cunning of the Caesar John,[65] but his ingenuity in the matter of advantageous marriages is called into question by Bryennios's witness that the astute mind who saw the benefits of the Komnenos–Doukaina marriage was not that of the Caesar John, but that of Maria of Bulgaria, his daughter-in-law.[66] Given the vast benefits that would accrue to Maria by a re-marriage to the usurper, is it too much to suggest that the scheme might have been her idea? The Caesar was very willing, since Botaneiates's choice seemed to be veering towards the last woman that the Caesar could afford to have back in the palace: Eudokia Makrembolitissa.

Maria fulfilled her goal, and her legitimising function, on that occasion, but was unable to repeat her method and pull off a third marriage to Alexios Komnenos on his accession, despite the possible support of Anna Dalassene and Alexios himself. Maria and Botaneiates's marriage was criticised as adultery, particularly by Skylitzes Continuatus, because Maria's former husband Michael had been forced into a monastery against his will, a circumstance that was not accepted as a qualification for divorce.[67] At the time, Maria broke the law without incurring penalty, although the priest who blessed the marriage was deposed. Most of the current criticism was reserved for Botaneiates, who was contracting a third marriage.[68]

Maria incurred criticism once again for remaining in the palace after the Komnenian coup, and the gossip of the streets whispered of another marriage. Anna Komnene, the great defender of imperial women at all times, was quick to exonerate Maria from this accusation, alleging her own credentials for knowing the truth of the matter, and justifying Maria's conduct as concern for her porphyrogennetos son.[69] In the end, Maria and Constantine left the palace, with Constantine's rights defined, and set up court in the Mangana.

Maria survived the conspiracy that overthrew her first husband, and actively participated in the conspiracy that overthrew her second. She gave her support to the Komnenoi, warning them of plots hatched against them, but only after Botaneiates began to groom a relative of his own as a successor, instead of Maria's son Constantine. In Anna Komnene's eyes, she was perfectly right to do this: the mother acting in the best interests of her son.[70]

Remaining unattached, either legally or illegally, was the only sure route to power, and one woman managed it. Anna Dalassene never exchanged her widow and motherhood for a wifely role. She remained a mother, exercising the functions that her son put into her hands for at least twenty years. Her success and her fame as the most powerful Byzantine woman of the eleventh and twelfth centuries demonstrate admirably the possibilities that the ideology of the widowed mother contained. She controlled the whole civil government, and since Alexios was frequently campaigning on the frontiers of the empire in company with his brother Isaac, she had no checks on her power.[71] The secret of her success was her constant presentation of herself as a mother. Her seals, in constant use, bore the legend 'mother of the basileus'.[72] In the documents that she promulgated she described herself as 'mother of the basileus', and Alexios's documents ratifying her requests always named her as his well-beloved despoina and mother.[73]

The contemporary speech to Alexios Komnenos by Theophylact of Ohrid demonstrated that she was perceived as a mother first and foremost by those around the court. He ended his praise of Anna by describing the peaceful and loving division of power between the mother and son. That the praise was for a mother and not for a woman on her own is clear from the conflating of Anna and Alexios: when Alexios was absent, he was still there, for his mother safeguarded his government. The power was hers, entrusted to her completely by him, but its source was the emperor, and it was to be kept for him. Unlike the other imperial women, who were compared with regularity to the moon, Anna was equal with Alexios: they were the new luminaries created by God as the second and fresh creation.[74]

Anna broke new ground in her role as a mother, but her actions were perceived as appropriate because she never attempted to set her son aside. The limits to which the ideology of the mother could be stretched were illustrated, and Anna knew it. Yet even this ideal mother was not entirely free from criticism. Zonaras recorded unrest about her rule, although it did not concern her sex, but her policies, which was a triumph in itself, and indeed may have been the typical scapegoating of the visible holder of power which protected the young and popular emperor.[75] There must also have been criticism of her position in terms of a transgression of gender boundaries because Anna Komnene defended her grandmother's position in what must have been a reaction to current slanders of her father's mettle.[76] One of her strategies was to present Anna Dalassene as a mother of the emperor rather than as a woman holding power. At the very beginning of the *Alexiad*, we heard of her relation to Alexios before we heard her name, and every reference to Anna Dalassene in the book referred to her as the mother of the emperor.[77] She was endowed with such a strong desire to enter a monastery that Alexios had to keep his intentions secret from her, and only her overriding love for her son and her duty as a mother kept her at his side, for she set little store by secular matters.

The aim of presenting Anna Dalassene as a mother was furthered by the omission of a physical description. All other major characters in the *Alexiad* were given physical descriptions, including Anna Komnene's maternal grandmother, whose beauty Anna herself could not have remembered. None of these women required the special pleading that was the reason for Anna Komnene's abandonment of her usual practice. Given the duty of a widowed mother to guard her young, Anna Komnene could present Anna as dutiful rather than powerful. Anna Dalassene was portrayed as being outside the usual categories of womanhood: she was no need of comfort in danger, she could see through the wiles of the enemy, she was a credit to the whole human race, not just to women.[78] Anna Dalassene never transgressed the gender boundaries to leave herself open to the nastier accusations of witchcraft that often dogged powerful women, but her demise is shrouded in obscurity and a possible rumour of heresy, which is at least a poor relative of witchcraft.[79] The only details that are clear show Anna Dalassene retiring strategically to the monastery of Pantepoptes at this point, living in honour for the rest of her life, surviving with her reputation intact. Anna Komnene never mentioned whatever scandal forced her grandmother into retirement: a silence that proclaims loudly that there was something to be hidden.[80] Anna Dalassene's fate was kinder than that of Eudokia Makrembolitissa, threatened with the unrestrained violence of the soldiers, or of Maria of Antioch, beheaded on the orders of a tyrant from whose authority her conduct had left her no refuge. Anna Dalassene fulfilled the ideology of the widowed mother to perfection, exercising great power for many years, demonstrating what a justification such an ideology provided.

Maria of Antioch abandoned the protection of the ideology of the mother when she took a lover; Eudokia Makrembolitissa was removed from under it when she married Diogenes. They both became invisible and powerless once they attached themselves again to men. Anna Dalassene remained powerful and relatively unscathed by criticism until her son decided he could do without her, when she too had to retire. But these women, no matter for how short a period, had the recognised right to direct the affairs and the fate of the empire. Irene Doukaina and Euphrosyne Doukaina, on the other hand, did not have that right, and although they could exercise power when the authority of the male to whom they were married was weak, they did not merit the same approval.

OUTSIDE IDEOLOGY

Irene Doukaina has a reputation as a powerful woman, and most of her visibility is due to the *Alexiad* which revealed the family life of the Komnenoi. Had we other *Alexiads* for other families, the same basic picture might also emerge. Wives can be credited with an influence on their husband's decisions, but this influence is private and does not appear in the sources. The evidence for Irene's role is mainly as a nurse and guardian of her husband, rather than as a partner in politics. Although she may have had some influence on the foreign marriages made by her children, as the number of foreign brides adopting Irene as their Byzantine name may suggest, evidence for the kind of marriage brokery in which Anna Dalassene and Eudokia Makrembolitissa engaged is lacking.[81]

Irene accompanied Alexios on campaign, a practice that was

productive of criticism in the form of letters thrown into their tent, warning Alexios to send Irene home.[82] Here she was seen as transgressing the gender boundaries for women, and Anna Komnene had to make much of her father's need for his wife to nurse his gout and guard his sleep in order to excuse and justify her presence there.[83] Zonaras was scornful of Alexios's habit of travelling with the gynaikonitis in tow, but did not record any other acts of Irene's that would set her beyond the pale. At the end of Alexios's life, when he was bed-ridden, he entrusted the management of affairs to Irene.[84] She immediately made Bryennios responsible for the administration of justice.[85] Irene was not criticised for her acts at this time because she was acting on Alexios's wishes.

Criticism was reserved for her interference in the succession, particularly by Niketas Choniates, who recorded her very un-attractive nagging of Alexios, and his patience in dealing with it.[86] Why Irene preferred Anna and Bryennios to John as the successors of the empire is unknown, but what is certain is that she did not succeed. John was able to drum up support from the nobles who had sworn loyalty to him as a child, and was able to seize the palace, although that act prevented him from attending his father's funeral.[87] After John was secure on the throne, Irene would have no part in any plot to overthrow him.[88] She retired to the monastery of Kecharitomene, where she pursued her intellectual interests in peace, continuing to be a person of some influence in the land.[89] She remained in John's good graces to an extent that his rebellious sister Anna did not because she recognised the limitations of her power and was content to be loyal once an emperor was firmly established. She did not have the backing of the ideology of the widowed mother to support her attempt to exercise power, so she failed and was criticised savagely by Choniates for her unfeminine behaviour.

Choniates exercised his full powers of denunciation in relation to Euphrosyne Kamatere Doukaina, the wife of Alexios III Angelos. Euphrosyne was the real decision maker of that reign, exercising authority to which she had no right at all by any ideology. Alexios III appears as such a weak character that it is unsurprising that any stronger character could dominate him. Euphrosyne seemed to be endowed with qualities that would ensure her success in the twentieth century: she could communicate very well, had a very persuasive tongue, was self-controlled in the matter of revenge, was an organiser, could appoint good ministers, and had the resolution to deal with crises when they arose and to cut out the dead wood of an organisation.[90]

In the twelfth century, however, a woman who was also a wife could not be praised for using such talents. Choniates, searching for the causes of the disaster of 1204, was critical of both Alexios and Euphrosyne, and he was able to present these two as a subversion of the natural order, a signpost that his readers would recognise as an explanation of the ruin of the public good. Choniates was able to imply this state of affairs time and time again: Euphrosyne had a wily tongue, eloquent and honeyed, Alexios hardly said anything at all;[91] Alexios knew nothing of what was happening in the empire, nothing could exceed Euphrosyne's inquisitiveness.[92] Eventually he clarified his hints: Euphrosyne had a manly spirit and Alexios was a womanly man.[93] Choniates stoked up his fire of accusations against Euphrosyne – she had overstepped the boundaries and treated the conventions of former Roman empresses with contempt, she had destroyed old customs and innovated new ones, she was a lover of money so she could spend on her pleasures, all activities improper in women – and let Euphrosyne remember that she was no more than a woman![94] The old accusation, well tried and never failing, of adultery, was levelled against her by her own family, eager to neutralise the power she was using to curtail their activities.[95] Alexios fell for it and had her banished, to the discomfiture of her family, who were reviled for dishonouring the bonds of kinship. Choniates did not believe that she had committed adultery, for he was unsympathetic to her accusers, opining that they should be ashamed of themselves.[96] Sympathy with Euphrosyne did not prevent him from using another trusty accusation against powerful women, the one Anna Dalassene escaped because of her mother image: the accusation of witchcraft.[97] Euphrosyne's dreadful practices, her excessive zeal, her unspeakable rituals, were detailed.

Choniates represented the opinions of Byzantine men about the powerful wife who is able to control her husband: Euphrosyne the mad, the excessive, the witch!

CONCLUSION

The differing opinions held of these women, who, in many cases, were fulfilling exactly the same functions, illustrates the strength of ideology. The ideology of the widowed mother was the strongest foundation for women's power. As a recognised, culturally legitimated activity, the mother's role in guarding and training her children, particularly her sons, brought approval for an exercise of authority that in any other woman was criticised as unseemly. Mothers, whatever their actions, were fulfilling an ideology of protecting their young that left their femininity intact. Wives, doing the same things, were branded overbearing and autocratic.[98] Those women acting as mothers were not escaping the modest woman ideology of their culture, but were fulfilling another strand of ideology which defined them as modest while they appointed magistrates and concerned themselves with public business. It was not in a negation of the dominant ideology that power was to be found and held, but in a fulfilment of it. Ideology itself conferred the power.

This is true also of Zoe and Theodora. As women, they were not suitable to rule the empire, but as the daughters of Constantine VIII they had imperial blood flowing in their veins, and the ideology of inheritance by blood guaranteed them loyalty and respect which they would never have received as women.

A viable explanation of the ambiguity of the historians' opinions on powerful women and a corresponding explanation of imperial women's power in Byzantium is made possible only by investigating ideology as a tool before approaching the historical evidence. Such a method is particularly important when studying women, whose role and place in our own society is far from resolved.

NOTES

1 L. Garland, 'The life and ideology of Byzantine women: a further note on conventions of behaviour and social reality as reflected by eleventh and twelfth-century historical sources', *B* 58 (1988), 361–93.

2 Ibid., 393.

3 Ibid., 391.

4 The only text of reasonable length surviving from the pen of any of these women is the *Alexiad*, which is often charged with perpetuating male ideas about women. See C. Galatariotou, 'Holy women and witches: aspects of Byzantine conceptions of gender', *BMGS* 9 (1984/5), 155–94, esp. 167–8; V. Bullough, *The Subordinate Sex: A History of Attitudes towards Women* (Chicago, 1973), chap. 6. The typikon of Theotokos Kecharitomene, composed on the orders of Irene Doukaina and no doubt reflecting her own wishes, deals with the usual areas of property and piety and tells us nothing about Irene's consciousness of her ideology.

5 The only indication that there are complex issues at stake is the unfootnoted statement that '. . . while it is dangerous to accept conven-

tions as reality, it is equally so to ignore their implications for historical truth'. Garland, 'Life and ideology', 365.

6 See Galatariotou, 'Holy women and witches', for the best detailed discussion of the views on women held by these segments of Byzantine society

7 See B. Hill, 'The ideal Komnenian imperial woman', forthcoming.

8 Motherhood was the 'greatest and most glorious function of a woman'. A. Laiou, 'The role of women in Byzantine society', *JÖB* 31/1 (1981), 233–60, esp. 236.

9 See B. Hill, L. James and D.C. Smythe, 'Zoe: the rhythm method of imperial renewal', in P. Magdalino, ed., *New Constantines: The Rhythm of Imperial Renewal, 4th–13th Centuries* (Aldershot, 1994), 215–30.

10 The wife of Alexios III Angelos.

11 Wives of Isaac I Komnenos, John II Komnenos, Manuel I Komnenos, Alexios II Komnenos and Andronikos I Komnenos, Isaac II Angelos, respectively.

12 J. le Goff, 'Mentalities: a history of ambiguities', in J. le Goff and P. Nora, eds, *Constructing the Past* (Cambridge, 1985), 175; G. Duby, 'Ideologies in social history', in *Constructing the Past*, 151–4, esp. 151; G. Greene and C. Kahn, 'Feminist scholarship and the social construction of women', in G. Greene and C. Kahn, eds, *Making a Difference: Feminist Literary Criticism* (London, 1985), 1–36, esp. 18.

13 Greene and Kahn, 'Feminist scholarship', 18; J. Dubisch, 'Introduction', in J. Dubisch, ed., *Gender and Power in Rural Greece* (Princeton, 1986), 21, 31; D. Kandiyoti, 'Bargaining with patriarchy', in J. Lorber and S. Farrell, eds, *The Social Construction of Gender* (London, 1991), 104–18.

14 T. Parsons, 'The superego and the theory of social systems', in T. Parsons, R.F. Bales and E. Shils, eds, *Working Papers in the Theory of Action* (New York, 1953); S. de Beauvoir, *The Second Sex* (London, 1953).

15 E. Janeway, *Man's World, Women's Place* (Harmondsworth, 1977).

16 J. le Goff, 'Mentalities', 175.

17 For Zoe, Psellos, *Chronographia* IV, 16 (Michael IV) in *Chronographie*, E. Renauld, ed. and tr., 2 vols (Paris, 1926–8); for Theodora, Psellos, *Chron.*, VI, 1–16 (Theodora).

18 Hill, James and Smythe, 'Zoe: the rhythm method'.

19 John Skylitzes, *Ioannis Scylitzae Synopsis Historiarum*, I. Thurn, ed. (Berlin, 1973), 373–4. See A. Laiou, 'Imperial marriages and their critics: the case of Skylitzes', *DOP* 46 (1992), 167–9.

20 Psellos, *Chron.*, III, 19 (Romanos Argyrus).

21 Skylitzes, *Historia*, 389.

22 Psellos, *Chron.*, IV, 16 (Michael IV).

23 Ibid., V, 4 (Michael V); Skylitzes, *Historia*, 416.

24 Attaleiates describes Michael's fate as divine punishment and does not condemn those who dragged the emperor and his uncle from the sanctuary of the church of Prodromos in Stoudios to their blinding in the market place. Michael Attaleiates, *Historia*, I. Bekker, ed. (Bonn, 1853), 17.

25 Psellos, *Chron.*, V, 25–51 (Michael V); Skylitzes, *Historia*, 417–20. The

people called out that they wanted the 'κληρουμον' Zoe: Attaleiates, *Historia*, 17. It would be a mistake to assume that all that is recorded in the sources took place in support of Zoe's cause. Self-interest and the chance to loot riches from the relatives of the erstwhile emperor must have been a factor. But these considerations do not affect the value of the opinions of the historians, who presented the riots as an expression of outrage at the treatment meted out to the person they considered the legitimate ruler.

26 Skylitzes, *Historia*, 422.

27 Psellos, *Chron.*, VI, 1–3 (Zoe and Theodora).

28 Ibid., 5 and 11 (Zoe and Theodora). It should be noted that feminists have detected this particular type of accusation in many societies. It works by placing a woman in a certain situation without giving her any choice and then blaming her for the results. In this case, the two imperial women had not been given the education to rule an empire but were criticised for their lack of knowledge. Psellos's change of mind must also be seen in connection for his support for Constantine Monomachos on a personal level. Monomachos was the emperor with whom Psellos exercised most influence.

29 Skylitzes presented Zoe as the person who ordered the tonsure of Theodora, *Historia*, 384, as the poisoner of Romanos Argyros, 389, as the author of a plot to poison John the Orphanotrophos, 403, and as the initiator of Michael V's selection, 416.

30 Monomachos was Psellos's hero, yet he was disgusted at his behaviour in importing his mistress into the palace and giving her an imperial title. But this offence alone was not enough to make him suggest that Zoe should get rid of Monomachos and rule alone. *Chron.*, VI, 58–60 (Constantine IX).

31 Ibid., 3 (Theodora); Skylitzes, *Historia*, 479.

32 Ibid., VI, 1 (Theodora).

33 Ibid., VI, 4 (Theodora).

34 Psellos had to retire to a monastery just before the death of Monomachos and was therefore not in the front rank of Theodora's advisers. He was reticent on the reason for this retirement: Ibid., 10 (Theodora). For Psellos's criticism of Leo Parasondyles, Ibid., 6 (Theodora). For Attaleiates's remarks, see *Historia*, 51.

35 Psellos, *Chron.*, VI, 15 (Theodora).

36 Garland, 'Life and ideology', 392.

37 E. Patlagean, 'L'histoire de la femme dèguisèe au moine et l'évolution de la sainteté féminine à Byzance', *Studi Medievali*, 17.2 (1976), 597–624.

38 Greene and Kahn, 'Feminist scholarship and the social construction of women', 6.; J. Mitchell, *Women: The Longest Revolution* (London, 1984); S. Firestone, *The Dialectic of Sex: The Case for Feminist Revolution* (New York, 1970); V. Walkerdine, 'Post-structuralist theory and everyday social practices: the family and the school', in S. Wilkinson, ed., *Feminist Social Psychology* (Milton Keynes, 1986); A. Rich, 'Compulsory heterosexuality and lesbian existence', *Signs*, 5.4 (1980), 631–60.

39 There has been debate among feminists concerning the amount of power conferred by the fulfilment of the ideal. Some feel that only favourable

conditions confer power; they have been accused of being materialistic and ethnocentric. Others believe that the realisation of the ideal provides women with a measure of power because they symbolise the ideal and are recreating the ideology and therefore have control over it. They contend that politics and economics are conventional sources of power but that feminists must include control over the individual psyche and ideology in their analyses. The fulfilment of the ideal may bolster a woman's sense of worth and must not be dismissed as collusion with the oppressor. See J. Dubisch, 'Introduction', in J. Dubisch, ed., *Gender and Power in Rural Greece* (Princeton, 1986), 22–3; M. Dimen, 'Servants and sentries: women, power and social reproduction in Kriovrisi', *Gender and Power*, 53–67.

40 J. Beaucamp, 'La situation juridique de la femme à Byzance', *Cahiers de civilisation médiévale*, 20 (1977), 145–76. J. Beaucamp, *Le statut de la femme à Byzance (4e–7e siècle)*, I (Paris, 1990). G. Buckler, 'Women in Byzantine law around 1100AD', *B* 11 (1936), 391–416. A prescription in law does not always guarantee that the law is being carried out and is sometimes an indication of the opposite. The ideal can therefore be stated, but not the actual situation in reality.

41 Theodore Prodromos, LXIV, W. Hörandner, ed., *Theodoros Prodromos, Historische Gedichte* (Vienna, 1974), 405–12.

42 Laiou, 'The role of women in Byzantine society', 236.

43 The tendency to define women in terms of their bodies and their reproductive capabilites, thereby condemning them to the operation of the 'natural' function, is one of the factors identified by feminists as a contributor to women's oppression in society. The bibliography is large. Some suggestions are: S. Ortner, 'Is female to male as nature is to culture?', in M. Rosaldo and L. Lamphere, eds, *Women, Culture and Society* (Stanford, 1974), 67–88; C. Fouquet, 'The unavoidable detour: must a history of women begin with a history of their bodies?', in M. Perrot, ed., *Writing Women's History* (Oxford, 1992), 51–60; J. Revel, 'Masculine and feminine: the historiographical use of sexual roles', in Perrot, ed., ibid., 90 105.

44 Theophylact of Ohrid, P. Gautier, ed., *Théophylacte d'Achrida. Discours, traités et poésies* (Thessaloniki, 1980), 190.

45 George Tornikes, J. Darrouzès, ed., *Georges et Démètrios Tornikés, Lettres et discours* (Paris, 1970), 247.

46 Theophylact, ed. Gautier, 190.

47 Nicephoros Bryennios, 1, 6, *History*, P. Gautier, ed. and tr., *Nicéphore Bryennios, Histoire* (Brussels, 1975), 86: Theophylact, ed. Gautier, 190. Even the political verses of Prodromos which mentioned Irene the sebastokratorissa only briefly expected that she would prepare her son to be a soldier. Prodromos, LXIV, ed. Hörandner, 407.

48 For Ignatios and Symeon, see *La Vie de S. Cyrille le Philéote par Nicholas Katasképenos*, E. Sargologos, ed. (Brussels, 1964), 91–3; for Little John, *Alexiad*, I. viii. 2, B. Leib, ed. and tr., 3 vols (Paris, 1937–45).

49 Janeway, *Man's World*, 87.

50 *Alexiad*, II. ii. 1.

51 For example, Irene the Athenian, Theodora the iconodule, Theodote, Theophano.

52 Psellos, *Chron.*, VII, 1 (Eudokia). Skylitzes Continuatus, E. Th. Tsolakes, ed. (Thessaloniki, 1968), 118, says that Eudokia was highly self-controlled and accustomed to men, wonderful at child raising and most excellent at managing state affairs.

53 Ibid., VII, 7–8 (Eudokia).

54 Ibid., 4 (Eudokia). Attaleiates, *Historia*, 100; Skylitzes Cont., 121.

55 Psellos, *Chron.*, VII, 1 (Eudokia).

56 Ibid., III, 1 (Romanos Diogenes).

57 John Zonaras, *Epitome historiarum*, L. Dindorf, ed., 6 vols (Leipzig, 1868–75); Byzantine section ed. T. Büttner-Wobst (Bonn, 1897), 685–7.

58 Attaleiates, *Historia*, 101; Psellos, *Chron.*, VII, 7–8 (Eudokia); Skylitzes Cont., 124.

59 Attaleiates, *Historia*, 168; Skylitzes Cont., 152; Zonaras, 704. Zonaras characterised the Caesar John and his sons as 'savage-minded'.

60 Psellos, *Chron.*, VII, 20 (Romanos Diogenes), relates that the empress lost her nerve and hid in an underground crypt on hearing the clamour of the soldiers.

61 Niketas Choniates, *Historia*, J.A. van Dieten, ed., *Nicetae Choniatae Historia* (Berlin, 1975), 225.

62 Choniates makes this clear, ibid., 224–5.

63 Choniates, ibid., 231.

64 Zonaras, 722.

65 B. Leib, 'Nicéphore III Botaniatès (1078–1081) et Marie d'Alania', *Actes de VIe congrès international d'études byzantines* (Paris, 1948), I, 129–40. Bryennios recounts the Caesar's cunning in the actual moment of marriage when the priest appeared to hesitate: Bryennios, *Histoire*, III, 25, ed. Gautier, 252–4.

66 Bryennios, *Histoire*, III, 6, ed. Gautier, 220 ff.

67 Skylitzes Cont., 182.

68 Botaneiates's most fervent supporter, Attaleiates, says nothing about the marriage at all, the most potent proof that it was considered sullied. See Laiou, 'Imperial marriages', 174.

69 *Alexiad*, III. i. 4.

70 Ibid., II. ii. 1. For the later career of Maria of Alania, see M.E. Mullett, 'The "Disgrace" of the ex-basilissa Maria', *Byzantinoslavica* 45 (1984), 202–11.

71 Isaac was in charge of keeping order in the capital, but all accounts of the family seem to show mother and sons working together amicably. N. Oikonomides, 'L'évolution de l'organisation administrative de l'empire byzantin au XIe siècle (1025–1118)', *Travaux et Mémoires* 6 (1976), 125–52, has argued that the logothete created by Alexios was the real decision maker in Constantinople and that Anna Dalassene was merely a rubber stamp, but see P. Magdalino, 'Innovations in government', in M.E. Mullett and D.C. Smythe, eds, *Alexios I Komenos* I (Belfast, 1996), for a counter-argument that the logothete could not have

had that power at that time because he was not of sufficiently high social standing.

72 N. Oikonomides, *Dated Byzantine Lead Seals* (Washington, DC, 1986), no. 102.
73 See, for example, F. Miklosich and M. Muller, *Acta et Diplomata Graeca Medii Aevi Sacra et Profana*, 6 vols (Vienna, 1866–90), 6, 32, 34.
74 Theophylact, ed. Gautier, 240.
75 Zonaras, 746.
76 *Alexiad*, III. vii. 2.
77 Ibid., II. v. 2 is the first time she is named; III. viii. 10 is the first time she is called empress.
78 Ibid., IV. iv. 1; III. viii. 2.
79 See Galatariotou, 'Holy women and witches', 55–94, on accusations of witchcraft. S. Runciman, 'The end of Anna Dalassena', *Melanges H. Gregoire: Annuaire de L'institute de philologie et d'histoire orientale et slave*, 9 (1949), 517–24.
80 B. Leib, 'Les silences d'Anne Comnene', *Byzantinoslavica* 19 (1958), 1–10.
81 For the argument that women can be seen to be powerful only when male authority is weak, and that this explains the changing role of women under the Komnenoi, see B. Hill, *Patriarchy and Power in the Byzantine Empire from Maria of Alania to Maria of Antioch, 1080–1180* (unpub. Ph.D. thesis, Belfast, 1994). For a more detailed argument on Alexios I Komenos and the power of the women surrounding him, see B. Hill, 'Alexios I *Komenos* and the imperial women', in Mullett and Smythe, eds, *Alexios* I Komenos, I, 37–54.
82 *Alexiad*, XIII. i. 6–10.
83 Ibid., XII. iii. 4–10.
84 Zonaras, 753 and 747.
85 Ibid., 754.
86 Choniates, *Historia*, 5.
87 Zonaras, 748 and 763–4.
88 Choniates, *Historia*, 8.
89 Italikos felt that an appeal to Irene's wishes would move the emperor John in his favour. Michael Italikos, 43, P. Gautier, ed., *Michel Italikos. Lettres et discours* (Paris, 1972), 239–70, esp. 269.
90 All from Choniates, *Historia*, 456–7, 460, 489, 455, 484 and 519 respectively.
91 Ibid., 456.
92 Ibid., 484.
93 Ibid., 460, 549.
94 Ibid., 460.
95 Ibid., 485–7.
96 Ibid., 489.
97 Ibid., 497, 519–20.
98 Zonaras, 766, on Irene Doukaina.

5

GENDER AND ORIENTALISM IN GEORGIA IN THE AGE OF QUEEN TAMAR[1]

Antony Eastmond

Queen Tamar dominates the history of Georgia. When she died in 1213, her loss was mourned by all her subjects. The impact on her nation was summed up by the author of the *Life of Tamar, King of Kings*, one of the chronicles that makes up *Kartlis Cxovreba – The Annals of Georgia*:

> In those times we had nothing but the name of Tamar on our lips; acrostics in honour of the queen were written on the walls of houses; rings, knives and pilgrims' staves were adorned with her praises. Every man's tongue strove to utter something worthy of Tamar's name; ploughmen sang verses to her as they tilled the soil; musicians coming to Iraq celebrated her fame with music; Franks and Greeks hummed her praises as they sailed the seas in fair weather. The whole earth was filled with her praise, she was celebrated in every language wherever her name was known.[2]

The chronicler goes on to paint a picture of a country that was at the peak of its military and cultural power, a 'Golden Age' in the history of Georgia.[3] It has given the queen an unrivalled place in the pantheon of her country's heroes, far surpassing her male medieval rivals, Vaxtang Gorgasali (*c*.447–*c*.522) and Davit IV Ağmašenebeli (the Builder) (1089–1125).[4] This chapter examines the role that gender has played in creating and enhancing this reputation over the centuries since her death. It is largely a historiographical study. It examines the impact that Tamar's sex has had on perceptions of her rule and on assessments of her reign. It is a curiously vague, even mystical, field of study. Very little has been concretely written on this subject, yet much has been hinted, assumed and implied through omission. Queen Tamar's reputation has evolved from a series of often contradictory facts, rumours and reapplied ancient myths. These elements appear to have been almost deliberately intermingled, and it is the very impossibility of unravelling or analysing them that has done so much to create the aura that surrounds her reign.

It is possible to ascribe much of queen Tamar's reputation to external factors. She ruled over the largest territory that Georgia has ever controlled, gained as a result of the military victories of her second husband, Davit Soslan, and her generals Zakare and Ivane Mxargrdzeli. Art and architecture flourished during her reign,[5] agriculture and science were improved,[6] and Georgia's greatest epic poem, Šota Rustaveli's *Vepxist'q'aosani* (*The Knight in the Panther's Skin*), is traditionally dated to this period.[7] These achievements are made more poignant by the fact that Tamar was the last of the great Bagrat'ioni rulers of Georgia; within twenty years of her death, the Mongol invasions destroyed the governmental and military system that had paved the way for expansion. Although there would be later periods of national revival, such as the reign of Giorgi the Brilliant (1299–1346) which was ended by Tamurlane,[8] nothing matched the combination of wonders that appeared in Tamar's reign.

Underlying all these factors the question of gender is ever present. Curiously, however, all the modern histories of queen Tamar acknowledge the problem only obliquely. This partly lies in the nature of the historical literature which, especially in the west, tends to be popular in nature. Given the general ignorance of Georgian history, even among Byzantine scholars,[9] these popular histories carry far more weight than is perhaps the case for their equivalents in Byzantine studies. Even in Georgian/Soviet studies, which have been far more rigorous in their analyses of Tamar's reign, the impact of gender has been underplayed. This is apparent in Roin Metreveli's biography of queen Tamar, which is the only full-length modern study of the reign (in Georgian).[10]

For the historians Alexandre Manvelichvili and Mariam Lord-kipanidze, gender seems to have been regarded as an irrelevance, the latter simply asserting that Tamar wielded supreme power as a king.[11] There is no debate as to how this might have been achieved, especially given the patriarchal, military nature of Georgian society. We know that traditional male attitudes to gender did determine many of the events and attitudes of Tamar's reign. At her accession, Tamar faced a revolt by her nobility. This was sparked by a reaction against the extreme and repressive policies of her father, king Giorgi III (1155–84), but it was encouraged by the supposed weakness of the female succession. Soon after her coronation, Tamar was forced into a marriage that later proved disastrous, in order to provide an heir. The nobility regarded her constitutional role in very limited and traditional terms: to them she was little more than the dynastic continuator – the conduit by which royal legitimacy could be conferred on other men, first in her own generation, and then in the next. The second reason they gave for demanding the marriage was to provide a husband to act as leader for the army, so giving voice to another gendered limitation placed on the queen's power and ability. That such constraints continued to be a liability to the queen can be seen in two later episodes: in 1187 Tamar's estranged first husband, Iurii Bogoliubskii, launched a coup against the queen which attracted the support of half of the Georgian aristocracy who sought traditional male-centred rule;[12] and in 1205 the Seljuk ruler, Rukn ad-Din, gave Tamar's sex as the only justification he needed to invade Georgia.[13] There was clearly a perception of women and power common to all the societies of Anatolia and the Caucasus at this time that saw women rulers as an impediment that weakened the authority and military standing of the whole kingdom. These facts have been noted by Kalistrat Salia, but he implies that once the initial revolt was diffused there was no further trouble over Tamar's sex.[14] Gaiane Alibegašvili, who has written two books on the known contemporary portraits of Tamar, nowhere mentions gender as a factor in the presentation of the queen (except in terms of physiognomy and beauty).[15] The arguments in these works imply that the proven success of Tamar's reign derived from the fact that it was unaffected by her sex. Behind this application of modern sexual equality there seems to lie a more medieval distrust of women and power: Tamar's rule is great because of her asexuality and her ability to negate what were regarded as typical female traits.[16]

Gender has played a more important role in western writing on queen Tamar, and it appears most conspicuously in Antonia Fraser's *Boadicea's Chariot. The Warrior Queens*:

Queen Tamar succeeded lawfully to her father to the acclaim of her people; [she] added to both the prestige and the dominions of her country, and died leaving a legally begotten male heir to succeed peacefully in his turn. *In actual fact, her gender, so far from detracting from all this glory, seems to have added to it.*[17]

Given the proclaimed purpose of the book – to celebrate and explain 'warrior queens' – it is a statement that might be expected, yet it is one that is never quantified or explained. W.E.D. Allen had tried to express a similar sentiment in words in his 1932 history, but the results were no more illuminating: 'The curiously maternal influence which a good woman ruler exerts over the minds of men was forceful throughout her reign . . .'.[18] Gender is seen to be a major contributory factor to the success of Tamar's reign. Indeed, these writers single out gender as *the* factor that makes Tamar's 'Golden Age' a unique event, but only in a mystical and ill-defined capacity. This mythologising of gender is no more credible than the view of sexual equality implied by Georgian writers, but it is perhaps more historically interesting. The appeal to gender and maternal power as explanations looks back to nineteenth-century images of the queen.

Many of the modern perceptions of queen Tamar and of Georgia were first formed in the nineteenth century. The Tsarist annexation of Georgia in 1801 opened the country safely to outside (mostly Russian) scholars and travellers. As a frontier land that had been under Islamic domination for much of the past 400 years, it brought another small corner of the Orient into the Russian empire, and was used as a place of exile by the Tsars. It held an uneasy position within the empire: as a largely orthodox Christian society it was politically and culturally a natural ally of Russia, especially against the rebellious Moslem states of the north Caucasus; but its history of foreign occupation and location in the Caucasus made it a more exotic and dangerous society.

The interest raised by queen Tamar and Georgian medieval history in the nineteenth century provoked two opposing reactions to the position of the queen. At one extreme is the romantic poetry of Mikhail Lermontov. The poem *Tamara* was written in the last year of Lermontov's life (1841) while he was in exile in the Caucasus. It presents the wildest interpretation of the effect of gender on Tamar's reign:

> That tower on the desperate Terek
> Belonged to Tamara, the Queen;
> Her beautiful face was angelic,
> Her spirit demonic and mean.[19]

The queen's innate female desires, given free rein by her power, have taken her over, requiring her to seduce a new man every night to satisfy her lustful needs. At dawn the luckless lover is hurled into the river Terek below. The poem was set to music by Mily Balakirev between 1867–82 and was introduced to new audiences in London and Paris in 1912 when the Ballets Russes turned it into a one-act choreographic drama.[20] Léon Bakst designed the grandiose, brooding set and erotic, oriental costumes to underlie the exoticism of the tale. The ballet fitted in well with the company's tradition of oriental productions such as *Scheherazade* or *Cleopatra*. The critic of the *Pall Mall Gazette* picked up on all these oriental cues: 'One is oppressed by the endlessness of this orgy of perverted desire.'[21]

Lermontov's conception of gender, and the siren-like destructive power of women, when given access to power and freedom of action, betrays the poem's romantic origins (although its view of women would not, I suspect, have been entirely out of place in the twelfth century).[22] It might seem odd to quote Lermontov as a source for queen Tamar's reign, especially as the poem has no apparent historical grounding, but it has been remarkably influential.[23] *Tamara* has raised the question of Tamar's sexuality, a question that later historians have been unable to resist commenting upon, if only to discount.[24] However, the very fact that the majority of western authors have felt it necessary to mention Lermontov's poem has cast a shadow over the queen's sexuality, and has given it far more prominence than is warranted by the medieval evidence with all its declarations of Tamar's purity. This interest in sexuality is markedly less strong with regard to all Georgia's male rulers, whose sexual preferences were often more extreme and better documented.[25]

However, within ten years of Lermontov's poem, we find the opposite construction of Tamar, as depicted in one of the many engravings of the queen produced for a mass audience in Georgia from the 1840s on (Plate 2).[26] Again the queen has been romanticised, but very differently from Lermontov's Tamara. The engravings present Tamar in the other extreme manifestation of her sex: as a passive, gentle, saintly (asexual?) woman. Her features have been softened and she is given a shy and modest expression. It is a coy and sentimental portrayal of the medieval ruler of a country permanently at war – a veritable 'queen of hearts'. This new image was probably encouraged by the growing nationalism of Georgian intellectuals in the mid-nineteenth century, reacting to their new Tsarist overlords and the accompanying suppression of national institutions.[27] The

Plate 2 Mid-nineteenth-century painting of queen Tamar
Source: K. Salia, History of the Georgian Nation (Paris, 1980)

immediate inspiration for the pictures was certainly the rediscovery of a contemporary, thirteenth-century wall painting of Tamar in the then ruined monastic church of Betania, which was uncovered and restored by Prince Grégoire Gagarin at this time (Plate 3).[28] The church is only 15km from the centre of Tbilisi and so became the closest of the images of queen Tamar for Georgians to visit and venerate. The portrait was heavily restored and 'improved' by Gagarin, but by comparing it and the engravings with one of the unaltered medieval images of the queen, such as that at Vardzia (Plate 4), it is possible to see the transformation that Tamar has undergone. The Persian ideals of beauty that informed the thirteenth-century paintings (visible in the queen's oval face, pale colouring and pearl-shaped eyes) have been subtly altered to show a more European,

Plate 3 Wall painting of queen Tamar from north transept of the monastery of Betania (painted *c.*1207; restored by G. Gagarin *c.*1851)

Source: Courtesy of the Conway Library, Courtauld Institute of Art

Plate 4 Wall painting of queen Tamar from north wall of the monastery of
Vardzia (1184–6)
Source: Courtesy of the Fixation Laboratory for the Restoration of Ancient
Monuments of Georgian Art

gentler face.[29] In 1887, the nationalist poet Grigol Orbeliani wrote
romantic verses about the queen while sitting beneath this wall
painting.[30]

No one, of course, would suggest that either of these nineteenth-
century reinventions of Tamar is at all 'realistic' or 'truthful', but
their ubiquitous presence in modern histories of queen Tamar has
meant that they have had a pervasive, if unconscious, influence on
popular perceptions of the queen. While Lermontov is now mentioned only to be dismissed, the very fact that he is there at all can
only lead one to suspect that there is no smoke without fire. The
impact of the engravings has been rather more insidious. These have
been used to illustrate otherwise serious accounts of the reign.[31] The
choice of nineteenth-century images, rather than one of the surviving
medieval portraits of the queen, inevitably has an impact on how the
reader assesses the queen. The engravings do not act as mere
illustrations to the texts they accompany (which is, no doubt, how
the authors and publishers envisaged them) but rather as glosses on
those texts of, at best, dubious relevance. They colour the texts with

107

their sentimental visions of youthful grace, European gentleness and almost virginal beauty. It becomes difficult not to picture this nineteenth-century Tamar, with these qualities, as the figure described in the more factual accounts in the histories. This image of a modest and saintly queen Tamar has perhaps been as influential on modern historians and popular views as the first images of Tamar were on their intended audiences.[32]

The contrasts between the two nineteenth-century views of Tamar, one Russian and the other Georgian, have shown how dependent our modern views are on these popular images, especially in a field as remote as Georgian studies. The opposing tides of 'siren' or 'saint' envelop all literature on Tamar, so that it is almost impossible to avoid them. However, these are only the most visible manifestations of a far deeper dichotomy which underlies the framework within which gender in Georgia must be discussed. This is the problem of the way in which Georgian medieval society itself should be characterised. All accounts of Tamar's reign rely in the end on an assessment of the society from which she came and its attitudes towards women. To Lermontov, Georgia was an exotic, 'oriental' society with all the attraction and excitement associated with those terms; it was the 'other' to the Eurocentric sophistication of the St Petersburg to which he belonged. This orientalist view was adopted by many other nineteenth-century writers.[33] At the same time, on the other hand, Georgians were being encouraged by their new Tsarist government to emulate Russian and especially St Petersburgian social models. There were, thus, two very different, contradictory constructions of society within Georgia itself, both of which could be applied back to the age of queen Tamar.

Georgia's position on the easternmost fringe of the medieval Christian world has left it in a geographical, socio-historical and cultural chasm.[34] It lies between Europe and Asia (often in neither)[35] and between the cultural mainstreams of Islam and Byzantine Christianity. It is a position far more precarious than Byzantium's on the eastern fringe of Europe.[36] The evidence from Tamar's reign itself does little to alleviate the confusion. On the one hand is the visual material from the orthodox churches built in the reign which show a great affinity to Byzantine models. This is supported by the Byzantine, Christian morality of the historical chronicles and contemporary theological writings. On the other hand is the literary evidence of Šota Rustaveli's *Vepxist'q'aosani*. Although the poem seems to reflect the life of queen Tamar, being about an unmarried princess destined to inherit her father's throne, the narrative is set in India and nowhere even mentions Christianity.

This indeterminacy has affected how questions relating to gender have been approached. With no easily categorisable identity of its own, Georgia is defined by other pre-existing models, whether western/feudal,[37] or oriental/despotic,[38] and so adopts their prevailing models of gender roles. As a result the image of Tamar has been usually constructed according to one of these models. The modern image of Georgia may be divided between western/Russian and Georgian writings. In the western world view, medieval Georgia is included in the Orient.[39] These views were largely arrived at by transposing the modern image of Georgia back onto its past. Visitors in the nineteenth century saw a country only recently brought under Tsarist rule after centuries of domination by either the Ottoman Turks or the Safavids; and it was these cultures that determined much of Georgia's outward appearance (Plate 5). The stereotypes of gender roles in an orientalist world view are well known, and this is where Tamar's sex becomes so important as it enabled her to be portrayed outside this standard image of arbitrary despotism. Indeed, Eugène d'Auriac, writing in 1892, saw Tamar's reign explicitly as an exception to the 'normal' actions of the oriental and cruel Bagrat'ioni kings.[40] The implication here is that it is Tamar's sex that makes her exceptional by nullifying the usual oriental characteristics of male rulers.

What is interesting about these nineteenth-century views is that they exactly parallel the ways in which Tamar's reign was justified and glorified in the thirteenth century in the chronicles of *Kartlis Cxovreba*, which were probably written in the 1220s or 1230s, as Georgia's power waned. As noted at the beginning of this chapter, these were written to give full expression to the idea of Tamar's reign as a 'Golden Age'. However, what makes this 'Golden Age' so unusual is the way in which it is oriented so closely around the person of the queen. The introduction to Šota Rustaveli's poem declares that the poem was written out of love for the queen, to whom the whole work is dedicated.[41] And in *Kartlis Cxovreba* every action is inspired by Tamar, or carried out in her honour. What is noticeable is the chronicles' insistence on Tamar as the focal point of the reign, and also the claim that this was realised at the time: we are told that on Tamar's deathbed, her subjects offered to sacrifice themselves in her place so that her reign could continue.[42] To achieve this impression, the chronicles have written the history of the reign in a way that

Plate 5 Les Terrasses de Tiflis. Engraving by G. Gagarin *c.*1851
Source: Courtesy of the British Library

re-evaluates the effect of Tamar's sex, and they give no hint that female leadership could have acted to the detriment of the country. Iurii Bogoliubskii's attempted coup of 1187 and Rukn ad-Din's attack of 1205 are both presented in a very different light in which their views are made to seem perverse, rather than Tamar's position to be weak. What Rukn-ad-Din saw as a common, 'inevitable' weakness is reinterpreted in the chronicles as an exceptional slight, and Iurii Bogoliubskii's ambitions are similarly disparaged. Both attackers are made to seem greedy and unstable, and their ambition extreme. Their base (oriental?) behaviour is contrasted with Tamar's stability and Christian good sense and, interestingly, both men's sexuality is brought into question.[43]

Although the chronicles re-express the events of Tamar's reign in a way that re-establishes her importance through gender, they do so in a way that still firmly locks the queen in a 'traditional', passive role. Although she is the focus of her 'Golden Age', she is so in a very different way from, for example, Augustus or Charlemagne.[44] These men are depicted as active participants in the acts of their courts and the creation of their glory. Tamar, on the other hand, is shown as a passive muse; the cultural efflorescence is in response to her existence and presence, not her actions. Even in the previous Georgian 'Golden Age', that of Tamar's great-grandfather, Davit IV Ağmašenebeli, the king is shown as the active centre: he initiates the policies of renewal and seeks out men for his court and new academy.[45] In Tamar's reign, the scholars, poets and artists, all men, gather together on their own initiative to celebrate the queen. Her role is inspirational and passive, not innovative or active. The second main chronicle of Tamar's reign, the *Histories and Eulogies of the Sovereigns*, even records that men went mad out of love for her, including one poor soul, a son of the king of Osseti, who pined to death.[46] These men were not lured to their deaths like Lermontov's love-lost victims of that other Tamara; quite the opposite: it is her chastity and the purity of her beauty that drives them to their deaths. Again, Tamar is not the instigator of the actions of the men around her. We are faced with an image of the queen as figurehead and personification, rather than active creator or participant. As Fraser pointed out, the structure of Tamar's 'Golden Age' is dependent on her gender; it is in fact the cause of it.

The figure of the queen is exploited to make the most of her sex. Its image of a passive, inspirational figurehead was not open to a male ruler. In descriptions familiar from Psellos, or Anna Komnene,[47] Tamar comes across in the chronicles as the ideal woman in that she adheres to all the gendered virtues of femininity: humility, love of mercy, devotion to family, faithfulness, hatred of violence, and purity.[48] This is a woman who never ordered anyone to be executed, and who pardoned her own ex-husband twice after his attempted coups. She helped monasteries throughout the east Christian world, from Libya to Bulgaria, Cyprus to Sinai,[49] and would permit no injustice in her realm. In fact, the queen's sanctity is almost too good for her kingdom's benefit, and her second (good) husband, Davit Soslan, has to execute one particularly evil brigand in secret, since he knows her clemency would be abused in this case.[50] However, the image of queen Tamar in the chronicles is more complex than this. Not only is she presented as an ideal woman, but she can also act as an effective man too. She is described as a wise and capable leader, and goes on campaign and even forms battle-plans.[51] These are all normally seen in Byzantine society as 'male' virtues, and are rarely applied to Byzantine women, without some form of qualification.[52] Indeed the only thing Tamar cannot do is actually fight. After addressing her troops, and leading them towards the battlefield, she has to retreat to a church or monastery, where she prays and weeps incessantly to help her troops. The image presented, then, carefully manoeuvres the queen between the pitfall of presenting her as a leader with only the passive qualities of the ideal woman, in which case she would be unable to feature prominently in her own reign, and that of assigning to her too many 'male' qualities which would undermine the positive aspects of her gender.[53]

The personification of the 'Golden Age' in the form of the queen, and her sanctification in the chronicles, was further accentuated by the portrayal of Tamar's successors, her children Giorgi IV Laša (1213–23) and Rusudan (1223–47). Their reigns coincided with the incursions of first the Khwarazmians and then the Mongols, which brought the Georgian ascendancy to an abrupt halt. Tamar was idealised as the model ruler and her virtues were contrasted with those of her children. Allen, basing his account on *Kartlis Cxovreba*, summed up the children thus: 'The adored sister of the splendid Lasha, she (Rusudan) shared his carnal tastes, but lacked his swash-buckling courage. She was fearless only in her lusts, and her polity was confined within the cruel and lurid meanness of an erotic woman.'[51] Here we can see again that the inclusion of gender pushes the interpretation to an extreme: men, it seems, can be splendid despite their sexual proclivities; women cannot. Gender is once more used as a means of identifying rulers with the historical events of their reigns. Just as Georgia's successes are seen as an expression of Tamar's saintliness, so its failures under the Mongols are personified by Rusudan's personal morality. Rusudan has been set up by the chronicles as a rhetorical foil to her mother.

It was the chronicles' desire to identify the morality of these women rulers with the fate of their country that required them to use gender and orientalism so forcefully. Whereas male rulers could be fitted in to a more traditional historical scheme, women rulers had to have their reigns explained in a different way which would take into account common notions of their supposed strengths and weaknesses. These stereotypes have echoed down the centuries to produce the various pictures of the queen that we see today. Perhaps the only exception to this is the depictions of queen Tamar set up during her lifetime, which I have examined in detail elsewhere.[55] As was seen earlier in the poetry of Šota Rustaveli, these royal portraits also provide a far more complex vision of the nature of Georgian society and the execution of power by a woman. The influence of Persian aesthetic and literary models, and our knowledge of the many close links between Tamar and the Moslem states around Georgia,[56] suggest that contemporary ideas of Georgia and orientalism could fit none of the simple patterns that were already being applied by the 1230s and which were later built upon by the nineteenth-century romantics.

NOTES

1 I wish to acknowledge the support of a postdoctoral fellowship from the British Academy while writing this chapter.
2 *Kartlis Cxovreba* II, S. Q'auxčišvili, ed. (Tbilisi, 1959), 146/13–22 (hereafter *KC*); K. Vivian, tr, *The Georgian Chronicle. The Period of Giorgi Lasha* (Amsterdam, 1991), 91–2. (*Kartlis Cxovreba* literally translates as *The Life of Kartli.*)
3 On the history of queen Tamar's reign, see: K. Salia, *History of the Georgian Nation* (Paris, 1980); W.E.D. Allen, *A History of the Georgian People* (London, 1932); A. Manvelichvili, *Histoire de Géorgie* (Paris, 1951), 181–98; M. Lordkipanidze, *History of Georgia in the XI–XII Centuries* (Tbilisi, 1987).
4 J. Aves, *Paths to National Independence in Georgia, 1987–1990* (London, 1991), 4.
5 See A. Alpago-Novello, V. Beridze and J. Lafontaine-Dosogne, *Art and Architecture of Medieval Georgia* (Louvain-La-Neuve, Milan and Tbilisi, 1980), 95–8, and R. Mepisašvili and W. Zinzade, *Die Kunst des Alten Georgiens* (Leipzig, 1977), 173–80.
6 Salia, *History*, 185.
7 Šota Rustaveli, *Vepxist'q'aosani*; M. Wardrop, tr., *Shot'ha Rust'haveli: The Man in the Panther's Skin* (London, 1912). Doubts as to the dating of the poem are raised in D.M. Lang, 'Popular and courtly elements in the Georgian epic', *Bedi Kartlisa* 27 (1970), 148. On other medieval literature, see J. Karst, *Littérature géorgienne chrétienne* (Strasbourg, 1934), 124–36.

8 D.M. Lang, 'Georgia in the reign of Giorgi the Brilliant', *Bulletin of the School of Oriental and African Studies* 17 (1955), 74–91.

9 One needs only glance through the indexes of general histories of Byzantium, such as G. Ostrogorsky, *History of the Byzantine State* (New Jersey, 1957), to see the absence of any consideration of Georgia (especially when compared to the attention given to Byzantium's other neighbours, such as Armenia, Bulgaria or Serbia).

10 R. Met'reveli, *Mepe tamari* (Tbilisi, 1991) (in Georgian, with Russian and English summaries).

11 Manvelichvili, *Histoire*, 197–8; Lordkipanidze, *Georgia*, 141. The influence of Georgian nationalism has also affected this portrayal of the reign.

12 *KC* II, 119/4–120/12; Vivian, *Georgian Chronicle*, 59–60.

13 *KC* II, 133/14–134/2; Vivian, *Georgian Chronicle*, 77–8; M. Canard, 'Les reines de Géorgie dans l'histoire musulmanes', *Revue des Études Islamiques* 1 (1969), 7.

14 Salia, *History*, 177–8.

15 G. Alibegašvili, *Četyre portreta Caricy Tamary* (Tbilisi, 1957), which was revised and extended in 1979 as *Svetskii portret v gruzinskoi srednevekovoi monumental'noi živopisi* (Tbilisi, 1979), 12–29. Alibegašvili deals with only four of the portraits of Tamar as the fifth image was discovered in 1982.

16 On contemporary attitudes to women in the Byzantine world, see, for example, Psellos, *Chronographie*, ed. E. Renauld, (Paris, 1928), 6 (Zoe and Theodora), 1–14; 7 (Eudocia), 1–9. For recent work on Byzantine concepts of gender, see C. Galatariotou, 'Holy women and witches: aspects of Byzantine concepts of gender', *BMGS* 9 (1984/5), 55–94. Some authors have even seen a hint of Georgia's legendary Amazonian past in the supposed equality of women in medieval Georgia. The link has been made most explicitly by Vivian, *Georgian Chronicle*, 160–1.

17 A. Fraser, *Boadicea's Chariot, the Warrior Queens* (London, 1986), 167 (italics mine). A similarly obscure link between gender and success is made by G. Gaprindašvili, *Ancient Monuments of Georgia: Vardzia* (Leningrad, 1975), 7.

18 Allen, *History*, 103.

19 A. Liberman, tr., *Lermontov: Major Poetical Works* (London, 1983), 264 (stanza 2). Another Tamara also features in *The Demon* (*Lermontov*, 354–414), in which the heroine's desire for chastity is slowly worn down by the Demon and, in the end, she willingly surrenders her body to him and then dies. The poem was toned down by Lermontov for his imperial audience, with the result that her actions were eventually sanctified; see L. Kelly, *Lermontov: Tragedy in the Caucasus* (London, 1977), 105.

20 M. Pozharskaya and T. Volodina, *The Art of the Ballets Russes. The Russian Seasons in Paris 1908–29* (London, 1990), 16 and plate on 107. The choreographer was Mikhail Fokine. I am grateful to Marion Lynden-Bell for these references.

21 Quoted in R. Buckle, *Diaghilvev* (London, 1993), 230.

22 See, for example, the misogynist world view of Neophytos the Recluse in Galatariotou, 'Holy women and witches', 55–94.

23 Kelly, *Lermontov: Tragedy*, 78, conjures up his own romantic vision of

Lermontov, 'doubtless' hearing the story from 'some wily red-haired Ossetian hunter' on the Georgian military highroad, and embellishing it 'with scant regard for history'! Libermann, *Lermontov*, 562, also discusses the possible folklore origins of the poem. The Arabic account of Ibn-Bibi does question Tamar's sexuality; see M. Canard, 'Les reines de Géorgie dans l'histoire musulmanes', *Revue des Études Islamiques* 1 (1969), 6–8 (this also discusses possible links with Lermontov's poem). Other folklore stories about the queen are mentioned in R. Métréveli, 'La Reine Tamar dans le folklore géorgien', *Bedi Kartlisa* 27 (1970), 126–34.

24 For example, Allen, *History*, 103; Fraser, *Boadicea's Chariot*, 167–9.

25 This is particularly clear in discussions of the reign of Tamar's father, Giorgi III.

26 More nineteenth-century images can be found in J. Mourier, *L'art au Caucase* (Brussels, 1912), part 1, 207–8, which shows two almost identical engravings by Fritel and an anonymous postcard artist which are clearly based on Gagarin's original publication of the wall painting, and in N.V. Romanovskaia, *Gruzinskaia Carica Tamara i eia vremia* (Moscow, 1915), 4.

27 On Georgian nineteenth-century history, see Salia, *History*, 385–93; R. Suny, *The Making of the Georgian Nation* (Indiana, 1988), 63–95; D.M. Lang, *A Modern History of Georgia* (London, 1962), 70–115.

28 Prince G. Gagarin and Comte E. Stackelberg, *Le Caucase Pittoresque* (Paris, 1847), note to plates XXXVI–XXXIX. Gagarin discovered and cleaned the image of Tamar at Betania in 1851, and published his drawings and reports the same year. The debt of the engravings to the wall painting is apparent. Gagarin was a close friend of Lermontov, both being members of the 'Circle of Sixteen', and his other engravings of the Caucasus (and especially life in Tbilisi) show a similar romantic affinity to Lermontov's views: Kelly, *Lermontov: Tragedy*, 114.

29 I. Hilgendorf, 'The complex investigation of the fresco portraits of Queen Tamar', *IVe Symposium international sur l'art géorgien* (Tbilisi, 1984), 10pp., has shown that the original painting at Betania, visible in ultraviolet luminescent and x-rayemissiographic photographs beneath the present nineteenth-century surface, was similar in style to that at Vardzia.

30 V. Gvaharia, 'La musique en Géorgie au temps de la grande reine Tamar', *Bedi Kartlisa* 35 (1977), 204–35. On Grigol Orbeliani's nostalgic and patriotic verse, see D. Rayfield, *The Literature of Georgia. A History* (Oxford, 1994), 153–5.

31 The most striking modern examples are Salia, *History*, plate 22; Fraser, *Boadicea's Chariot*, unnumbered plate between pp. 144–5 (who shows an engraving from 1859); and Manvelichvili, *Histoire*, 183 (who also gives similar nineteenth-century images of St Nino [93] and Šota Rustaveli [212]).

32 I have addressed this question more fully in A. Eastmond, *Royal Imagery in Medieval Georgia* (Penn State, 1997 forthcoming), chap. 3.

33 The one notable exception to this is the work of Marie-Félicité Brosset, the great French translator of *Kartlis Cxovreba* (as *Histoire de la Géorgie*

depuis l'antiquité jusqu'en 1469 de J.-C. (St Petersburg, 1849) and *Additions et éclaircissements à l'histoire de la Géorgie* (St Petersburg, 1851).

34 In Great Britain, the Caucasus has not yet earned a distinct identity, and is included on the fringes of either Central Asian or ex-Soviet studies, neither of which it entirely fits. Georgia has also lacked the diaspora that has given Armenian studies such prominence in the west (especially in France and the USA).

35 Compare, for example, the cataloguing systems of the Bodleian Library, Oxford, and the British Library. These place Georgia in Asia and Europe respectively.

36 The case for Byzantium as 'other' has most recently been made by Averil Cameron, 'The use and abuse of Byzantium', *Changing Cultures in Early Byzantium* (Aldershot, 1996), Study XIII.

37 The best exponent of this view is Lordkipanidze, *Georgia*, 5–27 (the book has a strongly Marxist approach which the author would not, perhaps, adopt today). Art historical texts also seek to infiltrate Georgian art into the discourse of the western Renaissance, often in a wildly ahistorical way; see O. Pirališvili, *Qintsvisi Murals* (Tbilisi, 1979), 51–72, esp. 71, who compares the works of Michelangelo, Raphael and Leonardo da Vinci unfavourably with the 'humanism' of the wall-paintings of the church at Q'inc'visi (*c.*1207), which features one of the portraits of queen Tamar.

38 For western conceptions of the Orient, particularly in the nineteenth century, and their implications for views about the position and characteristics of women, see R. Kabbani, *Imperial Fictions: Europe's Myths of Orient*, 2nd ed. (London, 1994), 26, 48–53, 74–8; E. Said, *Orientalism. Western Conceptions of the Orient* (Harmondsworth, 1995). On the Russian orientalism and feminisation of Georgia in the nineteenth century, see S. Layton, 'Eros and Empire in Russian Literature about Georgia', *Slavic Review* 57 (1992), 194–213; now expanded in S. Layton, *Russian Literature and Empire. Conquest of the Caucasus from Pushkin to Tolstoy* (Cambridge, 1994), 174–211. (I am very grateful to Steve Rapp for these references.)

39 The 'oriental' tendencies of Georgia were clearly implied by Gagarin and Stackelberg, *Le Caucase Pittoresque*, 6: 'Les Ivères, ou Khartvels, ont subi l'influence de relations fréquentes avec les nations de l'Occident, dont le contact leur à inculqué les premiers éléments d'ordre et de civilisation. L'esprit du christianisme, l'habitude du régime monarchique les ont préparés à recevoir une organisation stable et une administration régulière.' ('The Iberians, or Khartvels, experienced the influence of frequent contacts with western nations. This contact instilled in them the first elements of order and civilisation. The spirit of Christianity, the custom of a monarchical regime prepared them for stable organisation and lawful administration.') In western Europe, Georgia has been seen as similarly oriental. When seeking a return to the excitement and mysticism of the Orient after a 'dull' period as consul in Trieste, Sir Richard Burton requested a transfer to Tiflis (Tbilisi); see Kabbani, *Europe's Myths*, 94. Even H.F.B. Lynch, *Armenia: Travels and Studies*,

vol. 1 (London, 1910), 69, bemoaned Caucasian Christian habits in familiar terms when exasperated: 'it was Oriental, it was pathetic . . .'. These nineteenth-century views have continued to exert influence on the popular perceptions of Georgia; see, for example, V.S. Naipaul, *Among the Believers: An Islamic Journey* (London, 1981), 177, who writes that his impression of the Orient was determined by Tolstoy and Lermontov's writings from the Caucasus.

40 E. d'Auriac, *Thamar: Reine de Géorgie 1184–1212* (Angers, 1892), 1. His standard characterisation of the Georgians, against which he contrasts queen Tamar, is quite unambiguous: 'Mais ni la religion des Géorgiens, ni leur civilisation avancée ne les avaient encore fait renoncer à ces habitudes barbares des peuples, et surtout des souverains de l'Orient, qui ne connaissent d'autre droit que la force et ne parviennent le plus souvent au trône que par le massacre de leur parents.' ('But neither the religion of the Georgians nor their advanced civilisation made them give up these barbaric customs of the people and above all of the rulers of the Orient, who knew of no other law than force and who usually only succeeded to the throne by slaughtering their parents.') Equally, the decision to ascribe Georgia to an 'oriental' sphere has led modern western writers to apply radically different sets of values to their analysis than they might apply to a western society. Thus W.E.D. Allen, a Mosleyite Unionist MP before the Second World War, was prepared to say in defence of Giorgi III that: 'if later kings had used the blinding iron and knife with the same cold brutality against the Jaqelis and the Imerian Bagratids [Georgian rebels], the history of the Georgian people might have been less bloody and more fortunate' (Allen, *History*, 103); and his view has recently been repeated by Vivian, *Georgian Chronicle*, 159. Such a view is alien even to twelfth-century writers, such as Niketas Choniates, who lamented the Byzantine emperor Andronikos I Komnenos's excessive use of violence in the maintenance of his rule (Niketas Choniates, *Historia*, J.L. van Dieten, ed. [Berlin, 1975], 354).

41 Wardrop, *The Man in the Panther's Skin*, 1–6.

42 *KC* II, 145/7–15; Vivian, *Georgian Chronicle*, 90.

43 Iurii Bogoliubskii is condemned for his sexual deviance: *KC* II, 120/12–121/17; Vivian, *Georgian Chronicle*, 60–1; and Rukn-ad-Din for his polygamy.

44 P. Zanker, *The Power of Images in the Age of Augustus* (Michigan, 1988), 101 ff.; Einhard and Notker the Stammerer, *Two Lives of Charlemagne* (Harmondsworth, 1969), 79 ff.

45 *KC* I, 330–2; Vivian, *Georgian Chronicle*, 13–14.

46 *KC* II, 37/16; Brosset, *Histoire de la Géorgie*, 413.

47 For Psellos's description of his daughter, see K. Sathas, *Mesaionike Bibliotheke*, V (Paris, 1876), 62–87. For Anna Komnene's description of her mother, see her *Alexiad*, B. Leib, ed. (Paris, 1945), XII, 3.

48 All these virtues are applied to queen Tamar in *Kartlis Cxovreba*: *KC* II, 134–43; Vivian, *Georgian Chronicle*, 78–87.

49 *KC* II, 141/24–8 and 142/3–7; Vivian, *Georgian Chronicle*, 85–6; and *KC* II, 91/10–17; Brosset, *Histoire de la Géorgie*, 455.

50 *KC* II, 141/12–20; Vivian, *Georgian Chronicle*, 85.

51 *KC* II, 134/3–11; Vivian, *Georgian Chronicle*, 78.
52 This is particularly clear in, for example, Psellos's *Chronographia*, which covers the personal rule of several women. Thus, Zoe and Theodora, although capable, are never wise, and Eudokia Makrembolitissa's military abilities are circumscribed by her sexuality; see Psellos, *Chronographia*, E. Renauld, ed. and tr. (Paris, 1926–8), VI, 5 (Zoe and Theodora); VII, 1–9 (Eudokia); also B. Hill, L. James and D. Smythe, 'Zoe: the rhythm method of imperial renewal', in P. Magdalino, ed., *New Constantines. The Rhythm of Imperial Renewal in Byzantium, 4th–13th Centuries* (Aldershot, 1994), 215–29.
53 It is interesting to note how similar this account of the nature of Tamar's rule is to that of Elizabeth I of England. Both women cultivated a cult around their person that minimised the importance of men, and although they both espoused peace, they rallied their troops before battle, and personally reaped the rewards of their generals' victories. See Fraser, *Boadicea's Chariot*, 203–25 (this overplays the differences between Tamar and Elizabeth I by exaggerating Tamar's martial desires).
54 Allen, *History*, 111. In a similar vein see Mourier, *L'art*, 212 n. 2.
55 Eastmond, *Royal Imagery*, chap. 3.
56 V. Minorsky, *Studies in Caucasian History* (London, 1953), 135.

6

SALOME'S SISTERS: THE RHETORIC AND REALITIES OF DANCE IN LATE ANTIQUITY AND BYZANTIUM[1]

Ruth Webb

INTRODUCTION

One approach to the understanding of women's lives and of conceptions of gender in societies of the past, represented by several of the studies in this volume, is to look for evidence of women performing traditionally male roles: as rulers, patrons, artists or writers. An alternative is to concentrate on more humble occupations, on aspects of daily life or less prestigious activities (often considered a female preserve). The area I have chosen for this study is dance and specifically women's participation in dance, either as professional entertainers or informally as part of the social fabric of their daily lives.

Dance is a potentially rich area of study for the cultural historian. Recent interest in gesture, ritual and the social significance of the body has provided a background against which to explore the role of dance in society and in the construction of gender.[2] The burgeoning literature on the anthropology and sociology of spectacle and the theatre in all periods of antiquity provides a backdrop to the study of dance as performed on the public stage.[3] Away from the formal stage, Peter Brown has also drawn attention to the importance of physical presence and bodily performance in rhetoric and in daily life.[4] This interest in the use of the body stems ultimately from the work of the French anthropologist Marcel Mauss, who was the first to observe that the way we perform such apparently natural activities as walking, swimming or eating is as culturally specific as language and that these seemingly banal actions have their own meanings within a given culture.[5] As Pierre Bourdieu has suggested, the ways in which different groups conceive of and use the body reflect the ways in which they structure the wider environment, including, of course, the construction of gender.[6] Dance is one part of this continuum of bodily practice and dance forms belonging to different cultural contexts differ greatly in the conceptions of the body that they express and confirm.[7]

The occasions at which dance is performed and the manner of the performance also have a part in their wider social context. Here the work of Jane Cowan has shown how dance events in contemporary Greece both reflect and influence social interactions.[8] But the type and range of evidence available to the anthropologist is far beyond the reach of the historian. Dance has never enjoyed great prestige in the western tradition, and this lack of prestige is compounded, and perhaps caused, by the fact that the dancer, like any performance artist, leaves behind no direct monumental or textual traces.[9] Dance and performance in general, particularly by women, have rarely been the stuff of history: in the second century Lucian censured one historian for recording such banalities as the performance of a flute-girl rather than concentrating on reporting battles.[10]

The evidence that we do have for professional and non-professional dance by women in late antiquity is scattered but, I think, sufficient to indicate that it is an area worth examination. The sources discussed in this chapter are from a large geographical and chronological span: from the second to the seventh centuries AD and from rural Egypt to Constantinople. I have included in my survey references to 'women of the stage' (*thumelikai, scaenicae*) as well as to performers specifically identified as dancers or mimes (*choreutriai, orchestrides, mimades*); the problems raised by a woman dancing in public are much the same as those raised by any female performer. The type of evidence varies greatly. Some visual representations of dance and dancers do remain, on textiles for example, but interpreting the visual traces of dance or gesture in the visual arts is a notoriously difficult enterprise.[11] The documentary sources are scarce: one papyrus contract provides tantalising information about the economics of dance; the provisions of the Theodosian Code show the regulations imposed on 'women of the stage', while various Church councils attempt to restrict performance, particularly by women.[12]

As Lucian's comments suggest, history is not rich in references to dance and dancers. Procopius's lurid portrait of Theodora in the *Secret History* illustrates the difficulties involved in interpreting the evidence for female performers where it does exist. Other literary sources such as epigrams, hagiography and sermons contain indications that dance and performance more generally were professions open to women. The *Life of Pelagia*, for example, portrays the dramatic repentance of a celebrated performer in the fifth century, while the civic world of Symeon the Fool in the later sixth century was still inhabited by 'women of the stage' with whom he danced as proof of his immunity to sexual desire.[13] One of the richest sources, alongside the repeated prohibitions of the Church councils, is represented by Homilies. Those of John Chrysostom in particular contain many references to the stage and popular entertainment.

It is clear from the sources that there were many forms of public or semi-public context for dance performance in the first centuries of the Christian era. Women performed mime but not, it seems, the more serious pantomime.[14] Pelagia is described as 'the leading mime-actress (*mimas*) of Antioch who was also the leader of the chorus-girls (*choreutriai*) of the pantomime performer'.[15] That some such women might attain considerable wealth is suggested by the extravagant account of Pelagia's retinue. Within the narrative of the *Life*, the description of Pelagia's wealth serves a particular purpose, highlighting the wanton luxury of her worldly existence, then underlining the drama of her conversion as she orders all her gold and ornaments to be given to the Church. The presentation of this woman suggests, however, that some female performers might in fact attain considerable economic power. Some such reality may lie behind the figure (familiar from modern mythology) of the humble performer who, through her art, comes to mix with the powerful, a *topos* found not only in Procopius's representation of the empress Theodora but also in one of Aristainetos's fictional *Letters*, probably composed in the early sixth century.[16] Pelagia's *Life* also highlights the imprecision in the use of terms to describe such performers. The same performer may be described as 'mime' (*mimas*) and 'dancer' (*choreutria*), often the broader term *scaenica*, 'woman of the stage', or its Greek equivalent, *thumelike*, is used as in the life of Symeon.

Some of Chrysostom's criticisms of dance introduce us to a different phenomenon: the participation in dance by ordinary women as part of celebrations such as weddings.[17] It is against this background that I will consider the figure of the daughter of Herodias, wife of Herod. She is nameless in the earliest accounts of the death of John the Baptist, only later acquiring the name under which she continues to exert a fascination: Salome.[18] Although her notorious performance is in many ways a very public act, it is still set within the context of family relationships and might give us some insight into the less public function of dance in women's lives.

Sources such as hagiography, history and sermons are rarely, if ever, neutral in their presentation of dance and entertainment. Most of the references to these activities occur in contexts of disapprobation or prohibition. Public performers were, by definition, highly visible and, as such, attracted comment from vocal individuals like Chrysostom who felt that this visibility violated the norms of their ideal of society.[19] The terms of such criticisms can tell us about the systems of values in operation, and it is possible to set these comments against the wider background of conceptions of gender and the body current in antiquity.

In addition to the 'rhetoric' of the condemnation, I am also interested in looking beyond the sources to the realities of women's lives in late antiquity, to the experience of the performer or the importance of dance to women. Here we encounter the perennial problems that face the historian in search of 'the realities of female existence' in ancient and medieval societies.[20] The sources cast a veil of misrepresentation, or silence, around their subjects. They are far from representing women's experience, except in so far as the prohibitions may have been internalised by them.[21] Yet the very need for the polemic is clear proof that there were other voices to be heard. If the representatives of the Early Church felt the need to reiterate their prohibitions, there was presumably a public demand for performance and a general tolerance of women dancing at weddings and other festivals. Such tolerance, and enjoyment, can only be deduced from our sources. But it is possible to take some tentative steps further, to at least suggest some ways in which we might try to fill in a wider context in which the polemicists were simply one strand of opinion.

The results of such reading between the lines are, of course, very tentative, and can only be suggestions of what might have been. In trying to outline the context for late antique performance I have used the model of dance in the modern Middle East. I would suggest that the aesthetics of dance in our sources recall something close to the dance styles of the modern Middle East which may, or may not, be directly descended from women's dances of our period and earlier.[22] A term that recurs in Greek accounts of dance is *lugisma*, suggesting fluid, winding movements of the torso. The descriptions of Salome's dance in Early Christian writers, Greek and Latin alike, insist on the sinuous motion of her body.[23] What is important is not the reconstruction of movement, but the way in which this aesthetic of dance is part of a wider aesthetic of the female body in the ancient Mediterranean world. It is the sinuous motion of the servant girl Photis's torso and the vibration of her hips as she works that first attract the hapless narrator in Apuleius's *Metamorphoses*.[24] Centuries later, the eleventh-century Byzantine author Kekaumenos uses the word *gurisma* (twisting, turning) to describe the characteristic motion of the female body, which should be kept concealed from strangers' eyes.[25]

However, there are other ways in which dance in the contemporary Middle East might be relevant to the subject of this chapter. The work of Karin van Nieuwkerk on female entertainers in modern Egypt is particularly rich in suggestions as to how our sources may originally have been situated within a wider spectrum of opinion and practice. Her interviews with informants from a variety of social backgrounds reveal the diversity of opinion that can exist within a society. While members of the upper classes are likely to condemn dancers as immoral women, those of the lower classes, closer in status to the dancers themselves, tend to present them in a more banal light, as working women. Interviews with the performers themselves reveal that these 'dishonourable' women in fact have their own strict moral codes. The interviews also illustrate the complex ways in which a society's codes of shame and honour can accommodate apparent contradictions, allowing a dishonourable activity like dance to be enjoyed and condemned at one and the same time, one strategy being to attribute all the blame incurred to the performer.[26]

Once alerted to such strategies, we can detect something very similar in our sources. Seen in this light, the frequent assimilation of performers to prostitutes (*pornai*) appears as a way of expressing moral disapprobation rather than as a statement of fact about the status of performers. Following Fatna Sabbah, van Nieuwkerk further notes the way in which Muslim culture tends to ignore the economic aspects of women, defining them instead as essentially sexual beings.[27] Again this is a valuable reminder of the aspects of performance that are almost entirely ignored by our sources.

The historiography of dance in the medieval and modern Middle East also offers some instructive parallels to the problems involved in the history of dance in antiquity, showing how a rich tradition may be almost entirely ignored by official literature and even documents. Very few references to dance exist in Arabic literature, but those that do, combined with the iconograpic evidence, such as the unique depictions of dancers in the richly decorated Umayyad 'palace' at Qusayr Amra, provide glimpses of a long and rich courtly tradition.[28] Apart from a fascinating account of dance, placed by the tenth-century encyclopaedist Al-Mas'udi in the mouth of a male musician, this tradition is largely ignored by classical Arabic texts.[29] The stigma attached to women who performed in public meant that dancers were rarely mentioned even in official records as late as the nineteenth century.[30] A different type of evidence, which has no precise parallel for the ancient world, does exist but poses further problems of interpretation. Since the seventeenth century, European travellers had remarked on the public dancing girls of Egypt.[31] These western writers hinted at scenes of scandalous immorality, an idea developed by orientalist writers and artists in the nineteenth century, in their use of the dancer as the epitome of the languid, sensual exoticism of the East.[32]

The accounts of dance left by male European travellers to the Orient ignore a vital dimension of dance in society. Only the most public performances of dance would have been accessible to them as foreign males. However, certain professional dancers were also invited to perform for respectable women at family celebrations, a fact that reveals, once again, a rather more complex set of attitudes to professional dancers.[33] More important still is the existence of an almost entirely unrecorded tradition of female dance, an art passed down from mother to daughter and performed privately in the home, away from the male gaze and thus as invisible to the outside observer as to the historian.[34] This popular practice forms the background to the public, professional dancers and informs the female viewer's appreciation of a professional performance. What is more, it is as a vital means of expression for women that this dance takes on its real importance.[35]

I will be suggesting that this model may allow us to guess at a hidden context behind the evidence for female dance in society and the role of dance in women's lives. It should also lead us to question the almost total silence that falls on the female performer in the Byzantine period. After the fourth century, references to dance and dancers become few and far between, so much so that a pell-mell accumulation of references of vastly differing dates and types such as that offered by Koukoules seems the only option.[36] While the existence of some form of dance is hardly in doubt for the later centuries, it is more difficult to establish the existence of professional female performers or the contexts for performance. Does this mean that, once the first flurry of Christian denunciation had died down and the secular spectacles of the Late Roman cities had declined, professional dancers disappeared? Or is this silence on a delicate subject only to be expected?

Such questions are, of course, ultimately unanswerable. But, in what follows I will try to show how dance, as bodily practice and as spectacle, occupies a space intersected by questions of gender, viewing and social values and can thus provide a starting point for just such questions which can never be answered but which are well worth asking. In some cases I believe that such questions lead us to surprising answers, illustrating the pitfalls of applying modern theories, feminist or otherwise, directly to ancient sources. In particular, premonitions of modern concerns with 'the gaze' have also been traced in John Chrysostom, who will be one of our main informants.[37] I believe, however, that the network of attitudes to the female body in motion that our sources on dance reveal may indicate an alternative dynamic between viewer and viewed to the one dominant in modern critical discourse. After examining the inter-linked questions of gender and viewing I will be asking yet another unanswerable question, this time of the literary depictions of the most notorious female dancer of all antiquity, Salome. How far can we see in this figure, not simply a projection of male desire, but a representation of a specifically female form of expression?

DANCE AND GENDER

Dance emerges from even a cursory overview of the sources as a gendered activity and it is this aspect that I will explore first of all. In practice, dance performance, including mime, was staged publicly in late antiquity by men and women, and both male and female performers suffered from the disabilities imposed by Roman law.[38] Culturally, however, dance was considered a 'feminine' activity, as opposed to a 'masculine' activity such as rhetoric, the gendered nature of which is unambiguously illustrated in Artemidoros's discussion of the interpretation of dreams in which he interprets the penis as a sign of speech and education.[39] The accusation of effeminacy was constantly levelled against male mime artists: in the opening lines of Lucian's dialogue on dance (*orchesis*), the art (mime) is described as 'a worthless and womanish affair' whose male performers are 'effeminate beings'.[40] Male participation in dance was condemned by Christians and pagans alike as 'unbecoming' (*aprepes*) or 'unmanly' (*anandros*).[41] Nor did they need to participate actively in dance to put their virile status at risk. The mere perception of spectacles could have this debilitating effect, and various types of entertainment are described in Patristic and Byzantine texts as quite literally 'feminising' those who see or hear them.[42]

The fact that the performance of rhetoric in antiquity was very much a physical activity, a point that has been stressed in several recent studies of culture, rhetoric and the theatre in later antiquity, reinforces the parallel between the verbal and non-verbal performance arts.[43] As will be seen below in the story of Salome, the parallel of kinetic and verbal discourse could be presented as a contrast, even an antagonism, between the two.

Another culturally 'masculine' activity that was explicitly presented as the antithesis of dance was athletics. In one epigram by Rufinus, probably composed at the end of the first century AD, the speaker describes his transferral of interest from boys to women in terms of his abandonment of the discus and of the delicate skin of young boys in favour of *krotala* (wooden or metal clappers), the sign of the dancer in art and literature, and the artificially whitened complexion of the dancer.[44] The *krotala* appear as the attribute of the female entertainer in the fifth-century AD epigram by Claudianos mocking Machlas, an ageing dancer, who uses rouge and dyes her hair to hide the marks of mortality.[45] The discus is the symbol of boys' athletic training.[46] In the light of the gendered nature of the discus and *krotala* as male and female respectively, it is tempting to see a visual pun in the intriguing mosaic depictions at Piazza Armerina of 'bikini-clad' women wielding the discus and other athletic instruments. The similarity in shape between the round bronze *krotala* often depicted in dancers' hands and the discus reinforces the ironic reference. There was, moreover, surely a certain piquancy in the sight, in life or art, of these women wielding the symbols of virility – the ancient Sicilian equivalent of the semi-naked model astride a motorbike.[47] The Christian appropriation of *athletes* to mean 'martyr' allowed further development of this antithesis. In an epigram arguing against the practice of feasting at the martyrs' tombs, Gregory Nazianzen presents dance and the endurance of martyrdom as complete opposites.[48]

One element that recurs in Christian tirades against dance, and indeed all the performance arts, is the fear of feminisation, the fear that in watching, or even listening to, a spectacle a man might lose his grip on virility. This is one example of the way in which attitudes to dance form part of a larger social continuum and points towards an important feature of ancient and indeed Byzantine conceptions of gender, in particular the nature of masculinity. This latter was seen as a fragile achievement, a state attained through training and constant self-control, summed up in the notion of *paideia*.[49] Young men were considered in some respects similar or equivalent to women. In the lives of the Desert Fathers, beardless youths present the same temptations to the monks as do women.[50] Eunuchs, of course, who never developed masculine characteristics, retained the womanly nature of the young boy.[51] Catharine Edwards has shown how the rhetoric of effeminacy in Roman society served to define the behaviour expected of the Roman male.[52] But is there anything in these conceptions of gender roles that may help us to understand female experience? The assimilation of youths and eunuchs to women is perhaps unsurprising. It is significant, however, for it suggests that the female was considered to be a state that men left behind through puberty and, for the upper classes, through the rigours of *paideia*. Moreover, it was a state into which they were always in danger of falling. Indeed, the notion that the female was a prior, if imperfect, state of the male made the danger of a man lapsing into womanhood more acute.[53]

There is nothing surprising in a set of oppositions within which women are set firmly on the side of 'nature' rather than 'culture'. But might the notion of the female as primary have wider implications for the construction, and even the experience, of female sexuality? It is important to note, in particular, how radically different this conception of gender is from the Freudian notion of the woman as an ex-male still struggling to repress the last vestiges of masculinity within her.[54] It is precisely this Freudian notion that underlies current theories of sight and female sexuality whose relevance to the understanding of antiquity will be discussed, and questioned, below.

Although dance, whether performed by men or women, was, as we have seen, a culturally female activity, the biological sex of the dancer still influenced the significance of the act. One of the clearest expressions of such differences is to be found in the interpretation given to dreams of dance by Artemidoros in the *Oneirokritika*. As John Winkler has noted, Artemidoros reflects the 'common social assumptions' of the second century AD, particularly through his keen awareness of the difference that the gender and social status of the dreamer made to the significance of the dream.[55] For a man, dreams of dancing in a private setting, whether he dreams he is dancing alone, or that he sees his wife or relatives dancing, are of good omen, signifying well-deserved relaxation.[56] But dancing in public is a different matter; to dream of dancing in the presence of strangers is no good for anyone. Public performance here seems to mean the mime, and it is the characteristics of this art – splendid costumes, fictive characters and narrative plot – that underly the interpretation of such dreams when the dreamer is male. Depending on the status of the dreamer, they foretell wealth which will ultimately prove ephemeral, or alternatively legal embroilments as complex as the plot of a mime. But in the case of women, Artemidoros makes no such differentiation, nor do the external trappings of the mime's art play any part in the interpretation offered. For the female dreamer, whatever her social status, the very fact of appearing in public is sufficient to foretell 'great and infamous scandals'.[57]

PUBLIC DISPLAY

Conceptions and values surrounding dance can thus be seen as part of a wider cultural continuum. In this section I will first consider the evidence for the public performance of dance by women and its contexts. In most cases, of course, the evidence itself calls for careful interpretation. Procopius's notorious account of Theodora's up-bringing in the *Secret History* offers what purports to be a fascinating glimpse of the life of such *scaenicae* behind the scenes of the hippodrome at Constantinople.[58] Interestingly, he suggests that the skilled dancers were slightly more esteemed than a prostitute and stripper like the Theodora whom he portrays. Procopius is careful to note that she relied solely on her beauty and total lack of shame 'for she was neither a flute-player nor a harpist nor was she even practised in the dance' (*ta es ten orchestran*).[59] The place of even the skilled dancer in Procopius's hierarchy of the arts was clearly not elevated.

However, the importance of dance in particular in the ceremonial life of fourth-century Constantinople can be seen on the Theodosian Obelisk base, still standing in the hippodrome. On the east side a chorus-line of female dancers, accompanied by flutes and organs, is shown performing in front of the Emperor as he crowns a victor.[60] The stipulations concerning entertainers (*scaenicae*), presumably including dancers such as these, in the Theodosian Code show their vital importance to the state. Women of the stage were required to perform for the public good and any man who took a female performer away from her duty was subject to punishment.[61] This example of the rigid moral hierarchy in the Empire, and the inter-dependence of its highest and lowliest strata, sat uneasily with the tenets of Christianity. The Code attempted to negotiate between the needs of the State and individual morality by allowing performers to leave the profession on converting to Christianity. If they fell ill and took the sacraments but then recovered they could still leave the stage. But care was taken to avoid exploitation of this potential loophole, and the Code stipulated that they should not take the sacraments unless their illness was really serious.[62] It appears that attitudes to performers were just as complex and riven with apparent contradictions as those displayed by van Nieuwkerk's contemporary Egyptian informants.

Not all performance took place on an organised stage, and certainly not in such a regulated fashion. Male and female dancers were a feature of wealthy houses: Gregory of Nyssa lists a whole troupe of entertainers, including mimes, male and female musicians and female dancers (*orchestrides*), among the trappings of an extrava-gantly wealthy household.[63] In addition to the Gospel account of Salome, Josephus also mentions a dancing girl (*orchestris*) at a feast.[64] Otherwise, dancers could be hired for special occasions such as festivals or weddings. In some cases the same performers who appeared in organised civic spectacles may also have hired themselves out for such events.[65] But outside the cities there is some evidence for dancers who performed only at such private occasions in villages, such as the 'krotala dancers' (*krotalistriai*) whose contract to perform in a private house in early third-century Egypt is preserved on papyrus.[66]

The papyrus contract mentioned above provides us with a rare insight into the lives of these women. The dancer named in the contract, Isidora, is requested to bring another with her, suggesting that some kind of organisation existed among such entertainers.[67] In the case of Isidora and her companion, we are also made aware of everyday problems such as transport and security: they are to be provided with donkeys and any costumes and gold ornaments are to be kept safely in the hirer's house during the six-day festival. What makes this document still more precious, given the overwhelmingly masculine point of view of our other references to dance and dancers, is that the hirer in this case is another woman, by the name of Artemisia.

These pieces of evidence suggest the wide range of the sources but also illustrate the problems of interpretation they pose. Few of our texts are as concrete as the contract between Artemisia and Isidora, or as matter-of-fact as Josephus's mention of the dancer at the feast. Yet even these demand further questions and interpretation. Beyond the details mentioned above, we know nothing of the nature of Artemisia's festival or of her background. What is more, the unusual extent of economic independence enjoyed by women in Egypt, in comparison with other regions of the Empire, limits the application of this precious information to the rest of the Empire.[68] In Josephus's narrative the (nameless) dancing girl is introduced only as a catalyst in an amorous intrigue. She is an object of desire for Joseph the Tobiad, who falls in love with her, but is forbidden to him as a 'foreigner'.[69]

Church councils provide some of our most eloquent testimonies to the popularity and frequency of dancing and watching dance at private functions. But these references are always in a context of prohibition and control and the picture they present of dancers is of dangerously sexual beings, far removed from the humble realities revealed by the papyrus contract. In the fourth century, for example, the council of Laodicea forbade Christians from dancing or other-wise behaving indecorously at weddings and ordered clerics to ensure that they did not see the organised entertainments by leaving before the entertainers (*thumelikoi*) arrived.[70] In the seventh century, the council in Trullo banned 'public dances by women which are able to cause much impurity and harm'.[71] The unease that these and other references suggest clearly stems from concern about the effect of the sight of a woman dancing on the (male) viewer. The blame, it would seem, lies mainly upon the performer.

While the points of view voiced in these acts are at several removes from the experience of female dancers and represent what was doubtless one extreme among a complex range of contradictory attitudes towards dance and dancers, they do contribute to our understanding of the construction of gender. It is precisely because female entertainers were by definition visible that they provided a focus for the expression of ideas and prohibitions, particularly concerning the female body, which must have affected all women to a greater or lesser extent. The concerns expressed in our sources, particularly the relation of the female performer to the male viewer, intersect with modern interests in spectacle and 'the gaze'.[72] What is most interesting, however, is the extent of the difference in the dynamics of viewed and viewer between ancient sources and modern theory.

WOMEN AND SPECTACLE

As Artemidoros's interpretation of dreams of dancing shows, performing in public, while problematic for either sex, involved different stakes for men and women in the second century. For women the very act of appearing on stage in public was a source of scandal. Our sources indicate that this remained true in later centuries for it is taken for granted that women who display themselves in this way are morally lax in general. In other words, the condemnation of their profession is expressed as a statement about their moral character.[73] The biographical accuracy of such expressions of disapproval of public display should naturally be assessed with caution; Procopius's account of the young Theodora in the *Secret History* is the most notorious example. The description of the as yet unrepentant Pelagia's first appearance in her *Life* contains the telling detail that her veil remained around her shoulders and did not cover her head as it should.[74] In the *Life* this gesture, which carries Pelagia's visibility on stage into the rest of her life, is presented as a sign of her immorality. John Chrysostom also tells the story of a nameless repentant actress (referred to simply as a *porne*, 'harlot') whom he claims to have encountered personally. Her refusal to allow her lovers the slightest glimpse of herself after her baptism, in contrast to the promiscuity of her former visibility, is presented as a paradox equal to, and thereby proving, the statement that the 'last will be first and the first last'.[75]

The most common argument in Christian sources against viewing female dance, or indeed any type of secular spectacle, is the effect on the viewer. In his twelfth-century commentary on the council of Trullo, Zonaras elaborated on the explicit reasons given there for banning public dancing – the idea of the harm it could work on the hapless viewer – explaining that such sights were liable to incite wantonness (*akolasia*) in the audience. Indeed his comments are of particular interest in the present context for the distinct reasons he gives for prohibiting men and women from dancing in public. It is unseemly and indecorous for men to move sinuously (*lugizo*), but dancing women corrupt the viewer.[76] Though writing several centuries after the council, Zonaras echoes the concerns we find in earlier texts. And it is on this theme of the effect of the sight of a female performer on the male viewer that our sources are most informative. While not expressing directly any female experience of dance, either as performer, participant or spectator, they can still tell us something about prevailing attitudes and may, on occasion, afford glimpses of women's life. Before turning to this area, however, I would like to discuss the presentation of the (male) viewer of the (female) performer or dancer in John Chrysostom and others.

Concern for the moral safety of the viewer is a recurring theme in the patristic sources on the theatre. John Chrysostom, whose writings provide by far the richest source of material, returns again and again to the effect that the sight of a performer, whether a female performer or male mime artist, could work on an audience. This provided one of his strongest arguments against those Christians who would claim that the theatre was simply a harmless form of entertainment.[77] One of the most striking passages of Chrysostom's polemic shows clearly and forcefully the place that individual mimes and their art held in the minds, hearts and imagination of their audiences. The mere sound of a famous mime's name, he says, will be sufficient to conjure up the image of the performer, his roles and his attributes in the mind of the listener.

> As soon as the tongue has spoken the name of the [male] dancer the soul creates an image of his face, his hair, his delicate apparel, the man himself who is more effeminate even than these. Another again rekindles the flame in a different way, introducing a harlot (*porne*) into his discourse, along with her words, her gestures, her glancing eyes, her voluptuous appearance, her curled hair, her rouged cheeks, her dark-rimmed eyes.
>
> Did you not feel some effect (*epathete ti*) even as I recounted that?[78]

The passage is remarkable for its demonstration of the power of words to affect the imagination and to stir feelings in the audience.[79] It is unclear from the description of the *porne* in this passage whether she is to be thought of as a stage performer like Chrysostom's unnamed repentant or not. Elsewhere, however, Chrysostom is more precise, indeed he makes clear that the combination of the sight of a woman and of a performer in the person of an actress could have a devastating effect on the male soul.

In his discussion of this subject Chrysostom places the experience of the theatre audience against the background of everyday experience. He begins by admitting that 'often if we meet a woman in a public place we are troubled'.[80] How much more so, then, he goes on to argue, should one avoid the sight of a harlot (*porne*), her head bared, singing lewd songs. Such sights enter the viewer's mind and it is impossible not to be affected by them.[81] Above all, once the show is over and she has left the stage, an image (*eidolon*) of her remains lodged in the viewer's soul: her words, her gestures, her glances, her movement, the rhythm, the lewd songs. All of these elements that make up the pernicious image are described by Chrysostom as 'wounds in the soul'.[82] Thus scarred and afflicted the spectator goes home, unwittingly accompanied by this 'whore' and ready to sow the seeds of strife in his own family.

Once again, Chrysostom demonstrates his own powers of evocation. The display is not gratuitous for it illustrates the power of the imagination to conjure up the image of an absent sight as forcefully as if it were present. This idea has a long history in ancient rhetoric and psychology but Chrysostom adds a moral dimension: thinking of, and thus imagining, an act is as sinful as the act itself.[83] For Chrysostom, any woman in a public place risks exciting in a man feelings that are comparable, if perhaps less intense, to those he experiences (*paschein*) in the theatre. Moreover, the woman on stage represents all women. What the male spectator experiences in the theatre devalues his own wife in his mind: it is she whom he sees shamed in the person of the woman on stage.[84] In one respect, Chrysostom pleads in such passages for the human dignity of the performer, the abolition of distinctions of rank and context which allowed Christians to witness spectacles without any apparent sense of contradiction. He confronts his audience with their double standards, asking how, if they would be shocked to see a woman naked (or perhaps 'revealed', since nudity is a relative concept) in the agora or their own homes, they can watch her on stage.[85] The moral consistency that Chrysostom demands is a rare achievement in any time or place and his tirades shine a pitiless light onto the contradictory attitudes of his society.[86]

Chrysostom's main concern, however, reiterated by Zonaras several centuries later, was with the effect of the sight on the male viewer and on the contamination he brought from the theatre into his own household. The male is indeed the viewing subject, while, in our sources, the dancing woman is the viewed. But it is in the attribution of the 'active' and 'passive' roles between performer – and this includes the woman walking in the street – and the spectator that Chrysostom differs from the model used in much modern criticism. It might be expected that modern critical theory of viewing or 'the gaze' would be of relevance to unravelling our sources on female performers.[87] In analyses of viewing and the viewed based particularly on the cinema and following Laura Mulvey's seminal work, the viewed is presented as the passive object of the male, controlling gaze.[88] The underlying construction of sexuality is the Freudian dichotomy between the passive female and the active male.[89]

To what extent is this particular power relationship, and the view of human sexuality on which it is based, echoed in our sources on dance and on the ancient theatre in general? It is true that poor women were exploited in the civic spectacles of late antiquity and can therefore, in this broader social context, be seen as passive victims. It seems too that Chrysostom himself was protesting against the double standards that made this exploitation acceptable.[90] But, as Mulvey herself points out, the detached viewer of the cinema is not precisely equivalent to the audience of a live performance, even in the context of a modern theatre where the audience, separated from the stage by the proscenium arch and under cover of darkness, fulfil a quasi-voyeuristic role, seeing without being seen.[91] Theoretical models designed for the modern technology of cinema are still less likely to be applicable to the ancient theatre or to the private celebratory settings – weddings or feasts – in which dance was also performed.

Far from being the active source of a controlling gaze, the male spectator of the woman on stage, at a feast or even in the street, is presented in our texts quite literally as a passive victim, a prisoner; he suffers (*paschein*) and his soul is wounded.[92] Far from being the mere object of the male gaze, the woman is thought of as exerting a power over the men into whose field of vision, and thus into whose soul, she enters.[93] In some respects this difference may seem unimportant, a matter of interpretation. For in the passages discussed above the male is still the viewer; the end result is still that women's actions should be controlled in order to minimise their potentially dangerous effects on men. There is, however, a fundamental difference in the conception of female sexuality involved. Women, their bodies and their visibility need to be controlled because of the active sexual power that they exert over men. As Fatima Mernissi has pointed out, an implicit concept of active female sexuality is entirely consistent with a society in which women are kept secluded and under strict surveillance, as in Muslim societies, and also to a certain extent in Chrysostom's own society, where women were expected to conceal their bodies, if not to remain in total seclusion.[94] The idea of active female sexuality runs counter to the Freudian construction of the female body, a notion which was developed as a product of a particular modern culture.[95]

HERODIAS'S DAUGHTER AND THE DISCOURSE OF DANCE

The themes of dance, spectacle and the power relations involved in the display of the female body converge in the figure of Salome. For Early Christian and Byzantine writers she epitomised the evil of dance and its consequences; 'if you must dance,' urges Gregory Nazianzen, 'do not dance like the unseemly daughter of Herodias ... but like David'.[96] She dances at the intersection of public and private and may provide a glimpse of an otherwise hidden world of female dance.

The accounts of the events leading to John the Baptist's death in the Gospels of Mark and Matthew are sparse, but the narrative encapsulates powerful themes whose potential for development did not escape later writers.[97] Herodias, wife of Herod and widow of his brother, uses her daughter to take revenge on the Baptist for his criticism of her second marriage. Together the women trick Herod into executing the Baptist. Herod is depicted here with relative sympathy. He is saddened (*perilupos genomenos, lupetheis*) when he realises the consequence of his oath to grant Herodias's daughter whatever she desires as a reward.[98] The New Testament account of the Baptist's death thus contains the essence of a paradigmatic battle of the sexes in which the women use dance and trickery in response to the direct accusations spoken by the Baptist, the voice of Christ.[99] The ways in which later writers elaborate the narrative show that they were alive to the potential of this theme.

One such text is a sermon by Basil of Seleucia, written in the fourth century. His Herod is not evil, but a victim of his own weakness and slave to his passions.[100] Similarly, Augustine's Herod loved the Baptist, the man of God, but betrayed himself by his rash swearing of an oath to the daughter of Herodias.[101] The real opposition is between the Baptist and Herodias, ably assisted by her daughter. Basil of Seleucia insists upon the cause of this enmity: the words of the Baptist against Herodias's marriage, his freedom of speech (*parrhesia*), his voice.[102] Throughout the sermon, these attributes of the Baptist are set in opposition to the women's stratagems and trickery. From the very beginning, when he announces the theme and the *dramatis personae* of his sermon, Basil assimilates the 'voice' of the Gospel to that of the Baptist, stating that it too condemns the dance of the daughter of Herodias.[103] Through the text of the Gospel the women's attempt to silence John is made in vain, since not even in death was his voice stilled. The voice, discourse (and thus, of course, Basil himself) are on the side of God and the Gospel. In opposition are the women, the instruments of the devil. The weak link is Herod, the paradoxical leader of men made prisoner by his own passions.

The high point of Basil's sermon is his description of the dance itself. Mark and Matthew simply state that the daughter of Herodias danced (although the very idea of a princess of the royal house dancing in mixed company would no doubt have been scandalous in itself for the original audience). Basil, however, elaborates on the Gospel theme, painting for his audience a detailed picture of her performance:

> She was a true image of her mother's wantonness with her shameless glance, her twisting body, pouring out her emotions, raising her hands in the air, lifting up her feet she celebrated (*panegurizo*) her own unseemliness with her semi-naked gestures.[104]

In Matthew's lapidary account, Salome is simply said to have 'pleased' Herod. But Basil describes to us in fuller and now familiar terms the power that her performance exerted upon her audience: she drew all their eyes towards her until the weak and vulnerable Herod was overcome by the wonder (*thauma*) of the spectacle.[105] Like Chrysostom's spectators, Herod is a victim of his own susceptibilities; Salome is far from being the passive object of his gaze: she is an active participant in a scheme to ensnare him. Nor is she entirely without a voice.

In the first place Basil sets up a potent opposition between the Baptist's *parrhesia* and the women's schemes. The women use trickery to attain their ends.[106] What is more, they use the female body as a potent means of expression and, of course, persuasion. Salome persuades using an embodied rhetoric of dance, which turns out to be as effective as any speech could be. Indeed, Basil seems to play on this equivalence between Salome's dance and the male art of verbal discourse in the terms he uses to describe her. Her appearance, her gestures are referred to as *schemata*, a usual term for gesture or appearance, but also, of course, meaning figures of speech. Her figured movements are thus assimilated to artfully elaborated verbal forms of persuasion. Similarly the rhetorical connotations of *panegurizo*, meaning 'to make a speech' as well as 'to celebrate', are surely active in his description.

Basil is not the only author to suggest a parallel between the female body as symbol or means of communication and the (culturally male) art of rhetoric. In his speech against ascetic cohabitation, Chrysostom evokes a woman's bodily language, of gesture (*schema*), gait (*badisma*) and gaze (*ophthalmoi*), which are as eloquent as speech and thus as sinful as if the woman had pronounced lewd and provocative words.[107] In a secular context, Aristainetos, in an imaginary letter addressed to an imaginary female dancer, compares her art explicitly to that of the orator. Like Basil's Salome, she is a living image (*eikon*), this time of the subject matter of her dance, and in her powers of representation she resembles both the orator and the painter, adding another term to the traditional comparison between art and text.[108]

The female body in motion may be eloquent, even persuasive, but this non-verbal communication is not the moral equivalent of the word. Basil places his Herodias firmly outside the order of civil, eloquent and self-controlled society, through his depiction of her inhumane behaviour. Pronouncing the Baptist's death sentence, she exclaims, 'let his head be carried on a plate! let me feast on it with my eyes since I cannot with my teeth ... let me drink his blood!'[109] Several centuries later, Theodore the Studite attributed this behaviour to Salome herself, making her address her mother with the exhortation: 'eat, mother, the flesh of one who has lived without the flesh; drink the blood of the bloodless', adding, with an irony that would be clear to the reader of the Gospels, 'we have silenced for ever the tongue of our critic'.[110] Basil's Herodias makes clear the direct connection between the manner of the Baptist's death and his offence. Decapitation will silence his tongue, which he has used like the masculine weapon, the spear.[111]

The themes latent in the Gospel account of the death of John the Baptist clearly coincided with views of and anxieties about the female body in general and dance in particular in the Early Christian and Byzantine periods. Once again, what we find is a construction of the female dancer by an educated male author. In the parallels they draw between dance and rhetoric these authors hint at a potential female empowerment through the embodied discourse of dance. Or do they? Are the parallels between verbal and non-verbal communication merely 'rhetorical'? I would suggest that the recurrent comparison between dance and rhetoric is in fact significant, but that we might wish to put a different construction on it. Rather than being a morally imperfect substitute for speech, dance may, in fact, have had a value quite independent of the word. Dance is certainly presented as a communicative action, as indeed the very act of appearing in public might be for a woman. Chrysostom refers to such appearances – that of a bride at her wedding, or of mourning women at a funeral – as *epideixeis*, a 'revealing' of course, but also a rhetorical display, a statement, on the part of the woman.[112] The equivalence between such 'epideictic' performances by women and the show rhetoric that was an important part of civic culture is most clear in his condemnation of female mourners whose display (*epideixis*) of shrieks and lamentations (*threnoi, kokutoi*) and violent gestures rival, by implication, the male orator and his funeral speech.[113] There is another sense too in which the texts hint at an equivalence between dance and rhetoric, the product of male *paideia*. Dance, and of course bodily practice in the wider sense, are presented as the result of a female education that may, perhaps, take us closer to some elusive forms of female experience.

In the story of Salome the relationship between mother and daughter is all-important. Salome's dance is an art learned from Herodias. In Basil it is described as her mother's teachings (*didagmata, didaskalia*), for which Herodias now demands a return.[114] Theodore Stoudites also claims that Salome was schooled in dance (*pepaideusthai*) by her mother. Again dance, as a result of female education, is an alternative to the products of male *paideia*, producing figured, and persuasive, movement of the body. Naturally, from the point of view of the preacher, the guardian of the *logos* in all its senses, bodily discourse is an imperfect alternative, and one that is positively to be discouraged. Ambrose in his treatise *On Virgins* holds up Salome as a negative *exemplum*, a solemn warning to all mothers of the evils of teaching a girl to dance rather than to pray.[115]

Did this teaching exist outside our texts? Was dance for women a form of expression and communication independent of any comparison with the word? Might we be able to glimpse here, in the presentation of Herodias and her daughter, a tradition of female dance such as that mentioned in the discussion of dance in modern Middle Eastern societies? That is to say, is the presentation of Salome's dance a purely literary construction, or is it the reflection in a glass of a particular moral colour, of a common activity for women that becomes problematic, and hence a subject for discussion, only when it reaches the male gaze? Does the borrowing of terms from rhetoric suggest that there was no other form of discourse than the verbal, or simply that no other terms existed in which the non-verbal could be described, and condemned, when the need arose?

Chrysostom in fact pushes open the door to the domestic interior on several occasions when he complains about women dancing in front of men at weddings, and condemns the hiring of professional entertainers as a practice that brings the otherwise forbidden sights of theatre to the women inside their very homes.[116] Of course, his speeches take us inside this private sphere only on occasions when the symbolic divisions between public and private are breached: at weddings when even the chaste bride is displayed. We do not see through the eyes of the female viewer of the dancing female body, but she clearly existed in the domestic sphere; and while we cannot prove the existence of the tradition of female dance to which Basil, Theodore and Ambrose seem to refer in their depictions of Herodias and her daughter, neither can we deny the possibility of its existence.

Might we also glimpse the importance of dance for women as a means of expression, an alternative to the male discourse that was closed to all but the educated few? The mourning women criticised by Chrysostom represent one perennial form of female expression. The evidence provided by the figure of Salome for dance performing this role is slim but tantalising.[117] Another such insight might be seen in Basil of Caesarea's condemnation of women who celebrate with dance and song at the martyrs' tombs. For the Father of the Church these are shameless women who let the veils fall from their heads, show contempt for God and the angels and display themselves to the male gaze as they dance wildly, polluting the air with their lewd songs and the ground with their impure feet.[118] What might the women themselves, or their families, have said in response? The question is an impossible one, but might we not see, behind Basil's lurid evocation, an image of women expressing devotion in a way particular to them?[119] It should not be surprising that all these possible insights into female participation in dance are couched in terms of condemnation. For the only occasions on which this activity becomes visible to men, on whom we rely for our information, are the result of transgressions, of female appearance in public places or the invasion of the home by the world of the street and the theatre.

CONCLUSIONS

The construction of dance in our texts can therefore tell us something about the wider conceptions of gender and sexuality in the late antique period, conceptions that must have had some bearing on the lives and daily experience of both women and men. The prohibitions surrounding the public performance of dance by women can be seen to reflect wider anxieties, such as the fear that the viewing male might be feminised, and illustrate how the role of dance in society is part of a far broader social continuum. Though marginalised in history, dance has a vital contribution to make to our understanding of culture.

In particular, I have tried to show that the male depictions of dancing women reveal a concept of female sexuality as active, in contrast to the 'feminine' passivity that underpins many modern interpretations of viewing. In many ways the mode of presentation of our texts (men speaking about women) and their insistence on the implications of the act of viewing (again by men of women) do correspond to the preoccupations of our own age. But the underlying concepts appear to be very different. What is more, our texts need to be imagined in their elusive context if we are to get anywhere near to a glimpse of women's experience. This latter search is perhaps a rash enterprise and will often require a context to be read into a text, but I believe that it is worth attempting with all due caution. In their society, the voices that pronounced these texts were just one part of a polyphony of gradations of opinion, the complexity of which is merely hinted at by Artemisia's contract, or the moral compromises of the Theodosian Code. The writings that have survived until now were, of course, immensely influential and must reflect contemporary opinion, but not the totality of opinions. One way of at least reminding ourselves that these other voices must have existed is to make comparisons with modern societies (again with due caution), for which other forms of recording and documentation exist.

When we come to try to perceive these other voices, or even (one strand of) female experience, in the past we are as always faced with the lack of direct evidence. I have tried to suggest how we might read between the lines. There is a constant risk of finding precisely what one sets out to find in such an exercise and the results will always involve a certain degree of autobiography. Although I have chosen as my subject a non-verbal, unrecorded art form, I have still had to use texts and monuments as my sources. Can these really lead us to female experience, or is this an illusion? The Salome of the sermons is indeed a construct of language, a voiceless, objectified woman who exists only as viewed through male eyes. But my own reading of Salome suggests that, while she and her mother are indeed excluded from the male world of civilised discourse, this is not the only form of communication and persuasion available, and we would ignore a vital area of human experience to assume it was, or is, so.

NOTES

1 The study was begun while I was the holder of the Frances Yates research fellowship at the Warburg Institute and completed with the support of a British Academy Post-Doctoral Research Fellowship. I would like to thank seminar audiences in London, Oxford and Princeton and, in particular, Averil Cameron, Liz James and Dion Smythe for their comments.

2 See J. Cowan, *Dance and the Body Politic in Northern Greece* (Princeton, 1990), and, on the Classical period, S. Lonsdale, *Dance and Ritual Play in Greek Religion* (Baltimore, 1993).

3 See, for example, P. Brown, *The Body and Society* (London, 1989); F. Dupont, *L'acteur-roi ou le théâtre dans la Rome antique* (Paris, 1985); C. Edwards, *The Politics of Immorality in Ancient Rome* (Cambridge, 1993), 98–136; C. Roueché, *Performers and Partisans at Aphrodisias in the Roman and Late Roman Periods* (London, 1993); R. Scodel, ed., *Theatre and Society in the Classical World* (Ann Arbor, 1993); P. Ghiron-Bistagne, ed., *Anthropologie et théâtre antique* (Montpellier, 1987).

4 P. Brown, *Power and Persuasion in Late Antiquity* (Wisconsin, 1992), 48–61.

5 M. Mauss, 'Les Techniques du corps', *Journal de psychologie normale et pathologique* 35 (1935), 271–93, reprinted in M. Mauss, *Sociologie et Anthropologie* (Paris, 1968), 365–86; Cowan, *Dance and the Body Politic*.

6 P. Bourdieu, *Outline of a Theory of Practice* (Cambridge, 1977), 87–95.

7 For discussion, see A.W. Frank, 'For a sociology of the body: an analytical review', in M. Featherstone, M. Hepworth and B.S. Turner, eds, *The Body: Social Process and Cultural Theory* (London, 1991), 80–2, who notes the potential importance of dance for the understanding of 'the communicative body' but is unnecessarily dismissive of what traditional dance might offer. Frank bases his opinions of dance in traditional societies on J.L. Hanna, *Dance, Sex and Gender: Signs of Identity, Dominance, Defiance and Desire* (Chicago, 1988).

8 Cowan, *Dance and the Body Politic*.

9 See, for example, D.M. Levin, 'Philosophers and the dance', in R.

Copeland and M. Cohen, eds, *What is Dance? Readings in Theory and Criticism* (Oxford, 1983), 85–94, and F. Sparshott, 'Why philosophy neglects the dance', ibid., 94–102. An exception is perhaps the court ballet in the French Baroque period. See, for example, M. Franko, *Dance as Text: Ideologies of the Baroque Body* (Cambridge, 1993).

10 Lucian, *How to Write History*, 28, *Opera* 3, M.D. Maclean, ed. (Oxford, 1980), 305.

11 Several Coptic textiles represent dancers. One in Berlin is illustrated in K. Wessel, *Koptische Kunst: die Spätantike in Ägypten* (Recklinghausen, 1963), fig. 109. On the problems of reconstruction, see J.-C. Schmidt, 'The rationale of gestures in the west: third to thirteenth centuries', in J. Bremmer and H. Roodenburg, eds, *A Cultural History of Gesture from Antiquity to the Present Day* (Cambridge, 1991).

12 S. Andresen, 'Altchristliche Kritik am Tanz: ein Ausschnitt aus dem Kampf der Alten Kirche gegen heidnische Sitte', *Zeitschrift für Kirchengeschichte* 72 (1961), 217–62.

13 P. Petitmengin *et al.*, *Pélagie la Pénitente* (Paris, 1981); Leontios of Neapolis, *Vie de Symeon le Fou*, L. Rydén, ed. (Paris, 1974), 1724C. See also H. Magoulias, 'Bathhouse, inn, tavern, prostitution and the stage as seen in the lives of the saints of the sixth and seventh centuries', *Epeteris Hetaireias Byzantinon Spoudon* 38 (1971), 233–52.

14 Roueché, *Peformers and Partisans*, 26.

15 Petitmengin *et al.*, *Pélagie la Pénitente*, I, 78, 23–4: ἡ πρώτη τῶν μιμάδων ᾽Αντιοχείας· αὕτη δὲ ἦν καὶ ἡ πρώτη τῶν χορευτριῶν τοῦ ὀρχηστοῦ. Translation from Roueché, *Performers and Partisans*, 27.

16 Aristainetos, *Letters*, I. 26, O. Mazal, ed., *Epistualrum libri* II (Stuttgart, 1971).

17 O. Pasquato, *Gli Spettacoli in S. Giovanni Crisostomo: Paganesimo e Cristianesimo ad Antiochia e Constantinopoli nel IV secolo* (Rome, 1976).

18 Isidore of Pelusion was apparently the first to give the name 'Salome'. See H. Daffner, *Salome: Ihre Gestalt in Geschichte und Kunst* (Munich, 1912), 31.

19 See, for example, Pasquato, *Gli Spettacoli in S. Giovanni Crisostomo*; S. Andresen, 'Altchristliche Kritik am Tanz: ein Ausschnitt aus dem Kampf der Alten Kirche gegen heidnische Sitte', *Zeitschrift für Kirchengeschichte* 72 (1961), 217–62.

20 J. Herrin, 'In search of Byzantine women: three avenues of approach', in Averil Cameron and A Kuhrt, eds, *Images of Women in Antiquity* (London, 1993), 168. See also the comments of A. Rousselle, *Porneia. On Desire and the Body in Antiquity* (Oxford, 1988), 2.

21 C. Galatariotou, 'Holy women and witches: aspects of Byzantine conceptions of gender', *BMGS* 9 (1984/5), 55–94.

22 The origins of 'Turkish belly dance' (*tsifte teli*), which definitely involves *lugismata*, are a matter of controversy in Greece today. Some prefer to identify it as Turkish or Gypsy art while others claim it existed in Anatolia long before the Ottoman conquest. See Cowan, *Dance and the Body Politic*, 217, n. 29; T. Petrides, *Greek Dances* (Athens, 1975), 47.

23 The Greek sources will be discussed more fully below. In Latin, see Juvencus, *PL* 19, 219: 'alternos laterum celerans sinuamine motus'. For

further references, see T. Hausamann, *Die Tanzende Salome in der Kunst von der Christliche Frühzeit bis um 1500* (Zurich, 1980).

24 Apuleius, *Metamorphoses*, II. 7: 'lumbis sensim vibrantibus, spinam mobilem quatiens placide decenter undabat.' The undulating maid is already in the Greek version of the story, pseudo-Lucian, *The Ass*, 6.

25 Kekaumenos, *Strategikon*, B. Wassiliewsky and V. Jernsted, eds (Amsterdam, 1965), 44, ll.19–22. I am grateful to Catia Galatariotou for this reference.

26 K. van Nieuwkerk, '*A Trade Like Any Other': Female Singers and Dancers in Egypt* (Austin, Texas, 1996). One man is quoted as saying, 'Those jobs are shameful and detestable. I don't like it … but I do like to watch it. Once in a lifetime we invite them; it is *haram* (forbidden), but the fault is theirs', 121.

27 Ibid., 151, citing F. Sabbah, *Women in the Muslim Unconscious* (New York, 1984), 16–17.

28 On the recent history of dance in Egypt see van Nieuwkerk, '*A Trade Like Any Other*', 21–39; for the medieval Islamic world, see A. Shiloah, 'Réflexions sur la danse artistique musulmane au moyen âge', *Cahiers de civilisation médiévale* 5 (1962), 463–74. On Qusayr Amra, see M. Almagro *et al.*, *Qusayr Amra* (Madrid, 1975), and O. Grabar, 'La Place de Qusayr Amrah dans l'art profane du Haut Moyen Age', *Cahiers Archéologiques* 36 (1988), 75–83.

29 For French translation of the passage, see Shiloah, 'Réflexions sur la danse', 464–5.

30 See J. Tucker, *Women in Nineteenth-century Egypt* (Cambridge, 1985), 150.

31 See, for example, B. de Monconys, *Voyage en Egypte (1646–7)* (Cairo, 1973), and E.W. Lane, *Manners and Customs of the Modern Egyptians* (London, 1989), 372–6. On their modern descendants, the Ghawazi of Luxor, see J. Marre and H. Charlton, *Rhythms of the Heart* (London, 1985), 167–72.

32 R. Kabbani, *Europe's Myths of Orient* (London, 1986), 69. It is tempting to see the influence of this tradition at work in the tendency of historians of art and literature alike to qualify dancers depicted in late antique and Byzantine art and text as 'lascivious' even when there is nothing in the sources to warrant such a judgement. See, for example, the comments on the dance of Maryllis from Niketas Eugeneianos's *Drosilla and Charikles* in *ODB*, 'Humor'.

33 On the Egyptian *awalim*, see van Nieuwkerk, '*A Trade Like Any Other*', 26.

34 Hanna, *Dance, Sex and Gender*, 243, also ignores this phenomenon when she says of traditional dance, 'for the most part there is relentless male control over the production and reproduction of knowledge as it appears in the contours and quality of the kinetic discourse of dance'.

35 In a recently broadcast television interview, the Moroccan anthropologist Fatima Mernissi described the importance of dance as a means of expression before the alternative outlet of writing became available to her. Further discussion can be found in V. Lièvre, *Danses du Maghreb: d'une rive à l'autre* (Paris, 1987), and in T. Moubayed, interview with

Leila Haddad, *Dansons Magazine* 11 ('La danse orientale') (April, 1994), 13–17.

36 Ph. Koukoules, Βυζαντινῶν Βίος καὶ Πολιτισμός, 5 (Athens, 1952), 206–44, contains many useful references but the interpretation tends towards the literal. For additional representations of dance and dancers in a Byzantine context, see the illustrations in St Karakasis, Ἑλληνικὰ Μουσικὰ "Οργανα (Athens, 1970), figs 29–31, and A. Xyngopoulos, 'Σαλώη(;)','Επ.'Ετ. ΒυζΣπ. 12 (1936), 269–77. I am grateful to Roddy Beaton for the former reference.

37 See B. Leyerle, 'John Chrysostom on the gaze', *Journal of Early Christian Studies* 1:2 (1993), 159–74.

38 Dupont, *L'Acteur-roi*, 95–8, and C. Edwards, *The Politics of Immorality* (Cambridge, 1993), 123–6. Some of the penalties inflicted on the *infames*, such as the inability to serve as a magistrate or join the army, would have affected only men.

39 Artemidoros, *Oneirokritika*, R. Pack, ed. (Leipzig, 1963), 1.45; according to Artemidoros, this is because both are very fertile.

40 Lucian, *On the Dance*, 1 in *Opera*, 3, 26.

41 See, for example, Gregory Nazianzen, *Carmina*, 2.1.88.89–90, *PG* 37, 1438; Zonaras in *Syntagma ton theion kai hieron kanonon*, 2, G.A. Rhalles and M. Potles, eds (Athens, 1852), 425, refers to men ἀπρεπῶς λυγιζομένων καὶ ἀσχημονούντων ἐν τῶ ὀρχείσθαι.

42 Gregory Nazianzen, *Carmina*, 2.2.8, 101, *PG* 37, 1584, warns against 'songs which render the force of the heart effeminate'. See W. Weisman, *Kirche und Schauspiele: die Schauspiele in Urteil der Lateinischen Kirchenväter* (Würzburg, 1972), 97. Balsamon, in *Syntagma* 2, Rhalles and Potles, eds (Athens, 1852), 357, commenting on the council of Trullo states that monks should not witness any 'spectacle which renders the sense of sight effeminate'.

43 See Brown, *Power and Persuasion*. See also Dupont, *L'Acteur-roi*, 31–4, and B. Schouler, 'Les sophistes et le théâtre au temps des empereurs', in *Anthropologie et théâtre antique*, 273–94, on the comparison of rhetorical *actio* with stage performance.

44 Rufinus, *Epigrams*, D. Page, ed. (Cambridge, 1978), no. 6, 55 (= *Greek Anthology*, 5.19). Page places Rufinus in the generous period 150–400 AD, but Alan Cameron, 'Strato and Rufinus', *Classical Quarterly* 32 (1982), 162–73, argues for a date closer to 100 AD at the latest.

45 *Greek Anthology*, 9.139, W.R. Paton, tr. (Cambridge, Mass., and London, 1916).

46 See Page's comments in Rufinus, *Epigrams*, 77, for further references in the *Anthology*.

47 G. Clark, *Women in Late Antiquity: Pagan and Christian Lifestyles* (Oxford, 1993), 107, suggests a complementary reading of the Piazza Armerina figures' nudity as a sign of social lack of protection.

48 *Greek Anthology*, 8.166.

49 See Brown, *The Body and Society*, 11, and M. Gleason, *Making Men: Sophists and Self-Presentation in Ancient Rome* (Princeton, 1995), 59.

50 See, for example, Cyril of Scythopolis, *Lives of the Monks of Palestine*, tr. R.M. Price (Kalamazoo, 1991), 21, and other passages cited in the

index under 'Youths not permitted in laura'. See also Rouselle, *Porneia*, 147–8.

51 See, for example, Lucian, *Demonax*, 12–13, in *Opera*, 1, 49, on the eunuch Favorinus. In the first anecdote Demonax mocks Favorinus for his 'womanish' public speaking manner and, when asked for his own qualifications as a philosopher, retorts 'testicles'. Passage cited by A. Rousselle, 'Personal status and sexual practice in the Roman Empire', in M. Feher, R. Naddeff and N. Tazi, eds, *Fragments for a History of the Human Body*, 3 (New York, 1989), 313.

52 Edwards, *The Politics of Immorality*, 63–97.

53 Brown, *The Body and Society*, 10.

54 For a summary of Freud's views and the contrasting ideas of active female sexuality prevalent in Muslim society, see F. Mernissi, *Beyond the Veil* (London, 1985), 34–41.

55 J.J. Winkler, *The Constraints of Desire: the Anthropology of Sex and Gender in Ancient Greece* (New York and London, 1990), 24 and 29.

56 Artemidoros, *Oneirokritika* 1.76. English translation in Artemidoros, *The Interpretation of Dreams*, tr. R.J. White (Park Ridge, 1975), 55–6.

57 Artemidoros, *Oneirokritika*, 82, 16–18.

58 Procopius, *Secret History* 9.1–26, tr. H.B. Dewing, Loeb Classical Library (London, 1935).

59 Ibid., 9.12. For fuller discussion of the significance of Procopius's presentation of Theodora, see E.A. Fisher, 'Theodora and Antonina in the *Historia Arcana*: History and/or Fiction', *Arethusa* 11 (1978), 253–79, and Averil Cameron, *Procopius and the Sixth Century* (London, 1985), 67–83.

60 Alan Cameron, *Porphyrius the Charioteer* (Oxford, 1973), 38. Cameron notes that this ceremonial role of dance may also lie behind the dancers on the crown of Constantine Monomachos which have otherwise been seen as the result of Arab influence.

61 *The Theodosian Code*, 15.7, T. Mommsen, ed., 1, 2 (Berlin, 1954), 821–4; tr. C. Pharr (Princeton, 1952), 433–4. See Roueché, *Performers and Partisans*, 27.

62 Ibid. See also Clark, *Women in Late Antiquity*, 29.

63 Gregory of Nyssa, *De Pauperibus amandis*, I, A. van Heck, ed. (Leiden, 1964), 15. *Pace* D. Yannopoulos, *La Société profane dans l'empire byzantine du 7ième, 8ième, 9ième siècles* (Louvain, 1975); 275, dancing slave girls are not mentioned by Gregory of Agrigento in a similar catalogue of luxuries in *PG* 98, 805D–808A.

64 Josephus, *Jewish Antiquities*, 12.187.4.

65 See Roueché, *Performers and Partisans*, 25.

66 W.L. Westermann, 'The castanet dancers of Arsinoe', *Journal of Egyptian Archaeology* 10 (1924), 134–44. See also M. Lefkowitz and M. Fant, eds, *Women's Life in Greece and Rome* (London, 1991), 217. A papyrus dating from 231 BC, *Corpus Papyrorum Raineri*, XVIII (Vienna, 1991), 1, p. 24, records a contract between Olympias, a dancer from Athens, and a male flute player. I am grateful to Dominic Rathbone for this reference.

67 Westermann, 'The castanet dancers of Arsinoe', 138.

145

68 See Rouselle, *Porneia*, 184. I am grateful to Jane Rowlandson for discussion of this point.
69 For an analysis of this episode, see F. Villeneuve, '"L'histoire des Tobiades" chez Flavius Josèphe, *Ant.Jud.* XII, 154–241', in M.-F. Baslez *et al.*, eds, *Le monde du roman grec* (Paris, 1992), 249–57.
70 Council of Laodicea, Canons 53 and 54 in G.D. Mansi, *Sacrorum conciliorum nova et amplissima collectio* (Paris and Leipzig, 1901–27), 2, 571. For further references, see Andresen, 'Altchristliche Kritik am Tanz', 229.
71 Council in Trullo, Canon 62, *PG* 137, 728. See also J. Herrin, '"Femina Byzantina", The council in Trullo on women', *DOP* 46 (1992), 103. On a Byzantine festival that involved women dancing, possibly in the streets, see A. Laiou, 'The festival of Agathe: comments on the life of Constantinopolitan women', *Byzantion: Aphieroma ston A.N. Strato* (Athens, 1986), 1, 111–22.
72 See the comments of Leyerle, 'John Chrysostom on the gaze', 159.
73 The assumption that dancers were prostitutes is not confined to Christian sources. Libanios, *Apology*, 443.7, makes it clear that this was one of Aelius Aristides's accusations against female dancers in his lost speech against dance. See J. Mesk, 'Des Aelius Aristides Rede gegen die Tänzer', *Wiener Studien* 30 (1908), 63.
74 Petitmengin *et al.*, *Pélagie la Pénitente*, 1, 79.
75 John Chrysostom, *In Matthaeum 67 (68)*, *PG* 58, 636–7.
76 *Syntagma*, Rhalles and Potles, eds, 2 (Athens, 1852).
77 Similar arguments are used by Jacob of Serugh, writing in Syriac. See C. Moss, 'Jacob of Serugh's homilies on the spectacles of the theatre', *Le Muséon* 48 (1935), 90. The opposing view is set out in Chorikios, *Apologia mimorum* in *Opera*, R. Foerster and E. Richtsteig, eds (Leipzig, 1929), 345–80.
78 Chrysostom, *In Ioannem 18*, *PG* 59, 119–20: ἄμα γὰρ ἐφθέγξατο ἡ γλῶττα τοῦ ὀρχομένου τὸ ὄνομα, καὶ εὐθέως ἀνετύπωσεν ἡ ψυχὴ τὴν ὄψιν, τὴν κόμην, τὴν ἐσθῆτα τὴν ἀπαλήν, αὐτὸν ἐκεῖνον τούτων μαλακώτερον ὄντα. ἕτερος πάλιν ἑτέρωθεν ἀνερρίπισε τὴν φλόγα, γυναῖκα πόρνην εἰς τὴν διάλεξιν εἰσαγαγών, κἀκείνης τὰ ῥήματα, τὰ σχήματα, τῶν ὀμμάτων τὰς διαστροφάς, τῆς ὄψεως τὸ ὑγρόν, τῶν τριχῶν τὰς στρεβλώσας, τῶν παρειῶν τὰ ἐπιτρίμμητα, τὰς ὑπογραφάς. ἀρα οὐκ ἐπάθετέ τι καὶ ἐμοῦ ταῦτα διηγουμένου. The omission of several lines in the translation of this passage given in Leyerle, 'John Chrysostom on the gaze', 165, unfortunately gives the impression that the dancer and the harlot are one and the same and that Chrysostom is therefore referring only to women as objects of vision.
79 See R. Webb, *Imagination and the Arousal of the Emotions in Greco-Roman Rhetoric*, in S. Braund and C. Gill, eds, *The Passions in Roman Thought and Literature* (Cambridge, forthcoming), and L. James and R. Webb, '"To understand ultimate things and enter secret places": Ekphrasis and art in Byzantium', *Art History* 14 (1991), 1–17.
80 Chrysostom, *Contra ludos et theatra*, *PG* 56, 266.
81 Ibid. The troubling ability of 'lewd songs' to linger in a person's mind

against their will is also mentioned in the *Life of St Mary of Egypt*. See B. Ward, *Harlots of the Desert* (London and Oxford, 1987), 49–50.

82 Chrysostom, *Contra ludos et theatra*, *PG* 56, 267. See also *PG* 59, 333, for more 'wounds in the soul' caused by seeing women on stage.

83 See, for example, John Chrysostom, *Quod regulares feminae viris cohabitare non debeant*, *PG* 47, 515. See Leyerle, 'John Chrysostom on the gaze', 165, for further examples.

84 Chrysostom, *In Matthaeum 6*, *PG* 57, 71.

85 Ibid., col. 72. See P. Brown, *The Body and Society*, 316.

86 In contrast, Chorikios in his *Apologia* bases his defence of mime precisely on the common acceptance of such displays in practice.

87 Leyerle, 'John Chrysostom on the gaze', argues that Chrysostom anticipated feminist theory.

88 See L. Mulvey, 'Visual pleasure and narrative cinema', in L. Mulvey, *Visual and Other Pleasures* (London, 1989), 14–26.

89 For further discussion of the psychological background, see L. Mulvey, 'Afterthoughts on "visual pleasure and narrative cinema" inspired by King Vidor's *Duel in the Sun* (1946)' in *Visual and Other Pleasures*, 29–38, and J. Rose, *Sexuality in the Field of Vision* (London, 1986).

90 Brown, *The Body and Society*, 316.

91 Mulvey, 'Visual pleasure and narrative cinema', 25.

92 Leyerle, 'John Chrysostom on the gaze', 165, notes these images.

93 Edwards, *The Politics of Immorality*, 72–3, makes a similar point: that the attribution of 'active' and 'passive' roles in the act of penetration is largely a matter of point of view.

94 Mernissi, *Beyond the Veil*, 30–1. On veiling, see Clark, *Women in Late Antiquity*, 108–9. On female seclusion in Chrysostom, see Leyerle, 'Chrysostom on the gaze', 163–4. Leyerle notes the power that Chrysostom attributes to the woman viewed but does not step outside the model offered by feminist film criticism.

95 See the comments of Mernissi, *Beyond the Veil*, 34.

96 Gregory Nazianzen, *Contra Julianum 2*, *PG* 35, 709C.

97 Mark, 6.14–29; Matthew, 14.1–12.

98 Mark, 6.26; Matthew, 14.9.

99 Augustine, Sermon 288, *De voce et verbo*, *PL* 38, 1304.

100 Basil of Seleucia, *Oratio XVIII in Herodiadem*, *PG* 85, 228C.

101 Augustine, Sermon 308, *In decollationem beati Joannis Baptistae*, *PL* 38, 1408.

102 Basil of Seleucia, *In Herodiadem*, *PG* 85, 232AB.

103 Ibid., 225D–228A.

104 Ibid., 232C: ἀκριβὴς τῆς μητρικῆς ἀκολασίας εἰκὼν ἀναιδεῖ βλέμματι, καὶ περικλωμένῳ σώματι, ρεούσῃ ψυχῇ, χεῖρας εἰς ἀέρα πέμπουσα, πόδας εἰς ὕψος ἐγείρουσα, ἡμιγύμνῳ τῷ σχήματι, τὴν ἑαυτῆς ἀκοσμίαν πανηγυρίζουσα. I am grateful to Peter Kingsley for discussion of the translation of this passage.

105 Matthew, 14.7. Basil of Seleucia, *In Herodiadem*, *PG* 85, 232C.

106 See F. Malti-Douglas, *Woman's Body, Woman's Word: Gender and Discourse in Arabo-Islamic Writing* (Princeton, 1991), on the theme of womanly wiles and bodily discourse in Arabic literature.

107 Chrysostom, *Quod regulares feminae, PG* 47, 515.
108 Aristainetos, *Letters*, 1.26.
109 Basil of Seleucia, *In Herodiadem, PG* 85, 233.
110 Theodore Stoudites, *Or. 8 In decollationem S. Ioann. Bapt., PG* 99, 768.
111 Basil of Seleucia, *In Herodiadem, PG* 85, 233A.
112 Chrysostom, *In Epist. I ad Cor. Hom. XII, PG* 61, 104. See H. von Staden, 'Anatomy as rhetoric: Galen on dissection and persuasion', *Journal of the History of Medicine and Allied Sciences* 50 (1995), 47–66, for the suggestion that the term *epideixis* retains its full rhetorical implications when used by Galen to refer to scientific demonstrations.
113 Chrysostom, *In Ioannem Hom. 62, PG* 59, 346. See M. Alexiou, *The Ritual Lament in Greek Tradition* (Cambridge, 1974), 23.
114 Basil of Seleucia, *In Herodiadem, PG* 85, 233A and 233C.
115 Ambrose, *De virginibus*, 3.6.31, *PL* 16, 239–41.
116 Chrysostom, *In Epist. I ad Cor. Hom. XII, PG* 61, 105, and *In Epist. ad Coloss. IV*, Hom. XII, *PG* 62, 386–7; cf. Chrysostom, *Propter fornicationes 1, PG* 51, 212–13.
117 Much could rest on the meaning of ρεούση ψυχῆ in Basil of Seleucia, *In Herodiadem, PG* 85, 232C, which I have translated as 'pouring out her emotions'.
118 Basil of Caesarea, *In ebriosos, PG* 31, 445B.
119 For the importance of sanctuaries in female devotion in modern Morocco, see F. Mernissi, 'Women, saints and sanctuaries', *Signs* 3 (1977), 101–12.

7

WOMEN AS OUTSIDERS

Dion C. Smythe

A chapter on women as outsiders requires two definitions: what is meant by gender,[1] and what is meant by outsiders.[2] Once these definitions are clarified, evidence from Anna Komnene's *Alexiad* [3] is presented to prove the case that Byzantine women can be regarded as outsiders.

GENDER

Feminism's contribution to scholarship is that human beings are divided in two ways: biologically into male and female, the two sexes, and socially into feminine (like a female) and masculine (like a male), the two genders.[4] Arising from the debate over the origins of sexual social difference in nature or nurture, feminism identifies gender – socially, as opposed to biologically constructed sex – as a symbolic social construct, not bound in any 'natural' or necessary way to biological sex. From the recognition of gender as a social construct, feminist analysis moves on to see gender stereotypes as the product of the dominant social élite (normally men), who shape the stereotype roles available to women to fit their notions about the defective, other or second sex.[5]

The institutionalised imposition of these gender stereotypes, by which women are taught to be inferior and marginal, is termed patriarchy.[6] Some commentators have attempted to counter the marginalisation of women under patriarchy by stressing the idea of the two spheres: the public and the private.[7] Others reject this perpetual association of feminist analysis with patriarchy. In the early years of this century, Mary Ritter Beard held that 'women's history' misconstrued the experience of women in the past when it stressed the unchanging oppression of women, as women's active participation in historical events was underestimated.[8] According to Stuard, it was the espousal of a non-ideological stance on women by the *annales* school that resulted in a wholesale if unrecognised and perhaps unintended rendering of all social relationships in terms of self (male) and other (female). Such a definition places men within society, but women outside it, or related to society only functionally as a means of exchange.[9] To insist always on the centrality of the masculine–feminine oppressive dyad is to maintain men as the central actors, the definers of women's past, whilst the women themselves are reduced to reactors as best, objects at worst. Women's spheres of activity can be identified, but they are not public and do not have the *cachet* awarded by patriarchal society to men's activities. Rosaldo recognises the 'woman's sphere' – the quilting, the gossip, the centrality of the kitchen to psychological development – but stresses that scholars should turn to explore these aspects of human society where women are the main or only actors only after having made plain the exclusion of those same women from the public, highly valued areas of human interaction. The goal is a true women's history which identifies the complexity of women's experiences, making sure that events and processes that are central to those experiences assume historical centrality, and that women are recognised as active agents of social change.[10]

However, the nature of historical sources (written largely by men) means that we see women as their definers (men) saw them, not as they saw themselves. Little can be done to ameliorate this situation except to recognise that our sources do not document the entire story. Bynum, discussing Turner's liminal theory, remarks:

> In many places he suggests that women are liminal, or that women, as marginals, generate *communitas*. What I am suggesting is exactly that Turner looks *at* women; he stands with the dominant group (males) and sees women (both as symbol and as fact) as liminal to men. In this he is quite correct of course, and the insight is a powerful one. But it is not the whole story. The historian or anthropologist needs to stand *with* women as well.[11]

For anthropologists, a male–female pairing of fieldworkers is a possibility; for historians, evidence is dictated by the survival of sources, and even the rare occurrence of a woman-authored source such as Anna Komnene's *Alexiad* cannot be assumed to be the authentic voice of all Byzantine women. Indeed, given Anna

Komnene's particular circumstances, it would be most unlikely if it were.

OUTSIDERS

If the feminist definition of gender is one element of the discussion, the second is the sociological definition of the outsider. An outsider is someone who is not an insider; the outsider is the Other. I raise de Beauvoir's identification of 'Subject' and 'Other' to join gender to notions of otherness, alienation, outsiderness which sociological disciplines have used to explain how human societies are organised, and which Kristeva has widened out to include discussions of the individual psyche and general culture.[12]

Properly speaking, there is as yet no unified sociological theory of deviance (the dominant élite's term is autocentrically used in sociology to describe outsiderness). Rather there are orientations, sensitising concepts,[13] that help develop such a theory. The lists of deviants used in empirical studies of modern society – the nuts, sluts and preverts (sic) of undergraduate course titles in American institutions[14] – make interesting reading: felons, cheque forgers, embezzlers, murderers, robbers, convicts, drug dealers and addicts, motorcycle gangs, gamblers, alcoholics, prostitutes, homosexuals, adulterers, divorcees, widows and orphans, paupers, suicides, mystics, atheists, hippies, racially mixed couples, vegetarians, the mentally ill, the old, stutterers, village eccentrics, bohemian artists – and in case you were feeling left out – intellectuals.[15] It would seem that we are all deviants, we are all outcasts. If all these persons can be defined as deviant, what does it mean? Goode has pointed out that basically it means nothing.[16] Deviance in isolation is meaningless: a theory of sociological otherness must identify the dominant élite (the insiders) as well as the powerless (the outsiders), and clarify the relationship – one of differential power – between them.

The materialist view of deviance is that it has an objective reality that can be measured in some way. The stress is on norms, or their institutionalised variant, laws. The identification of the norm (usually with a sanction for the transgression of the norm), coupled with the action that contravenes it, is held to provide an objective definition of deviancy. Whilst the materialist–realist view has the appeal of simplicity, it fails to answer three questions: who does the defining? how is behaviour defined as deviant? and why is concealed deviant behaviour by the dominant élite treated differently?[17]

Furthermore, this orientation implies that outsiders are the dross of society, and that deviancy is somehow intrinsic to the outsider. This depersonalises outsiders and reifies them, turning them into objects upon which social processes operate, alienating them from human society, rather than seeing them as human actors engaged in social transactions, even if they are acting from a subordinate social position. Such matters are countered by labelling theory, which sees deviancy as an ascribed social construction.[18]

Labelling theory has much of the Holy Roman Empire about it: it is not a theory and it does not label. Goode finds no unified school espousing the research method – indeed he is hard pushed even to find one exponent.[19] The famous definition is Becker's: the deviant is one to whom that label has successfully been applied; deviant behaviour is behaviour that people label as deviant.[20] The dominant group defines certain behaviour as deviant; it defines persons who engage in such behaviour as deviants; it treats them in the appropriate fashion – applying sanctions of increasing severity, placing the individual in an outsider status.[21] Deviancy must be understood as the product of some sort of transaction between the rule-breaker and the dominant élite of society.[22] For Sumner:

> deviance is not best defined as a set of distinguishable behaviours offending collective norms but as a series of flexible ideological terms of abuse or disapproval which are used with varying regularity and openness in the practical networks of domination.[23]

This theoretical orientation helps explain the Byzantine outsider, the Other, by turning attention away from some supposed 'real' cause of deviancy, to locate its origins in the social interaction between the dominant élites (the powerful) and the mass of the powerless.[24] It is within this context that the treatment of women in Byzantium, cast into outsider roles by virtue of their socially constructed gender, may be viewed.

Defining – labelling – women as outsiders has a two-fold result. Individually, the women become marginalised to the dominant male society, and in their alienation – the product of the variance between their ascribed statuses and their self-aware achieved statuses – attain states reminiscent of Durkheim's *anomie*. Collectively, women may form a minority group, when their individual outsider statuses become institutionalised into the structure of society (patriarchy), and they are disadvantaged, the object of discrimination, either

objective or subjective. The important aspect is the subjective
awareness or self-awareness as members of a minority group. Awareness without actual objective discrimination will create a minority
but discrimination without awareness (either self-generated or ex-
ternally imposed) will not. Even though historically a crude numer-
ical majority of the human population, women manifest many of the
psychological characteristics, such as group self-hatred, that have
been imputed to self-conscious minority groups.[25] This self-hatred
is not countered by socialisation within the minority group, because
other ranks conferred by other roles – frequently a direct function
of the ranks held or achieved by the women's fathers, brothers,
husbands, lovers and sons – take precedence over their membership
of the minority group 'women'. On one level, the social distance
between men and women is much smaller than that between many
dominant élites and their other-defined minorities. The evidence
usually cited for this intimacy is the heterosexual pairing, codified
by many societies into marriage or at least cohabitation. However,
this takes no account of the physical intimacy between house-slaves
and owners in the ante-bellum South, which did nothing to reduce
the social distance between black and white.[26] The sexual intimacy
of marriage does not necessarily mean that a man treats his partner
as an equal. Many men are married but would not consult a woman
doctor or other professional.[27] Frequent and symbolically meaning-
ful social interaction with men curtails the development of women's
increased self-awareness as equally disadvantaged members of a
minority group.

The question of whether Byzantine women formed a disadvantaged minority group because their biological sex and feminine
gender-construct excluded them from access to political power and
the allocation of resources can be approached in two ways.[28] One
is to examine the institutional structures to see if women are
marginalised, cast into outsider roles. Within the Byzantine context,
such an examination is achieved by investigating the legal position
of women.[29] Joëlle Beaucamp provides a succinct summation:

le droit byzantin parle des femmes de trois manières: pour
formuler des incapacités qui ont leur contrepartie dans des
protections particulières, pour énoncer des règles morales qui
s'appliquent aux femmes d'une façon spécifique, enfin pour
délimiter le rôle des femmes dans la famille, que ce soit pour la
conclusion du mariage, la situation de femme mariée ou de
mère.[30]

The alternative is to examine women as outsiders in Byzantine society from the cultural perspective, using high-level historiography as an expression of that culture.

Literature is the product and mirror of experience. Words are symbolic information conveyors whose form is arbitrary, and whose meaning is determined by those who use them.[31] The use of symbols by persons in social interaction enables them to give meaning to transactions and to understand – at a socially defined level – what is going on, to create the symbolic environment in which they live.[32] Words and language are not passive reflectors of an observable, phenomenologically distinct object or range of objects *out there*, rather they are part of the symbolic screen that sifts, edits and rationalises sense-impressions and perceptions into a recognisable form.[33] The extreme theoretical position that maintains that the possession of a particular mother-tongue imposes an inescapable world view is perhaps overstated;[34] but ways of thinking *are* influenced by the ways in which those thoughts can be communicated. Studies carried out in Modern English have shown that English provides negative semantic space for women's experience.[35] What is meant by this is that the language is so dominated by the idea that the man is the One, the norm, and the woman the Other, the abnormal, the minus-man, that it is almost impossible to give voice to the concerns and interests of women in a serious way. Canonical (usually male) criticism marginalises literature written by women by stressing its emphasis on the limited particular at the expense of the general. Limited (not different, *limited*) experience produces limited literature. The question of women as outsiders can be restated: does Byzantine literature provide only a negative semantic space for women which marginalises their experiences and therefore their lives, making them outsiders to their own culture?

ANNA KOMNENE

It was my intention to expound the whole Bogomilian heresy, but 'modesty', as the lovely Sappho somewhere remarks, 'forbids me'; historian I may be, but I am also a woman.[36]

This quotation from Anna Komnene's *Alexiad*, the mid-twelfth-century account of the reign of the Byzantine emperor Alexios I Komnenos (1081–1118) written by his eldest child, introduces the problem. First the *Alexiad* was written by a woman – not a very

common event in the corpus of approximately 'two to three thousand
volumes of normal size'[37] of Byzantine literature that has come down
to us. Second it suggests that certain things were deemed by the
Byzantines of the eleventh and twelfth centuries not to be the
concerns of women. Is the *Alexiad*, therefore, limited literature in
that it omits in vocabulary or subject matter those concerns that are
held (by men) to fall outside a woman's proper sphere of interest?

Joanna Russ sets out the various ways used to marginalise women's
writing, to make of it the muted babblings of outsiders on the
margins of human (male) society.[38] The first and most drastic is the
complete denial of agency. Anna Komnene did not write the *Alexiad*,
her husband did. This explains the accounts of battles and wars,
which obviously women do not write about; this view has yet to
achieve full scholarly exposition.[39] The second method is to admit
that the woman did the writing, but to denigrate the product. Anna
Komnene's *Alexiad* is presented as a rather strange kind of history.
Less a history book than the title of an epic poem, the *Alexiad* was
written to celebrate a legendary hero.[40] Anna raises Alexios above
Constantine the Great, and makes him *isoapostolikos*. Despite the
overblown praise, however, 'grâce à elle nous connaissons bien
l'homme et pouvons voir ce qu'il fut'.[41] This is the problem: we know
the *man* and what *he* did, but the author is outsider to her own text.
Interpretation of the text is hijacked, and we do not ask the right
questions of a text written by a woman. Dieter Reinsch[42] has
suggested that it is of no consequence that Anna Komnene was a
woman:

> that the author was a woman lies outside consideration here, I
> mean in my interpretation as well as in the scholarly literature.
> In the case of Anna Komnene, beloved synonyms such as 'the
> princess', the 'emperor's daughter' or even the 'chronicler'
> function merely to suggest implicit and ill-considered pre-
> judices under the mantle of elegant variation.[43]

Scholarly literature of previous ages has the defence of ignorance;
Reinsch operates in a world where feminist writers have sensitised
us to gender as a legitimate tool of historical analysis. Whether
authorial biography is a necessary adjunct to the serious literary
treatment of texts is open to debate, but to the historian, the serious
treatment of literary texts as historical sources requires their proper
location in time, which includes addressing questions of author-
ship.[44] It *is* important that Anna Komnene was a woman writer and

serious historical interpretation must take account of that. The question of audience is more problematic. The nature and size of the readership of the high-level atticising Greek texts of the eleventh and twelfth centuries is still debated.[45] Indeed, there is a subsidiary question as to whether the destined recipients of the texts should be thought of as an audience or as a readership.[46] These questions are part of the wider context of the proper treatment of texts.

As *the* woman writer of Byzantium, it is a legitimate question to ask if Anna Komnene's writing has a specific quality that may be ascribed to her gender, if it exists in negative semantic space. A recurrent theme in the *Alexiad* is the ἀνδρεία, the male bravery or courage, displayed by male characters and on one occasion by Anna's mother Irene Doukaina, when she accompanied Alexios on campaign against Bohemond. Anna is careful to separate Irene's courage[47] from that of barbarian women; it lay elsewhere than on the battlefield, and if she were armed, it was with a relentless fight against the passions and a sincere faith.[48] Anna ends by reiterating that Irene was as peaceable as her name. Anna uses the notion of ἀνδρεία, but does not provide us with a positive substantive derived from it. This may be an example of negative semantic space limiting the expression of women's experience. However, the jury has yet to render its verdict. In my study of eleventh- and twelfth-century historiography, I can find no difference in Anna Komnene's choice of vocabulary or differences in sentence structure (as suggested by Virginia Woolf) when compared with the histories of Michael Psellos, Nikephoros Bryennios, John Kinnamos or Niketas Choniates to suggest a woman constrained by negative semantic space. Anna Komnene speaks not as a woman in an *écriture féminine*, but in the same full-blown atticising form of Greek favoured by the dominant élite of eleventh- and twelfth-century Byzantium.

If Anna Komnene's use of language provides no difference that may be ascribed to gender, what of her choice of topics to cover in her history? The main theme of the *Alexiad* is to offer her father's successful reign as a mirror for the reign of her brother John II Komnenos (1118–43), and that of her nephew Manuel I Komnenos (1143–80). Even though strictly public and political in theme, it is pivotal 'that the author [of the *Alexiad*] was a woman'.[49]

Anna Komnene was born the eldest child and first daughter of Alexios I Komnenos and Irene Doukaina. Most significantly, Anna was born in the porphyra chamber of the imperial palace, and her birth was associated with a miraculous happening.[50] This self-

conception as the eldest born of the Komnenoi–Doukai porphyro-
genitoi was an expression of her goal in life: 'nämlich dereinst als
Kaiserin den Thron zu besteigen'.[51] At first, this goal seemed within
her grasp. At an early age, Anna Komnene was betrothed to
Constantine Doukas, the son of Michael VII and Maria of Alania, but
her future became less bright with the birth of her brother John in
1087, and in 1092 she lost her priority in the succession to him. It
seems that Constantine Doukas died about two years later. By 1097
at the latest, she was married to Nikephoros Bryennios. The marriage
produced two sons and a daughter, though they receive no mention
in the *Alexiad*, and it seems to have lasted happily until Nikephoros
Bryennios's death in 1136–7. 'Anna's Caesar' was liked by his mother-
in-law, and with her daughter, Irene Doukaina attempted to replace
John Komnenos with Bryennios and Anna in the succession. All the
machinations came to nothing, and after her husband's death[52]
Anna retired to the monastery of Kercharitomene, founded by her
mother.[53] There she began work on completing the life of her father
begun by her husband at the request of her mother. Anna died in
about 1153–4. These brief details of Anna Komnene's life define her
as a daughter, a fiancée and a wife (but interestingly not as a mother).
She viewed herself as being as capable as her grandmother of running
the empire on her father's behalf, but she never got the chance. As
Hunger has remarked, 'die Hälfte ihres Lebens (seit 1118) hatte sie
fern von Macht und Einfluß verbracht'.[54]

However, if Anna spent half her life far from the centres of power
and influence, the same is not true of the women she portrays in the
Alexiad. This is most clearly seen in the women of Book II. The
women we see are from the upper layers of society – the empress
Maria, Anna Dalassene, the protovestiaria Maria the Bulgar, Irene
Doukaina and the Alanian Irene Komnene. Their social and political
importance – one might say their power – is shown by the fact that
when Isaac and Alexios Komnenos recognise the enmity of Borilas
and Germanos, they endeavour to create an alternate power base,
centred on the women's quarters of the palace. They were 'hunks of
the month',[55] able to melt hearts of stone. From the first, the empress
is shown as head of family, deciding on the marriages of the family
members – a role indicated for three out of the four women
mentioned. Family solidarity is emphasised;[56] just as Alexios helped
Isaac secure his bride, the empress Maria's niece Irene, so Isaac
helped Alexios gain access to the charmed circle of the empress
Maria, achieved by Alexios's adoption by Maria. The envy provoked

by Alexios's adoption was due to the empress Maria's role as the legitimiser of Botaniates's government. With the adoption of Alexios, Maria had two heirs presumptive under her control; she cannot be regarded as an outsider to political power.

The growing concern with the succession is emphasised in the next section. Badly advised, Botaniates adopted a relation, Synadenos, as his heir. This Synadenos receives a favourable description,[57] but in choosing him as the heir Botaniates passed over those with a better claim, notably the porphyrogenitos Constantine, son of Maria of Alania and Michael VII. Much of the empress's activities hereafter may be interpreted as attempts to preserve the rights of her son. She showed her sorrow to no one, but her concealment did not escape the notice of the Komnenoi.[58] Isaac said that she seemed changed, sad, and asked if she no longer felt able to confide in them.[59] Basically, she could not. Maria had to play off all possible claimants for the throne one against another, engineering it so that her son was left in sole command. This difficult task was made harder by the realisation that the Komnenoi wished to use her as a lever in a contrary direction. The failure of the Komnenoi to reveal fully the extent of their plans for fear that Maria would reveal all to the emperor shows that theirs was an alliance of convenience rather than one of congruent goals. The empress Maria was not an outsider in the Byzantine intrigues; rather she was playing the Great Byzantine Game for all she was worth. The Komnenoi returned the next day, and won her over to them when they promised to ensure, with God's help, that Constantine would not be deprived of his throne. The Komnenoi continued to court the empress, a policy that paid off when the Alan magistros revealed to them the plot being hatched by Borilas and Germanos.[60]

Just as the empress Maria is presented as an insider, so too Anna Dalassene, Anna Komnene's paternal grandmother, is presented as the matriarch of her family. In Book I, her sorrow could sway emperors when her youngest son, Alexios, was dismissed from the army and sent home to comfort her after the death of her eldest son.[61] She plays a central role in Book II. Like the empress Maria, her interest centres on her family, rather than on abstract power. In family deliberations she had the right to be consulted, to warn and to advise. She provided the pretext for Isaac and Alexios to visit the empress when the succession crisis was at its height,[62] and though it is not made explicit, it seems likely that it was her advice that caused the crucial change in the attitude of the Komnenoi between their two visits to the empress. Like knowing like, Anna Dalassene recognised the porphyrogenitos Constantine as the key to securing the empress Maria's help.

Anna Dalassene moves to centre stage in the fifth chapter of the book, and remains there. In common with the empress Maria, marriage negotiations are one of her major concerns. When the revolt of the Komnenoi becomes overt, she is involved in the arrangements for the marriage of her granddaughter (Manuel's daughter) to Botaniates's grandson. To conceal the commotion of the rebellion, she orders her household to prepare to attend church. She deals with the boy's inquisitive tutor, and the party reaches the sanctuary of Hagia Sophia in safety. When Botaniates dispatched Straboromanos and Euphemanos to bring the women to the palace, it is Anna Dalassene who justifies the revolt of her sons to the emperor's envoys. They have fled not in revolt, she says, but out of innocence, with a three-fold aim: to avoid humiliation, to draw attention to the jealousy that was rampant against them and to seek imperial protection. When pressed by the imperial envoys, she retorted with vigour that having come to the church to pray, she would pray to the Theotokos to intercede on her behalf, before God and with the emperor's spirit. She approached the chancel as if weighed down by age, and made genuflections at the iconostasis. However, on the third genuflection, she grabbed the holy doors and cried out loudly that she would not leave the place unless given a cross by the emperor as surety for her safety. Offered a cross by Straboromanos, Anna Dalassene refused it, specifying that the cross had to be from the emperor himself of a sufficient size so that everyone could see it.[63] These actions are public, and Anna Dalassene ensures that they are noticed: she speaks vigorously and loudly, and the cross demanded had to be visible to all. Nikephoros Botaniates, 'being honourable by nature', listened to the words of the woman – Anna Dalassene – and sent her the cross that she demanded. Anna Dalassene left the church, and on the orders of the emperor she, together with her daughters and daughters-in-law, was confined in the Petrion nunnery. Also placed there was the Protovestiaria Maria of Bulgaria, Anna Komnene's maternal grandmother.

Without realising the consequences of his actions, Botaniates placed the two leaders of the rebellion together. Paradoxically, though made physical outsiders by their confinement within the Petrion nunnery, these women were the political insiders, who knew how to manipulate the political system and who are depicted by

Anna Komnene as the two-stroke engine that powers the rebellion. Just as Anna Dalassene organised her household, confounded the menfolk (the tutor, Straboromanon, Euphemanos and the emperor himself) and gave public justification of the rebellion, so too Maria the Bulgarian directed her menfolk. When Isaac and Alexios Komnenos left the city on the night of 13 February, they encountered the Protovestiaria Maria and George Palaeologos (her son-in-law, as was Alexios Komnenos) at the monastery of Kosmidion. This was no chance meeting. Maria the Bulgarian wanted to have a man she could trust with the active revolt. Palaeologos was made to join the revolt, but only after dire threats from Maria the Bulgarian.[64] Anna Dalassene and the Protovestiaria Maria are not 'active' in the revolt in the sense that they do not storm the imperial palace. However, though outside the Chalke Gate, they are very much insider dealers in the Byzantine political process. Compare this determination of the women to succeed with the action men. Isaac and Alexios Komnenoi are shown agonising over what to do next. Not knowing what to say, they stand with their eyes downcast and their hands covered. They do not know what to do when faced with a suspected plot by the two Slavs. Pakourianos doubted their determination; in the midst of the rebellion, they need a message from Caesar John Doukas to remind them to proceed to the palace, rather than going to their mother.[65]

In Book III, the empress Maria of Alania continues to play the Byzantine Great Game. As the mother of a porphyrogenite heir, the empress Maria could easily have provided the focus for a new rebellion, all the more so because she remained inside the palace. Anna Komnene credits the empress with good reasons for staying in the palace, though she admits that not everyone saw it in those terms. Anna sees the reason for Maria staying in the palace as being not because of the charm of Isaac and Alexios, but because she was in a foreign country without friends, parents or even a single compatriot.[66] Anna goes on to reveal a deeper reason underlying this plausible excuse: she did not wish to leave the palace before she had secured the position of both herself and her son.[67] The image of the empress Maria alone against a hostile world is reinforced by the Caesar John Doukas. He had recommended Maria of Alania to Botaniates as a marriage partner on three counts: her physical beauty, her nobility of birth, and the fact of her foreign origin which would mean that there would be no mob of relatives to trouble the emperor.[68] Thus, though an outsider by her foreign birth and her gender, Maria of Alania was the insider with control of the heir presumptive within the palace.

In this same book, Anna Dalassene is presented as a paragon of virtue. This mighty stronghold[69] divided herself between concern for her son and the world, and for the hereafter.[70] Her power of discernment made it no surprise that Alexios entrusted the government to her.

> For my grandmother had such an exceptional grasp of public affairs, understanding how to arrange and govern that she seemed able to rule not only the Roman empire, but all other empires wherever they were found under the sun.[71]

Removing the taint of Romanos Monomachos, she made the palace take on the air of a monastery. Anna Dalassene was compassionate and generous to the needy. She was the embodiment of propriety, the due proportion of warm humanity and strict moral principles.[72] With these imperial and Christian attributes, and placed at the centre of the government, Anna Dalassene was no outsider.

The aristocratic woman as leader is shown by Irene Doukaina when she comes forward during the financial crisis, sending her own possessions to the mint in the hope of encouraging similar acts of generosity.[73] The story also serves to strengthen Irene Doukaina's position *vis-à-vis* Anna Dalassene. Irene is portrayed later as a forceful dominant character, very much her husband's equal, sharing with him the responsibilities of power, and yet showing her conformity to certain aspects of the stereotypical Byzantine woman. Thus Anna emphasises her mother's shy and retiring nature, an aspect developed further in the next paragraph. For the moment, however, she is described as retiring from public life and devoting herself to her own occupations. A list is provided of good orthodox occupations: reading books of the saints, and doing deeds of good works and charity towards men, especially to those who by their mien and way of life she knew to be devoted to God, both in prayer and in the chanting of hymns.[74] Anna guards against any suggestion of unseemly immodesty by describing how her mother blushed when she had to appear in public.[75] The modesty of Irene is stressed, and how she preferred for her voice not to be heard, never mind her elbow being seen. The modesty of the empress would have confined her to the palace had it not been for her great devotion to the emperor.[76] Reasons are given why this devotion caused Irene to accompany Alexios: from the domestic sphere, only the ministrations of the empress could ease the emperor's gout; from the public sphere, Irene acted as a bulwark against the numerous plots against Alexios.[77] Anna maintains that it was only natural that Irene would act as his very help-mate. However, this aid was not given in the public gaze, and the sight, silence and court (or rather lack of it) paid to Irene meant that no one realised she was there.[78] Thus she was an insider to the realities of power, but an outsider to its outward show.

What may we conclude? From the themes covered it is clear that Anna Komnene, in the *Alexiad*, writes on topics known and familiar to Byzantine men, namely wars, rebellions and struggles for the succession. There is no strong different women's experience presented in Anna Komnene's *Alexiad*. But what would we expect? What is women's experience? Childbirth and pre-menstrual tension are biologically determined and it would be a brave man, a possessor of ἀνδρεία indeed, who would suggest that they constituted women's experience. Gendered experience is a cultural variable and perhaps we attempt to see Byzantine women too much in terms familiar to ourselves. Hotspur's denunciation of Kate's mealy-mouthed oaths, suited to a comfit-maker's wife, rather than the mouth-filling oaths that befit a lady reminds us that nobility not gender may have been a more significant boundary in the articulation of Byzantine society. Anna declines to give a full account of the Bogomil heresy: 'But modesty forbids me, for though I am a historian, I am also a woman' – a woman held down by patriarchy perhaps? But then she continues: 'born in the porphyra, most honoured and first born of Alexios's children; what was common hearsay had better be passed over in silence'.[79] Anna Komnene's gender is important because it informs our understanding of the *Alexiad*. If Anna had been born male, as the eldest child she would have inherited the empire; as a woman she was displaced by John. Anna Komnene found herself cast into an outsider role (a porphyrogenite not permitted to rule and reign) because of her gender, and the *Alexiad* may be read as her response to that. Anna Komnene as a woman outsider is an individual case that shows that gender can have a strong cultural impact, assigning an outsider role. The other women of almost her station (but not quite as they were not born in the purple) are portrayed in the *Alexiad* as insiders to the Byzantine political élite. The paucity of sources means that the majority of women's experiences remain concealed from us. However, Byzantine women can be examined as outsiders to Byzantine society, not necessarily because of what they did or were (remember labelling?), but because gender along with race, class and religion is one boundary used by people in human societies to divide 'like me' from 'not like me'. Furthermore, gender is still an issue in Byzantium not only because of the way in which the Byzantines used gender to articulate their own society, but also because of the way in which we use gender to articulate our society, shaping how we see Byzantine society, whether through a glass darkly or directly face to face.

NOTES

1 J.W. Scott, 'Gender: a useful category of historical analysis', *American Historical Review* 91 (1986), 1053–75; I. Illich, *Gender* (London, 1983); O. Hufton, 'Women in history: early modern period', *Past and Present* 101 (1983), 125–41; Linda J. Nicholson, *Gender and History* (New York, 1986); Nikki R. Keddie and Beth Brown, eds, *Women in Middle Eastern History: Shifting Boundaries in Sex and Gender* (New Haven, 1992). For a Byzantine context, see Catia Galatariotou, 'Holy women and witches: aspects of Byzantine conceptions of gender', *BMGS* 9 (1984–5), 56–7; J. Grosdidier de Matons, 'La femme dans l'empire byzantin', *Histoire mondiale de la femme* (Paris, 1967), 3:11–43; and A. Laiou, 'The role of women in Byzantine society', *JÖB* 31 (1981), 233–60. Recent work has also been done on the social construction of masculinity: Robert Bly, *Iron John: A Book About Men* (Shaftesbury, 1990); Michael Herzfeld, *The Poetics of Manhood: Contest and Identity in a Cretan Mountain Village* (Princeton, 1985); Rosalind Miles, *The Rites of Man: Love, Sex and Death in the Making of the Male* (London, 1991); Brian Pronger, *The Arena of Masculinity: Sports, Homosexuality and the Meaning of Sex* (London, 1990); see also the chapter in this volume by Charles Barber. The possibility of the 'third sex' (as opposed to the grammarians' 'third gender') has a classical history (see s.v. 'Third sex', Robert Goldenson and Kenneth Anderson, eds, *Everything You Ever Wanted to Know About Sex But Never Dared Ask* [London, 1986]). In the Byzantine context, this could cover the eunuchs of the imperial service or the ideal of the ascetic removed from all physical desire, in addition to the modern usage referring to homosexuals of both sexes.

2 Helen Meyer Hacker, 'Women as a minority group', *Social Forces* 30 (1951), 60–9; I deal with these matters in my Ph.D. thesis, *Byzantine Perceptions of the Outsider in the Eleventh and Twelfth Centuries: A Method* (Unpub. Ph.D. thesis, St Andrews, 1992), esp. 41–80 and 103–226, using evidence drawn from Michael Psellos's *Chronographia*.

3 Text: Anne Comnène, *Alexiade*, Bernard Leib, ed. and tr. (Paris, 1967), with a fourth index volume prepared by Paul Gautier (Paris, 1976).

4 Ann Oakley, *Sex, Gender and Society* (London, 1972), 12; Josephine Lowndes Sevely, *Eves' Secrets: A New Perspective on Human Sexuality* (London, 1989).

5 Simone de Beauvoir, *The Second Sex*, H.M. Parshley, ed. and tr. (London, 1953).

6 Galatariotou, 'Holy women and witches', 56–7; Cheris Kramarae and Paula A. Treichler, eds, *A Feminist Dictionary* (London, 1985), s.v. 'Patriarchy', 323; Dale Spender, *Man-made Language*, 2nd edn. (London, 1985), 1; Marilyn French, *The War Against Women* (London, 1992); Neil Lyndon, *No More Sex War: The Failures of Feminism* (London, 1992).

7 Carroll Smith-Rosenberg, 'The female world of love and ritual: relations between women in nineteenth-century America', *Signs: Journal of Women in Culture and Society* 1 (1975), 1–29. Smith-Rosenberg has defended herself vigorously against the charge (made by Ellen du Bois) of seeing women's roles as a separate structuralist-functionalist sphere (Smith-Rosenberg, *Feminist Studies* 6 [1980], 55–64).

8 Quoted by Ellen du Bois in Judith R. Walkowitz *et al.*, 'Politics and culture in women's studies: a symposium', *Feminist Studies* 6 (1980), 28, citing Bernice Carroll, 'On Mary Beard's *Woman as Force in History*', in Bernice Carroll, ed., *Liberating Women's History* (Urbana, 1976), and Ann Lane, *Mary Ritter Beard: A Sourcebook* (New York, 1977).

9 Susan Mosher Stuard, 'The annales school and feminist history: opening a dialogue with the American stepchild', *Signs: Journal of Women in Culture and Society* 7 (1981), 135–43.

10 M.Z. Rosaldo, 'The use and abuse of anthropology: reflections on feminism and cross-cultural understanding', *Signs: Journal of Women and Culture in Society* 5 (1980), 414–17.

11 Caroline Walker Bynum, 'Women's stories, women's symbols: a critique of Victor Turner's theory of liminality', in Frank Reynolds and Robert Moore eds, *Anthropology and the Study of Religion* (Chicago, 1984), 108–9.

12 Julia Kristeva, *Strangers to Ourselves*, Leon S. Roudiez, tr. (Hemel Hempstead, 1991).

13 Erich Goode, 'On behalf of labeling theory', *Social Problems* 22 (1974–5), 582, citing Herbert Blumer, *Symbolic Interactionism: Perspective and Method* (Englewood Cliffs, 1969), 147–51.

14 Alexander Liazos, 'The poverty of the sociology of deviance: nuts, sluts and preverts', *Social Problems* 20 (1972–3), 111a.

15 Liazos, 'Nuts, sluts and preverts', 106b–107b.

16 Goode, 'On behalf of labeling theory', 579.

17 Jack P. Gibbs, *Norms, Deviance and Social Control: Conceptual Matters* (New York, 1981), 26. This is Liazos's 'covert institutional violence' ('Nuts, sluts and preverts', 104, 109 and 111–14). See also John I. Kitsuse and Malcolm Spector, 'Social problems and deviance: some parallel issues', *Social Problems* 22 (1974–5), 586.

18 Jonathan Dollimore, 'Masculine sexuality – 1: homophobia and sexual difference', in Robert Young, ed., *Sexual Difference, Oxford Literary Review* 8 (1986), 7.

19 Goode, 'On behalf of labeling theory', 570a–571b; cf. also John Hagan, 'Labelling and deviance: a case study in the "sociology of the interesting"', *Social Problems* 20 (1972–3), 447b–448a.

20 Howard S. Becker, *Outsiders: Studies in the Sociology of Deviance*, 2nd ed. (New York and London, 1973), 9.

21 Francis E. Merrill, *Society and Culture: An Introduction to Sociology*, 3rd ed. (Englewood Cliffs, 1965), 56.

22 Stanley Cohen, *Images of Deviance* (Harmondsworth, 1971), 14; Geoffrey M. White and John Kirkpatrick, *Person, Self and Experience: Exploring Pacific Ethnopsychologies* (London, 1985), 16.

23 Colin Sumner, 'Rethinking deviance', *Research in Law, Deviance and Social Control* 5 (1983), 188.

24 Fredrik Barth, *Ethnic Groups and Boundaries: The Social Organisation of Culture Difference* (Boston, 1969), 13–14; Rosemary Morris, 'The powerful and the poor in tenth-century Byzantium', *Past and Present* 73 (1976), 3–27.

25 Helen Mayer Hacker, 'Women as a minority group', in Nona Glazer-Malbin and Helen Youngelson Waehrer, eds, *Woman in a Man-made World: A Socio-economic Handbook* (Chicago, 1972), 40; Eugene Genovese, *Roll, Jordan, Roll: The World the Slaves Made* (London, 1975); Hortense Powdermaker, *After Freedom: A Cultural Study in the Deep South* (New York, 1969).

26 Mary Boykin Chesnut, *A Diary from Dixie*, Ben Ames Williams, ed. (Cambridge, Mass., 1949), 21.

27 The one 'professional' that men might engage a) confirms the tendency to see women as sexual commodities; and b) shows the extent to which English is a man-made language.

28 Contrast Judith Herrin, 'In search of Byzantine women: three avenues of approach', in Averil Cameron and A. Kuhrt, eds, *Images of Women in Antiquity* (London, 1983), 167–89.

29 Joëlle Beaucamp, 'La situation juridique de la femme à Byzance', *Cahiers de Civilisation Médiévale Xe–XIIe siècles* 20 (1977), 145–76; Joëlle Beaucamp, *Le statut de la femme à Byzance (4e–7e siècle) I Le droit impérial* (Paris, 1990); Georgina Buckler, 'Women in Byzantine law about 1100 AD', *B* 11 (1936), 391–416.

30 Beaucamp, 'La situation juridique de la femme à Byzance', 148. 'Byzantine law speaks of women in three ways: to draw up weaknesses which are compensated for in special safeguards, to set out the moral rules which can be applied to women of a certain kind, in order to define the role of women in the family, whether it be making a marriage, the situation of the married woman or of the mother.'

31 Gerhard Lenski and Jean Lenski, *Human Societies: An Introduction to Macrosociology*, 4th ed. (New York, 1982), 18.

32 'Symbolization constitutes objects not constituted before, objects which would not exist except for the context of social relationships wherein symbolization occurs. Language does not simply symbolize a situation or object which is already there in advance; it makes possible the existence or the appearance of that situation or object, for it is part of the mechanism whereby that situation or object is created.' (James B. McKee, *Introduction to Sociology* [New York, 1969], 61, quoting G.H. Mead)

33 McKee, *Introduction to Sociology*, 62; Mary Douglas, *In the Active*

Voice (London, 1982), 3, suggests that this speech determinism – only a step away from cultural determinism – is not the best corrective to mechanistic determinism. For an opposing view to McKee, see Cyril Mango, 'Byzantine literature as a distorting mirror', *Byzantium and its Image: History and Culture of the Byzantine Empire and its Heritage* (London, 1984), 3–18.

34 E.D. Hirsch, *Validity in Interpretation* (New Haven, 1967), 28–9. For example, because German has no word for bully, this does not mean that the concept does not exist; similarly, because English has no equivalent for *Weltanschauung*, this does not mean that English speakers have no world view.

35 Jennifer Coates, *Women, Men and Language: A Socio-linguistic Account of Sex Difference in Language* (London, 1986).

36 *Alexiad*, XV. ix. 1.

37 Cyril Mango, *Byzantium: The Empire of New Rome* (London, 1980), 233.

38 Joanna Russ, *How to Suppress Women's Writing* (Austin, 1983).

39 Now in print: James Howard-Johnston, 'duma Kouinene and the *Alexiad*' in M. Mullett and D. Smythe, eds, *Alexios I Kouinene 1: Papers* (Belfast, 1996), 260–302.

40 Charles Diehl, *La société byzantine à l'époque des Comnènes* (Paris: 1929), 8. See more recently, P. Magdalino and R. Nelson, 'The emperor in Byzantine art of the twelfth century', *Byzantinische Forschungen* 8 (1982), 129.

41 Diehl, *Société*, 8.

42 Dieter Roderich Reinsch: 'Ausländer und Byzantiner im Werk der Anna Komnene', *Rechtshistorische Journal* 8 (1989), 257–74.

43 Reinsch, 'Ausländer', 259.

44 Margaret Alexiou, 'Literary subversion and the aristocracy in twelfth-century Byzantium: a stylistic analysis of the *Timarion* (ch.6–10)', *BMGS* 8 (1982–3), 45; Susan R. Suleiman and Inge Crosman, *The Reader in the Text: Essays on Audience and Interpretation* (Princeton, 1980), 9; Ruth Macrides and Paul Magdalino, 'The architecture of ekphrasis: construction and context of Paul the Silentiary's poem on Hagia Sophia', *BMGS* 12 (1988), 47–82, esp. 81; Robert W. Uphaus, *The Idea of the Novel in the Eighteenth Century* (East Lansing, 1988), introduction, x; Averil Cameron, *History as Text* (London, 1989), 206–8.

45 Robert Browning, 'Byzantine scholarship', *Past and Present* 28 (1964), 3–22; Robert Browning, 'Literacy in the Byzantine world', *BMGS* 4 (1978), 39–54; Robert Browning, 'The Patriarchal School at Constantinople in the twelfth century', *Byzantion* 32 (1962), 167–201, and 33 (1963), 11–40; Alexander P. Kazhdan and Giles Constable, *People and Power in Byzantium: An Introduction to Modern Byzantine Studies* (Washington, DC, 1982), 96 and 102–4; Mango, *Empire of New Rome*, 237–40; M.E. Mullett, 'Aristocracy and patronage in the literary circles of Comnenian Constantinople' in Michael Angold, ed., *The Byzantine Aristocracy, IX to XIII Centuries* (Oxford, 1984), 173–201; Nicolas Oikonomides, 'Mount Athos: levels of literacy', *DOP* 42 (1988), 167–78; N.G. Wilson, 'Books and readers in Byzantium', in *Byzantine Books and Bookmen* (Washington, DC, 1975), 1–15.

46 Mullett, 'Aristocracy and patronage', 180; Roderick Beaton, 'Was Digenes Akrites an oral poem?' *BMGS* 7 (1981), 7–27; Kazhdan and Constable, *People and Power*, 103; E. Patlagean, 'Discours écrit, discours parlé. Niveaux de culture à Byzance aux VIIIe–XIe siècles', *Annales Economies, Sociétés Civilisations* 34 (1979), 264–78.

47 ἀνδρεῖον: *Alexiad*, XII. iii. 8.

48 *Alexiad*, XII. iii. 8.

49 Reinsch, 'Ausländer', 259.

50 *Alexiad*, VI. viii. 2.

51 'namely one day to ascend to the throne as empress'. Herbert Hunger, *Die hochsprachliche profane Literatur der Byzantiner*, vol. 1, *Philosophie, Rhetorik, Epistolographie, Geschichtsschreibung, Geographie* (Munich, 1978), 401.

52 Perhaps after 1138, according to Rae Dalven, *Anna Comnena* (New York, 1972), 66.

53 A later example of Leslie Brubaker's 'matronage', perhaps?

54 'she had spent half her life (since 1118) far from power and influence'. Hunger, *Hochsprachliche Literatur*, 403.

55 Ἐπαγωγοί: *Alexiad*, II. i. 4.

56 *Alexiad*, II. i. 4.

57 Ibid., ii. 1.

58 Ibid., ii. 1.

59 Ibid., 2.

60 These events are narrated in Ibid., i–iv.

61 Ibid., I. i. 1.

62 Ibid., II. ii.2.

63 Events told in Ibid., v.

64 Ibid., vi. 2.

65 Described in Ibid., ii–xii.

66 Ibid., III. i. 2.

67 Ibid., .2.

68 Ibid., 3.

69 ἡγιασμένῃ: Ibid., vi. 5.

70 Ibid., vi. 1–2.

71 Ibid., vii. 2.

72 Ibid., viii. 2–4.

73 Ibid., V. ii. 1.

74 Ibid., XII. iii. 2.

75 Ibid., 2.

76 Ibid., 4.

77 Ibid., 5.

78 Ibid., 6.

79 Ibid., XV. ix. 1. Compare this with previous exhortations to ignore the calumnies of the crowd if we wish to be numbered among the 'better sort' (Ibid., III. i.4).

8

BYZANTINE EUNUCHS: AN OVERVIEW, WITH SPECIAL REFERENCE TO THEIR CREATION AND ORIGIN

Shaun F. Tougher

That eunuchs were an integral part of the history of the Byzantine empire and its society is a fact well known both to the Byzantines and their medieval contemporaries, and to modern-day historians. A gift of 100 eunuchs was said to have been made to Basil I (867–86) by his Peloponnesian patroness Danelis, since she knew that there was always a place for eunuchs in the imperial palace.[1] The Abasgian kings knew there was a huge market in the exportation of eunuchs to the Byzantine empire, for as the chronicle tradition records, the Romans were infatuated with eunuchs.[2] Liudprand of Cremona notes with immense satisfaction that of all the gifts he brought to Constantine VII (913–59) on his diplomatic embassy of 949, the emperor prized that of four eunuchs above all the others.[3] Likewise Hopkins in his classic study of the presence and power of eunuchs at the imperial court in late antiquity justifies this exercise by the reflection 'because they were important'.[4] This point was previously voiced by Runciman in his study on the reign of Romanos I Lekapenos (920–44), though it was combined with the sharp observation that the significance of Byzantine eunuchs 'has never . . . been properly realised'.[5]

This comment was made in 1929; since then there has been some headway made in the study of Byzantine eunuchs, most notably by Guilland and the already mentioned Hopkins.[6] Guilland concentrated on the study of various offices held by eunuchs in the imperial administration, initially providing a very useful analysis of the position of eunuchs within the Byzantine empire, and the military, ecclesiastical and, above all, civil service roles that known eunuchs played throughout the entire span of Byzantine history.[7] Hopkins chose to focus on a shorter period, that of late antiquity, and tackled the crucial question of why eunuchs became a significant presence at the imperial court at this time, and also reflected on the nature and extent of their power.[8] Yet for such a crucial aspect of Byzantine history and society, such headway is extremely paltry, and overly preoccupied with the phenomenon of court eunuchs.[9] Such in-adequate consideration of the general history of eunuchs is reflected in Boswell's assertion that a major study on eunuchs is 'badly needed'.[10] One valuable addition to the bibliography on eunuchs that has appeared very recently, indeed during the evolution of this chapter, is Ringrose's study on Byzantine eunuchs and the issue of gender.[11] Ringrose engages with the notion of Byzantine eunuchs as a third sex, and contests that secular and ecclesiastical views differed on this point, the secular perception being that eunuchs did indeed form a distinct third sex, whilst the ecclesiastical view, as represented by Theophylact of Ohrid, 'undermined the distinct engendering of eunuchs', and asserted that 'eunuchs are neither a third sex nor a third gender; they are simply men'.[12] Ringrose is also extremely interested in the notion that eunuchs could possess magical powers, though she does not have the space to expand on this topic.[13]

Thus the study of eunuchs is beginning to broaden out, and in this chapter I wish to contribute to this process. First, I aim to establish certain key issues concerning the history of Byzantine eunuchs, and current thinking on these issues, and then, second, to focus on two crucial but often under-studied, or even ignored, aspects of the history of Byzantine eunuchs: how they were created, and where they came from.

Although both the societies of classical Greece and Rome were not at all unfamiliar with the phenomenon of eunuchs, it is quite clear that the period of late antiquity witnessed a dramatic upsurge in the visibility of eunuchs in Roman society, for at this time they appear to have become a vital element of the imperial court. This is what motivated Hopkins's classic study, for he sought to explain this development. The increasing presence of eunuchs at the court is generally linked with the emperor Diocletian (284–305), whose reign is said to have witnessed an 'orientalisation' of the Roman emperor and his court.[14] Certainly court eunuchs appear as victims of the Great Persecution,[15] whilst the *Historia Augusta* reflects that eunuchs had become a significant presence and influence at court.[16] Hopkins even wondered if this apparently sudden development owed something to the capture of the Persian king's harem by Galerius in 298.[17] The prominence of eunuchs at the late Roman imperial court is vividly illustrated by the reigns of Constantius II (337–61) and his successor Julian (361–63). When Julian came to power he ushered in his reign with a purge of his cousin's court, dispensing with its luxury and extravagance, at least as he saw it. Amongst the victims of this purge were the court eunuchs, whom Libanius said numbered more 'than flies around cattle in springtime',[18] and by whom it was widely held that Constantius was heavily influenced, in particular by his chamberlain Eusebius.[19] Most of the eunuchs simply found themselves out of a job, but the high chamberlain Eusebius, whom Ammianus describes as having 'risen from a mean station to a position of almost imperial power', and whom Julian credited with his poor relationship with his imperial cousin, was condemned to die and was burnt alive.[20] However, this anti-eunuch policy seems to have lasted only for the extent of Julian's reign, for following his death in 363 it is evident that eunuchs again became a vital component of the imperial court.

As to why most emperors were so keen to employ eunuchs at court, it is most often asserted that there were two main reasons for this: first that eunuchs could never aspire to be emperors themselves, and second that they were safe to have around females. These, in essence, boil down to the same fact: you can trust them. Such explanations are rather half-truths, for whilst eunuchs could not become emperors themselves, there was nothing to stop them assisting in the plots of others,[21] and it is clear that they could indeed engage in affairs with court females; it was just that there was no danger of impregnation.[22] A considerably more sophisticated analysis of the attraction of eunuchs for emperors is provided by Hopkins, whose observations have as much validity for Byzantine history as for that of late antiquity. He makes it clear that eunuchs were not merely oriental window-dressing, but had very real functions. They were useful in 'soaking up criticisms which might otherwise have fallen upon the emperor';[23] they 'acted as a lubricant preventing too much friction between the emperor and the other forces of the state which threatened his superiority';[24] and they met 'the need of a divine emperor for human information and contact'.[25]

Another key aspect of the history of Byzantine eunuchs that has received a certain amount of study is the functions and roles that eunuchs played within Byzantine society. In the popular imagination, eunuchs are linked primarily with domestic service, and above all with attendance upon, and guarding of, women. Certainly such roles were filled by Byzantine eunuchs, but this is not the full picture by any means. For instance, it is well established that eunuchs who served at the imperial court filled not only mundane domestic chores, but could also attain high office which gave them a degree of contact and influence with the emperor himself. In late antiquity, the figure of the grand chamberlain was one to be reckoned with, as we have already seen in the case of the emperor Constantius II and his chamberlain Eusebius.[26] Our knowledge of posts for eunuchs at the imperial court is especially good for the middle Byzantine period, thanks to the *Kletorologion* of Philotheos the atriklines which was composed in 899 during the reign of Leo VI (886–912).[27] An atriklines was an imperial official whose task it was to organise imperial feasts and ensure that the correct order of precedence was observed with respect to the guests who were invited to such occasions, and in his *Kletorologion* Philotheos sets out to describe for his fellow atriklinai those individuals that could be invited to the imperial feasts, their exact order of precedence at that moment in time, and the prominent feasts of the year to which various combinations of these people would be invited. In the course of his text Philotheos reveals much information about the specialised domestic offices that were available to eunuchs at the imperial court.[28] There were ten such offices in all, all of which reflect contact and even intimacy with the emperor. For instance, the very name of the highest of these, the office of parakoimomenos, highlights this degree of close proximity with the emperor, for it literally means 'the one who lies beside', or 'keeps watch beside'. The holder of this office was usually a key figure in the imperial regime, and it was held by such famous individuals as Samonas, Constantine the Paphlagonian and Basil Lekapenos. The other nine offices included such spheres as attending to the emperor's wardrobe, attending on the imperial tables, and seeing to the security of the imperial palaces. These offices were the preserve of eunuchs alone, they were unable to be filled by their non-eunuch counterparts (whom Philotheos designates as 'bearded'),[29] though it does seem that this exclusivity could sometimes be broken. The most famous case of this is the holding of the top eunuch office of parakoimomenos by Basil the Macedonian, an office he held prior to becoming Michael III's (842–67) co-emperor and adopted son in 866, and ultimate successor in 867. Yet Philotheos also makes plain that eunuchs in the imperial service were not limited to their 'exclusive' palace posts alone but, in sharp contrast to the 'bearded' who might occasionally fill a eunuch post, were also able to serve in all other administrative posts, including those of the strategoi, with the exception of three. The three posts that were reserved for the 'bearded' were those of the eparch, the quaestor and the domestic (which itself had several types).[30] Despite this bar it is thus clear that eunuchs in the imperial service had a wide range of functions open to them, a range in fact far exceeding those of their 'bearded' counterparts.

Much of the work done on Byzantine eunuchs has tended to focus on those who worked within the sphere of the imperial court.[31] In this context it has been noted that there appears to be a change in the phenomenon of the powerful court eunuchs in the eleventh century, with the advent of the Komnenian dynasty in 1081. Certainly the accession of Alexios I Komnenos (1081–1118) did witness a shift in the traditional balance of power, with the Komnenian family in its widest sense being installed in power at the expense of the traditional senatorial ruling élite. Lemerle remarks particularly on the passing of the paradynast, an unofficial designation of an official who happened to be the right-hand man of the emperor or empress, and was often perceived to be the real ruling force.[32] Listing paradynasts of the eleventh century from the time of the death of Basil II (976–1025), Lemerle names John the Orphanotrophos, Leichoudes, John the logothete, Leo Paraspondylos, John the metropolitan of Side, Nikephoritzes, and finally the famed Psellos. He then notes that the phenomenon of the paradynast ended with Alexios Komnenos and the establishment of the family regime, for the paradynast under Alexios was effectively his own mother Anna Dalassene, and then his wife Irene Doukaina.[33] What is particularly interesting for the student of Byzantine eunuchs is that most of the named paradynasts were in fact eunuchs: the three Johns and Nikephoritzes. This disappearance of the powerful court eunuch under the Komnenoi has also been noted and commented upon by Kazhdan,[34] though he also notes that at the end of the twelfth century with the accession of the Angeli and their restoration of the traditional powers, court eunuchs reappear.[35] For Guilland the real change is marked by the Palaiologan period, from the restoration of Constantinople to the Byzantines in 1261 to its fall to the Turks in 1453. Citing the Latinisation of Byzantine attitudes, and the security of the emperors in this period, he argues that the Byzantines no longer had the desire nor the need to employ eunuchs, and concludes that 'il est vrai-semblable de supposer que leur influence sur la politique et sur le gouvernement est moins importante que jadis'.[36] Undoubtedly this issue of the fate of eunuchs within the empire is one that requires much further study.

A less uncertain aspect of the history of Byzantine eunuchs is that as a group they were greatly reviled by other members of society. This is particularly marked in the period when eunuchs were emerging as a significant group at court in late antiquity. For instance, the *Historia Augusta* expresses gladness that an emperor has dispensed with their services at court,[37] whilst Lactantius notes that Constantine the Great escaped a murder attempt of his father-in-law by placing a 'worthless eunuch' in his bed in his stead, where the eunuch was then murdered.[38] However, it is the historian of late antiquity, Ammianus Marcellinus, who is the key exponent of anti-eunuch views in this period. Such feelings seem to have been kindled in him due to his experiences, and those of men he admired, at the hands of the court of Constantius II. Ammianus is particularly aggrieved about the treatment of the Master of Cavalry, Ursicinus, under whom he served, and the historian blames especially the chamberlain Eusebius for this. Ammianus says:

> Like a snake bursting with venom which sends out a swarm of its little ones to do mischief when they can scarcely crawl, Eusebius dispatched his subordinates the moment they reached maturity to assail the reputation of the hero [Ursicinus] with malicious suggestions, which their attendance in private gave them the chance of insinuating into the ears of the credulous emperor [Constantius] in the childish and reedy voices of their kind.[39]

Ammianus is thus revolted not simply by individual eunuchs like Eusebius, but by eunuchs as a whole, and such is his disgust that it even elicits praise for the usually reviled Domitian (81–96), since this emperor had 'forbade under threat of severe penalties the castration of a boy within the bounds of Roman jurisdiction', and Ammianus then comments further that if Domitian had not acted so, 'who could have endured the resulting swarms of eunuchs, since he can barely tolerate them in small numbers'.[40] Even when Ammianus feels moved to praise a eunuch, the chamberlain Eutherius who came to the support of another of Ammianus's heroes, Julian, during his

173

Caesarship, the historian makes it clear that this eunuch was a very unusual case. He states:

> It may perhaps sound incredible, because even if Numa Pompilius or Socrates were to speak well of a eunuch and back their statements with an oath they would be accused of departing from the truth. But roses grow in the midst of thorns, and among wild beasts there are some that grow tame.[41]

Ammianus also notes that Eutherius was able to retire to Rome in his old age, where he was cherished by all, and again the historian comments on the exceptional character of this case, saying 'in general men of his kind look out for a secret retreat in which to enjoy their ill-gotten wealth and hide like creatures who hate the light from the eyes of the multitude of those whom they have wronged'.[42] Such anti-eunuch sentiment is also famously reflected in Claudian's attack on Eutropius, a key figure at the eastern court of Arcadius (395–408), which is echoed too in Synesius's complaints on Arcadius's kingship.[43] According to Hopkins, the reasons for such vehement hatred of eunuchs on the part of the traditional élite stems from a revulsion at their physical condition, their lowly origin, but perhaps most of all from the perceived influence of the court eunuchs over the figure of the emperor himself.[44] Quite simply, traditional officialdom resented the physical barrier of eunuchs that had been placed ✓ between them and the emperor. Such distaste for eunuchs remained a constant feature of Byzantine social attitudes, which ultimately culminated in the production of a work in defence of eunuchs. This was crafted in the twelfth century by Theophylact of Ohrid, and was written at the request of one of his brothers who was himself a eunuch.[45] This brother, probably Demetrios, was tired of the insults that eunuchs had to suffer and wanted his brother to produce a work setting the record straight. Theophylact composed the requested piece in the form of a dialogue between a monk and a eunuch during a visit of the emperor Alexios I Komnenos to Thessalonike. The proponent of the anti-eunuch stance typically presents them as sources of all kinds of vice, and asserts that they are all homosexuals. Theophylact also wrote a short diatribe against a libidinous eunuch, which highlights that in popular opinion eunuchs were 'monsters' known for their corruption and sexual depravity.[46] The eunuch he assails is described as a libertine, a friend of prostitutes, a corrupter of virgins, more lustful than a billy-goat, and is compared to Priapis and Pan. However, Theophylact also contests that the libidinous eunuch is in fact the exception to the rule, and that purity is the natural privilege of eunuchs.

So far I have sought to delineate well-known aspects of the history of Byzantine eunuchs, but now wish to turn to aspects that are equally crucial, but as yet have not received, as far as I am aware, the comment that they deserve. The first of these aspects is the fundamental issue of castration. Despite being an obvious concern, it is one that is not discussed by most of the works that deal with eunuchs; although the recent work on eunuchs by Ringrose does raise the topic, it is confined to discussion in a footnote, and fails to describe the process. Perhaps part of the problem is that the Byzantines themselves tend to ignore the issue too; it is enough to describe someone as a eunuch without going into detail as to how they became one. It is assumed that the reader/listener will not need to be told, or perhaps is not interested in being told.

However, one Byzantine account of the operation of castration that does exist is found in the medical encyclopaedia (called the *Epitome of Medicine*) of a seventh-century doctor, Paul of Aegina.[47] Paul comments that the operation was one that he sometimes performed, even if it was against his will, and goes on to describe two methods of castration, the first by compression,[48] the other by excision. He writes:

> That by compression is thus performed: Children, still of a tender age, are placed in a vessel of hot water, and then when the parts are softened in the bath, the testicles are to be squeezed with the fingers until they disappear, and, being dissolved, can no longer be felt. The method by excision is as follows: let the person to be castrated be placed upon a bench, and the scrotum with the testicles grasped by the fingers of the left hand, and stretched; two straight incisions are then to be made with a scalpel, one in each testicle; and when the testicles start up they are to be dissected around and cut out, having merely left the very thin bond of connexion between the vessels in their natural state. This method is preferred to that by compression; for those who have had them squeezed sometimes have venereal diseases, a certain part, as it would appear, of the testicles having escaped the compression.

Whether everyone was as clinical and careful as a professional doctor is a moot point. Legislation of the emperor Justinian I (527–65) asserts that out of a sample of ninety people who were castrated only three survived.[49] The description of the roaring trade in eunuchs that the kings of Abasgia in the Caucasus did with the Byzantine empire up to and during the same Justinian's reign certainly makes one wonder as to the quality of care taken in performing the operation. Procopius notes that the Abasgian kings would

> take such boys ... as they noted having comely features and fine bodies, and dragging them away from their parents without the least hesitation they would make them eunuchs and then sell them at high prices to any persons in Roman territory who wished to buy them.[50]

'Cutting' is also mentioned as a method of castration by the widely travelled tenth-century historian Masudi, but he also mentions the ominous sounding practice of 'dragging'.[51] It should also be noted that sometimes it was not just the testicles that were removed, but the penis as well, though such eunuchs seem to have been a rarity in Byzantium.[52] When Liudprand of Cremona knew he was to fulfil a diplomatic mission to the Byzantine court in 949 he made sure he came with suitably impressive gifts. Amongst his chosen presents were four carzimasians; these were young eunuchs 'who have had both their testicles and their penis removed'.[53] However, not all eunuchs had to be purposely created. When in the ninth century the patriarch Methodios (843–7) was accused of having seduced a woman, an official inquiry was held. To prove his innocence, Methodios disrobed before the crowd and judges, revealing to them that he was physically incapable of what he had been accused of. He explained that many years ago he had been tormented by carnal desire, and that in answer to his prayer his body had been withered.[54] A case of an accidental eunuch in antiquity is provided by the Hellenistic eunuch Philetaerus, a key figure in the history of the principality of Pergamum.[55] Although Philetaerus is well known as a eunuch, Strabo reveals that his condition was accidental, for it was caused when as a child he was crushed in a crowd whilst with his nurse at a funeral.[56] Thus Philetaerus became a eunuch through accidental compression, and it is possible that such cases were found in Byzantium also.

Concerning the topic of castration, it is also essential to distinguish between those who were created eunuchs whilst children, and those who became eunuchs after having reached puberty. Those of the former category were presumably more prevalent, for only by being created a eunuch before puberty would one exhibit the classic physical characteristics of the group that denoted sexlessness. These characteristics were 'high-pitched voices ... faces with smooth glossy skins covered with a network of fine wrinkles', and a tendency 'to run to fat'.[57] According to Masudi, another distinguishing feature of eunuchs was that their armpits did not smell.[58]

As for eunuchs who were created after reaching puberty, much illumination is shed on this group by Rouselle.[59] She notes that those who had their testicles removed after reaching puberty still retained the signs of virility as 'other male hormones are produced ... by the suprarenal glands'; they could 'feel desire', and 'achieve erection and ejaculation of seminal fluid from the prostate and the seminal vesicles'.[60] She cites as an example of castration after puberty in the ancient world the case of the Galli, the worshippers of Cybele, whose aim had been to continue their sex life, but to be infertile. Rouselle then makes it clear that such eunuchs were also to be found in the Byzantine empire, quoting Basil of Ancyra writing in the fourth century advising virgins to avoid contact with eunuchs, for some of them had only been castrated after puberty and these 'burn with greater and less restrained desire for sexual union, and ... not only do they feel this ardour, but they think they can defile any woman they meet without risk'.[61] Given the differences between pre-pubertal and post-pubertal eunuchs, it does seem most likely that the former category were more prevalent, and the sources do tend to suggest that most eunuchs were created young.

The other fundamental issue of the history of Byzantine eunuchs that I wish to raise is that of origin. This is an issue perhaps even more overlooked than that of castration itself; even Ringrose failed to explore this avenue, simply qualifying the view that eunuchs originated both outside the empire and as slaves with the comment, 'By the eleventh century, it is apparent that castrations were regularly performed within the Byzantine empire and that youths who were castrated were often drawn from free-born families within the empire.'[62] Certainly there is an assumption that Byzantine eunuchs were of non-Roman origin and of servile status, and this is true up to a point.[63] Legislation initiated by Domitian was insistent that no Roman should be turned into a eunuch,[64] and such sentiments are echoed in the legislation of Leo I (457–74), who allowed the selling of eunuchs of barbarian stock within the empire, but outlawed the selling of eunuchs of Roman nationality.[65] Across the span of Byzantine history we do find eunuchs of obvious non-Roman origin.

For instance, the fourth-century chamberlain Eutherius was born in Armenia;[66] according to the sixth-century historian Procopius, 'most of the eunuchs among the Romans ... happened to be Abasgi by birth';[67] in the seventh century during the first reign of Justinian II (685–95), the emperor's right-hand eunuch, Stephen, was a Persian;[68] whilst at the start of the tenth century the chief eunuch of Leo VI was Samonas the Arab.[69]

There was clearly also an active and lucrative trade in eunuchs, highlighting that many indeed did have servile origins. The Armenian chamberlain Eutherius, although being born of free parents, was captured as a child by a neighbouring tribe who castrated him and sold him to Roman merchants, via whom he ended up serving in the palace of Constantine the Great.[70] We have already seen that the kings of Abasgia did a phenomenal trade in eunuchising the children of their own subjects and selling them on to the Byzantines. Samonas may have begun his career in Byzantium after being captured as a prisoner of war, and he was a lowly servant in the house of the family of the empress Zoe Zaoutzaina before entering the service of Leo VI and beginning his meteoric rise to the position of parakoimomenos. The oft-mentioned carzimasians of Liudprand were certainly of slave origin, for he bought them from the merchants of Verdun, whom he tells us perform the operation and 'take the boys into Spain and make a huge profit'.[71]

Yet it would be quite wrong to state that all eunuchs were of non-Roman origin, or that they all began life as commodities on the slave trade, and it would be equally wrong to suggest that the change in this phenomenon only occurred as Byzantine history evolved. Despite Domitian's ruling we do hear of Roman eunuchs, and free ones at that. Dio tells us that during the reign of Septimius Severus (193–211) the emperor's praetorian prefect Plautianus castrated one hundred noble Roman citizens, both youths and married men, in order that his daughter Plautilla should have only eunuchs as attendants.[72] Thus it seems clear that legislation could be ignored; indeed, the case of Leo I legislating against the selling of Roman eunuchs within the empire reveals that such trade was going on rather than that the emperor managed to stamp it out.

In the ninth century the imperial attitude towards castration was still that it should not be performed, though Leo VI does recognise that the operation should sometimes be performed for medical reasons.[73] Masudi openly acknowledges that the Byzantines, like the Chinese, did practise the castrating of several of their children.[74] This fact is reiterated and clearly illustrated in an account of the origin of the eunuch Constantine the Paphlagonian, who emerged as a significant figure in the early tenth century under Leo VI and his fourth wife Zoe Karbonopsina. This account states that Constantine's father was a farmer called Metrios who copied the practice of his neighbours; these castrated their sons, educated them, and sent them off to Constantinople to carve out lucrative careers.[75]

A similar case is found in the example of the early career of Symeon the New Theologian (949–1022), as well as the career of his own uncle.[76] Symeon too was a Paphlagonian, born in Galata, and after receiving a basic education from his parents he was then sent off to his grandparents in Constantinople where his education was taken to a higher level. His subsequent career in the imperial household, where he rose to the title of spatharokoubikoularios, was initiated through his uncle, who was himself a chamberlain (koitonites) in the imperial service.

Eunuchs could help members of their own family to attain social prominence. Under the empress Irene (c.800), one of her key officials, the eunuch Aetius, is said to have planned to make his own brother Leo emperor.[77] Constantine the Paphlagonian rose to such prominence that it seems that a member of one of the leading families of the day, Leo Phokas, married his sister.[78] A particularly famous eunuch known for the advancement of his own family is the eleventh-century figure John the Orphanotrophos.[79] A native of Paphlagonia,[80] he rose in the service of Basil II, and eventually guided his brother Michael (1034–41) and then his nephew, also called Michael (1041–2), onto the Byzantine throne.

Some eunuchs were even members of prominent Byzantine families themselves. From the early ninth century we have Theodore Krateros, one of the emperor Theophilos's (829–42) key officials, who became one of the forty-two martyrs after the Arabs captured Amorion.[81] One very well-known example is the tenth-century eunuch Basil Lekapenos. He was the illegitimate son of Romanos I Lekapenos (920–44), born to the emperor of a Bulgarian servant woman, and was castrated as a child. He went on to have a long and successful career, spanning the reigns of several emperors.[82] The case of Basil Lekapenos is also useful in that it reminds us that not all eunuchs were created simply to ensure that they had healthy career prospects, for Basil was castrated in order to prevent him from ever becoming emperor. This device of castration as a political weapon was common in Byzantium, and would often befall the surviving sons of deposed emperors. A notable instance of this is the fate of the sons of Michael I (811–13) on his deposition.[83] These sons, Theophylact and Niketas (the former being 20 years of age, the latter 14), were both tonsured and castrated and then exiled. They took the monastic names of Eustratios and Ignatios respectively, and although their imperial careers were terminated, Ignatios did later return to public life as patriarch of Constantinople (847–58 and 867–78), before going on to achieve sainthood. Other Byzantines who suffered unlooked-for castration could be prisoners of war, such as those captured in Italy in the late 920s by Theodbald the marquess of Camerino and Spoleto (929–36).[84]

In this chapter I have tried both to highlight what we already know about Byzantine eunuchs and to highlight and explore certain aspects that should be more well known, namely the issues of castration and origin. As such I have only been scratching the surface of this interesting and central subject, and can only end with the observation that much remains to be done before we can no longer call Byzantine eunuchs 'under-studied'.

NOTES

1 Theophanes Continuatus, I. Bekker, ed. (Bonn, 1838), 318.

2 For the export of eunuchs to Byzantium from Abasgia, see Procopius, *Gothic Wars* VIII.3.15–17. For the chronicle comment. see Zonaras, XV.1.6–7.

3 Liudprand, *Antapododis*, VI.6. The standard edition for Liudprand is J. Becker, *Die Werke Liudprands von Cremona* (Hanover-Leipzig, 1915); F.A. Wright, tr. *The Works of Liudprand of Cremona* (London, 1930).

4 K. Hopkins, *Conquerors and Slaves* (Cambridge, 1978), 172.

5 S. Runciman, *The Emperor Romanus Lecapenus and his Reign. A Study of Tenth-Century Byzantium* (Cambridge, 1929), 29.

6 See also H. Diner, *Emperors, Angels and Eunuchs. The Thousand Years of the Byzantine Empire*, trs E. and C. Paul (London, 1938), 62–72.

7 Guilland's articles on eunuch jobs and titles (including his general overview 'Les eunuques dans l'empire byzantin. Etude de titulaire et de prosopographie byzantines', *Revue des Etudes Byzantines* 1 [1943], 197–238) are collected in *Recherches sur les institutions byzantines*, I (Amsterdam, 1967), 165–380.

8 Hopkins, *Conquerors*, 172–96.

9 As also noted by K. Ringrose, 'Living in the shadows: eunuchs and gender in Byzantium', in G. Herdt, ed., *Third Sex, Third Gender* (New York, 1994), 85.

10 J. Boswell, *The Kindness of Strangers* (London, 1991), 113 n. 76. It is to be greatly regretted that Boswell will not be able to fulfil this task himself.

11 Ringrose, 'Eunuchs and gender', 85–109.
12 Ibid., 102, 107.
13 Ibid., 92–3.
14 On this supposed orientalisation, see Averil Cameron, *The Later Roman Empire* AD *284–430* (London, 1993), 42.
15 See, for instance, Lactantius, *De Mortibus Persecutorum* XIV.2–XV.3, ed. and tr. J. L. Creed (Oxford, 1984), 20–3; B. de Gaiffer, 'Palatins et eunuques dans quelques documents hagiographiques', *Analecta Bollandiana* 75 (1957), 17–46.
16 See Alan Cameron, 'Eunuchs in the "Historia Augusta"', *Latomus* 24 (1965), 155–8.
17 Hopkins, *Conquerors*, 192–3.
18 Libanius, *Orationes* XVIII.130, A.F. Norman, ed. and tr., *Libanius, Selected Works*, 3 vols, I, The Julianic Orations, Loeb Classical Library (Cambridge, Mass., and London, 1969), 362–5.
19 For Julian's purge and Constantius's dependence on his eunuchs, see Ammianus Marcellinus, XXII.4 and XXI.16, W. Hamilton, tr., *Ammianus Marcellinus. The Later Roman Empire (A. D. 354–378)* (Harmondsworth, 1986), 237–8, 232. It seems that Julian's anti-eunuch policy was a popular one, at least with his supporters: for Ammianus's views on eunuchs, see below; Mamertinus, *Panegyric on Julian* XIX.4, in S.N.C. Lieu, ed., *The Emperor Julian. Panegyric and Polemic*, 2nd ed. (Liverpool, 1989), 29; for Aurelius Victor, see H.W. Bird, *Sextus Aurelius Victor. A Historiographical Study* (ARCA, Classical and Medieval Texts, Papers and Monographs, Liverpool, 1984), Appendix V, 'Women, eunuchs and sexual morality', 116–21. This anti-eunuch stance was also shared by the *Historia Augusta*: see Cameron, 'Eunuchs in the "Historia Augusta"'.
20 Ammianus, XXII.3, tr. Hamilton, 237. For Julian on Eusebius, see his *Epistula ad Athenienses*, 274A, W.C. Wright, ed. and tr., *The Works of the Emperor Julian*, 3 vols, II, Loeb Classical Library (Cambridge, Mass., and London, 1980), 256–7.
21 For instance, at the start of the ninth century Aetius is said to have plotted to make his brother emperor, whilst in the eleventh century John the Orphanotrophos certainly secured the throne for both his brother and his nephew. For these episodes see below.
22 An example of a liaison, or at least a suspected one, between a eunuch and a female was that between Constantine the Paphlagonian and the empress Zoe Karbonopsina *c.*907: see Theophanes Continuatus, 869.
23 Hopkins, *Conquerors*, 174.
24 Ibid., 180.
25 Ibid., 187.
26 For instance, see ibid., 174–6.
27 For the text, see N. Oikonomidès, *Les listes de préséance byzantines des IXe et Xe siècles* (Paris, 1972), 65–235.
28 Philotheos also details the specialised titles that eunuchs could hold: see Oikonomidès, *Listes*, 124–35. See also J.B. Bury, *The Imperial Administrative System in the Ninth Century* (New York, 1958; orig. publ. London, 1911), 120–9. There were eight eunuch titles, in contrast to the

eighteen available to non-eunuchs. However, some of the titles were shared by both groups, namely those of protospatharios and patrikios. Notably eunuchs who held the title of patrikios preceded in eminence those non-eunuchs of the same title. This has been taken to signify that eunuch dignitaries had precedence over bearded dignitaries (Guilland, 'Les eunuques', 198), though it is salutary to remember that the highest eunuch title was that of patrikios, whilst non-eunuchs could ascend to the height of magistros, and indeed to the position of emperor.

29 Oikonomidès, *Listes*, 135.9.

30 Bury, *Administrative System*, 74, suggests that eunuchs were barred from these offices as they were posts with 'ancient associations and prestige', predating the formation and rise of a significant eunuch presence.

31 When talking about the functions that eunuchs could fulfil in Byzantine society there is a danger, as Ringrose has detected, that one does end up concentrating on those eunuchs in the imperial service. To a certain extent this is hard to avoid, as it is precisely these eunuchs that we know so much about. However, we should certainly also remember that the households of the social élite could also have a eunuch staff, probably based on the imperial model, but more than this we need to be aware of the range of functions and positions that eunuchs, both free and slave, can be found in across the spectrum of Byzantine society. Ringrose, 'Eunuchs and gender', 98–9, reminds us that eunuchs could be monks, priests, bishops, singers, actors, prostitutes and teachers. Thus when considering the roles that eunuchs played in Byzantine society we should be careful not to limit ourselves to the spheres of court service and domestic service alone.

32 P. Lemerle, *Cinq études sur le XIe siècle Byzantin* (Paris, 1977), 260–3.

33 Note, however, that B. Hill, 'Alexios I Komnenos and the imperial women', in M.E. Mullett and D.C. Smythe, eds, *Alexios I Komnenos* (Belfast, 1996), 37–54, esp. 53, questions the power of Irene Doukaina.

34 See A.P. Kazhdan and A. Wharton Epstein, *Change in Byzantine Culture in the Eleventh and Twelfth Centuries* (Berkeley, Los Angeles and London, 1985), 69–70.

35 A. Kazhdan and G. Constable, *People and Power in Byzantium* (Washington, DC, 1982), 136.

36 'It is reasonable to believe that their influence on politics and government is less important than formerly'. See Guilland, 'Les eunuques', 234.

37 See Cameron, 'Eunuchs in the "Historia Augusta"', 155–8.

38 Lactantius, *DMP* XXX.3–4, tr. Creed, 46–7.

39 Ammianus, XVIII.4, tr. Hamilton, 149.

40 Ibid.

41 Ibid., XVI.7, tr. Hamilton, 95.

42 Ibid., 96.

43 Claudian, *In Eutropium*, M. Platnauer, tr., *Claudian*, I, Loeb Classical Library (London and New York, 1922), 138–229; Synesius, *De regno*, C. Lacombrade, tr. and comm., *Le discours sur la royauté de Synésios de Cyrène à l'empereur Arcadios* (Paris, 1951). See also Alan Cameron and S. Long, with a contribution by L. Sherry, *Barbarians and Politics at the Court of Arcadius* (Berkeley, Los Angeles and Oxford, 1993), 107–9.

44 Hopkins, *Conquerors*, 195.
45 For the text, see P. Gautier, ed., *Théophylacte d'Achrida. Discours, traités, poésies* (Thessalonike, 1980), 288–331. For commentary on the text, see Ringrose, 'Eunuchs and gender', 102–7. See now also D. Simon, 'Lobpreis des Eunuchen', *Shriften des Historischen Kollegs Vorträge* 24 (1994), 5–27.
46 See Gautier, *Théophylacte*, 366–9.
47 Paul of Aegina, VI.68, F. Adams, tr., *The Seven Books of Paulus Aegineta*, 3 vols (London, 1844–7), II, 379–80.
48 For further reference to compression by Psellos, see Ringrose, 'Eunuchs and gender', 91 and n. 19.
49 Justinianus Imperator, *Novellae* CXXXXII, R. Schoell and W. Kroll, eds, *Corpus Iuris Civilis* iii.4 (Berlin, 1905); Guilland, 'Les eunuques', 199.
50 Procopius, *Gothic Wars*, VIII.3.15–16.
51 Masudi, *The Meadows of Gold. The Abbasids*, P. Lunde and C. Stone, eds and trs (London, 1989), 345–6. Masudi seems to have had a keen interest in eunuchs, and his lost *Historical Annals* included comment on 'eunuchs from the Sudan, the Slavic countries, Byzantium and China'.
52 See the comments of Ringrose, 'Eunuchs and gender', 91 and n. 21.
53 Liudprand, *Antapodosis*, VI.6.
54 See J.B. Bury, *A History of the Eastern Roman Empire from the Fall of Irene to the Accession of Basil I (A. D. 802–867)* (London, 1912), 151.
55 See, for instance, F.W. Walbank, *The Hellenistic World* (Glasgow, 1986), 123–4; R.B. McShane, *The Foreign Policy of the Attalids of Pergamum* (Urbana, 1964), 30–42.
56 Strabo, *Geographus* XIII.4.1, H.L. Jones, tr., *The Geography of Strabo*, 8 vols, VI, Loeb Classical Library (London and New York, 1929), 162–5.
57 Hopkins, *Conquerors*, 193–4.
58 Masudi, *Meadows*, 346.
59 A. Rouselle, *Porneia. On Desire and the Body in Antiquity*, F. Pheasant, tr. (Oxford and New York, 1988), 122–3.
60 Ibid., 123.
61 Ibid. I intend to explore the topic of eunuchs and sexual relationships in another paper.
62 Ringrose, 'Eunuchs and gender', 90 and n. 16.
63 For instance, Hopkins, *Conquerors*, 172.
64 See B.W. Jones, *The Emperor Domitian* (London, 1993), 31.
65 *Codex Justinianus* IV.42.2, P. Krueger, ed., *Corpus Iuris Civilis* II (Berlin, 1915), 179; Guilland, 'Les eunuques', 199.
66 Ammianus, XVI.7, tr. Hamilton, 95.
67 Procopius, *Gothic Wars*, VIII.3.17.
68 Patriarch Nicephorus, *History*, XXXIX.1–6, C. Mango, tr., *Nikephoros Patriarch of Constantinople. Short History* (Washington, DC, 1990), 94–5.
69 For Samonas, see R. Janin, 'Un arabe ministre à Byzance: Samonas (IXe–Xe)', *Echos d'Orient* 34 (1935), 307–18; R.J.H. Jenkins, 'The flight of Samonas', *Speculum* 23 (1948), 217–35, repr. in his *Studies on Byzantine History of the 9th and 10th Centuries* (London, 1970), X; L. Rydén, 'The portrait of the Arab Samonas in Byzantine literature', *Graeco-Arabica* 3 (1984), 101–8; S.F. Tougher, *The Reign of Leo VI (886–912). Personal*

Relationships and Political Ideologies (unpub. Ph.D. thesis, St Andrews, 1994), chap. 7.

70 Ammianus, XVI.7, tr. Hamilton, 95.

71 Liudprand, *Antapodosis*, VI.6.

72 Dio, *History*, LXXVI.14.4–6, E. Cary, tr., 9 vols, Loeb Classical Library, (Cambridge, Mass., and London, 1982), IX, 228–9.

73 Leo, *Novel* LX, P. Noailles and A. Dain, trs, *Les novelles de Léon VI* (Paris, 1944), 222–7. Leo VI deals with eunuchs in two other of his novels. In *Nov.* XXVI (trs Noailles and Dain, *Les novelles*, 100–5) the emperor decrees that eunuchs should be allowed to adopt children, whilst in *Nov.* LXXXXVIII (trs Noailles and Dain, *Les novelles*, 320–7) he maintains that eunuchs should not be allowed to marry.

74 Masudi, *Meadows*, trs and eds Lunde and Stone, 345.

75 *Synaxarion of Constantinople*, *Acta Sanctorum*, Proylaeum Novembris, 721–4. This is not the only story touching on Constantine's background, but this does not affect the fact that among Paphlagonian farmers there was the practice of castrating their sons. Note that the chronicle indicates that Constantine was a piece of property that could be passed from one owner to another: Theophanes Continuatus, 869. For his career under Leo VI, see Tougher, *The Reign of Leo VI*, chap. 7.

76 See R. Morris, 'The political saint of the eleventh century', in S. Hackel, ed., *The Byzantine Saint* (London, 1981), 44 and n. 9.

77 See P.E. Niavis, *The Reign of the Byzantine Emperor Nicephorus I (AD 802–811)* (Athens, 1987), 28. It is said that another of Irene's eunuchs, Staurakios, even planned to make himself emperor.

78 See R.J.H. Jenkins, 'A "Consolatio" of the Patriarch Nicholas Mysticus', B 35 (1965), 159–66, repr. *Studies*, XIX.

79 See R. Janin, 'Un ministre byzantin. Jean l'Orphanotrophe (XIe siècle)', *Echos d'Orient* 30 (1931), 431–43.

80 One does begin to wonder if Paphlagonia was a region particularly given to the production of eunuchs.

81 See M.W. Herlong, *Kinship and Social Mobility in Byzantium, 717–959* (unpub. Ph.D. thesis, Washington, DC, 1986), 140–1 (for Theodore Krateros), 140–3 (for the Krateroi).

82 See W.G. Brokkaar, 'Basil Lacapenus. Byzantium in the tenth century', *Studia byzantina et neohellenica neerlandica* 3 (1972), 199–234.

83 Bury, *Eastern Roman Empire*, 29; Herlong, *Social Mobility*, 52–3.

84 Liudprand, *Antapodosis*, IV.9.

9

HOMO BYZANTINUS?

Charles Barber

The conceptualisation of men in Byzantium is not a developed area
of study. For example, the *Oxford Dictionary of Byzantium*, which
presents an overview of present knowledge in Byzantine studies,
betrays such a lack.[1] Within the pages of the *Dictionary* it is possible
to turn to a section on Byzantine women (pages 2201–4). This reveals
a lively, recent and continuing literature that has identified women
and their social construction as a valid object of study. We cannot
turn to an equivalent section on men. I would suggest that this lack
reveals a problem for those of us who would wish to provide a
reading of Byzantium that is aware of the many implications of a
gendered framing of our visual and verbal materials. In particular,
the *Dictionary* makes no attempt to distinguish the category 'men'
from their institutional manifestations. We can find emperors,
monks, patriarchs, but we cannot find men. Instead, the introduction
to the *Dictionary* informs us that we can find *homo byzantinus*, the
'man in the street' of Byzantium, within its pages. It seems therefore
that Byzantine men are everywhere in the tome and yet nowhere are
they offered as a defined gender category.

An unwillingness to distinguish between homocentric discourse
and men is apparent in the construction of a figure such as *homo
byzantinus*, who is familiar to all Byzantinists. This totalising figure
was popularised by Alexander Kazhdan in his influential and
important study *People and Power: An Introduction to Modern
Byzantine Studies*, and was designed to encompass the experience of
the 'average Byzantine'.[2] In the introduction to this work Giles
Constable argues that the term *homo byzantinus* has been adopted
in order to escape the sexism of the term 'man'.[3] I would suggest that
this Latinisation makes a frail fig leaf. It masks the maintenance of a
theoretical framework that sustains a history free of considerations

185

of gender, namely a positivist reiteration of sources as deposits of fact more than as texts in their own right.[4] This reiterative gesture presents a problem to any gendered reading of the past: if we are to locate the validity of our discourses in the primary texts alone, then will our analyses necessarily be conditioned by the unspoken gendered expectations of our object of study? Central to this question are the ways in which *we* are to read texts. By not making men or rather masculinity an object of study, the secondary literature perhaps sustains a political construction that is written into our sources.[5] This is that Byzantine society can be written, seen and spoken of only in terms that correspond to the male world view. Men cannot be an object of analysis in this society because that would reveal that this necessarily partial patriarchal reading of the Byzantine world was a construct. *Homo byzantinus*, for instance, is an example of this extension of the patriarchal discourse to encompass this society as a whole. Born of texts that both construct and reflect a masculine reading of the world, *homo byzantinus* sustains the notion that men are the 'natural' embodiment of this Byzantine society. It can be argued that the conception of a Byzantine 'man in the street' is an accurate reflection of the male sources that we have. In which case, should we accept that Byzantium can be seen only through male eyes, and thereby maintain the silence that surrounds Byzantine masculinity, or should we attempt to make this masculinity an issue, and so develop a further strategy for the deconstruction of our sources and their particular patriarchal world?

This chapter will offer a reading of one verbal and one visual text. My intention is to raise the possibility of an investigation of masculinity in Byzantium, rather than to provide definitive answers on this subject. Certainly, the chapter will not claim to be a comprehensive survey of the forms of masculinity in Byzantium.[6] Rather it will attempt to investigate the process and implications of the naturalisation of the masculine as *the* voice of Byzantium in both our primary and secondary texts. My concern, in making men a proper object of study, is to suggest that the implications of gender studies, for long aimed at the recovery of women and female voices from the past, can be extended to men and a fuller investigation of the configuration of masculinity in Byzantium. As such, this chapter will necessarily make the texts of and on the past an issue. In Byzantine culture public discourse represented male values. This point has been well documented by feminist historians and their deconstruction of the textual treatment of women in Byzantium.[7]

This chapter will propose an analysis of the predominant homo-centric language of power in Byzantium from a different angle. Rather than analysing this masculine discourse in terms of its construction of the feminine and women, it will examine the pos-sibilities of a discussion of the relation of men to the male values that empower them.[8]

Before embarking on this preliminary historical essay, I wish to clarify the terminology and the theoretical stance of this chapter. My concern is with masculine identity in Byzantium. In order to investigate this topic I will distinguish three terms: *men, male* and *masculinity*. Such distinct categories are not unproblematic and their use will be returned to at the end of the chapter.[9] These distinctions will, however, help to define the issues under discussion here. By *men* I refer to the sex differentiated from women in terms of their distinct corporeal and sexual natures – that is a distinction based on physical difference. By *male* I mean the homocentric values produced from the construction of distinct gender categories around this named sexual and corporeal difference. By *masculinity* I describe the space of the discourse within which these *male* values are inscribed onto the *man*'s body, the body that will then both enact and validate the values ascribed to gender difference.[10]

A well-known imperial portrait provides an opportunity for the analysis of the relationship between men and the male notions of power in Byzantium. Such an analysis raises one of the fundamental issues in gender studies, that is the relationship between gender identity and power.[11] The imperial portrait of Basil II from the *Psalter of Basil II* (Marciana gr. 17 fol. 3r) suggests an identification of Byzantine politics with the men in that society (Plate 6).[12] The image dates, probably, from the early years of the eleventh century. It is a rich depiction of Byzantine imperial power. The figure of the emperor dominates the scene. He stands in military dress on a small podium. Above him is Christ, who reaches down from a reserved space, holding a crown above the emperor. This crown is placed on the emperor's head by the Archangel Gabriel. To the left, the emperor's lance is given him by a second Archangel, Michael. To either side of the emperor are images set within the image, six icons of military saints (Theodore Teron, Demetrios, Theodore Stratelates, George, Procopius and Mercurios). Beneath the emperor are a number of men in proskynesis, the full bow of the subject before his lord. Their lesser significance is suggested by the change in scale between the emperor and these figures. The inscriptions that are found to either side of the emperor can be translated as: 'Basil the Younger Emperor of the Romans Pious in Christ'. It is an image that has a wealth belied by its apparently simple structure. In particular, the natural and the supernatural are joined here in an expression that refers to no particular event, but rather constructs the political figure of the emperor.

Plate 6 The emperor Basil II, from the Psalter of Basil
Source: Courtesy of the Biblioteca Marciana, Venice, gr. 17, fol. 3r

This political portrayal of Basil betrays the gendered discourse of power in Byzantium. The image is exclusively masculine in its terms.[13] The emperor (a man) is crowned by Christ (a man). The emperor is then seen alongside military saints (men). We can assume an identity is being proposed between the emperor and these saints. Their common dress proposes such a link. This construction of a saintly identity for the military emperor is then addressed to a depicted audience made up of men. We witness them acknowledging this image of imperial power and being incorporated within it. Within the signifying field of the manuscript image there is a notion of power present that is unveiled in terms that are wholly masculine.

The key relationship in the Psalter image is that between the emperor and Christ. This is demonstrated in the act of Christ holding the crown above Basil's head. A poem is written on the folio opposite this portrayal and it elaborates on the visual material:

> A marvellous novelty is shown here. Christ from heaven offers in his life-bringing right hand the crown, the symbol of power, to the pious powerful lord Basil. Below (are) the foremost of the Incorporeal, one of whom has taken (this crown), brought (it) down, and joyfully crowned (the emperor); the other then adds victories to the (symbol of) power, bearing a lance, a weapon that frightens enemies, (and) places it in the hand of the lord. As a friend the martyrs are his allies, casting down those who should be (cast down).[14]

Christ is the source of power, here symbolised by the crown. The saints are the emperor's friends. Within this holy framework the emperor, raised above other men, is empowered over those other men. In Byzantine political ideology the relationship of the emperor to Christ-God was a fundamental aspect of the emperor's identity. This was given a classic definition by Eusebius in his *Tricennial Oration* to Constantine. The conception of the emperor as the image of God or Christ defined in this *Oration* was then repeated throughout Byzantine history:[15] heard in encomia, seen in images, embodied in ritual.[16] This relationship underpinned the Byzantine idea of monarchy in which the emperor's idealised links to Christ empowered his rule.

An expression of this relation between emperor and Christ was given by Michael Psellos in a poem addressed to Isaac Komnenos (1057–9):

You are an image of the signs of God. You are straight, true, stiff, exact, sweet, gentle, steadfast, firmly fixed, lofty ... a lantern of purity, a light-bringer of piety, an impartial judge unwavering in judgement ... there are no unseemly qualities in you, neither easily excited emotion, nor false speech, nor severity, nor a deceiving heart ... nor excessive toil, nor delight ...[17]

The emperor is here defined as a model of restraint. Being in the image of God, he is granted no excess of emotion or action. Rather he is refined beyond the flaws of humanity into an image of God, who is beyond such flaws. Such restraint was a standard topos of Byzantine descriptions of the ruler. The self-mastery proposed in this restraint was a prior necessity to the mastery of others.[18] It lifted the emperors above ordinary men, a distinction perhaps shown in the portrait of Basil II, where the emperor towers over the other men and is now seen among the saints.[19] The emperor, master of himself, is fit to rule.

But should this superman figure be interpreted as a product of a gender-neutral political ideology, or is the image of the emperor to be interpreted as an exemplar of a notion of power that within Byzantine homocentric discourse *has to be* inscribed onto a man's body? In his *Chronographia*, Psellos wrote of Basil II in this way:

To most men of our generation who saw the emperor Basil he seemed austere and abrupt in manner, an irascible person, who did not quickly change his mind, sober in his daily habits and averse to all that is delicate, but if I am to believe the historians of that period who wrote about him, he was not at all like that when his reign began. A change took place in his character after he acceded to the throne, and instead of leading his former dissolute, voluptuous sort of life, he became a man of great energy. The complete metamorphosis was brought about by the pressure of events. His character stiffened, so to speak. Feebleness gave way to strength and the old slackness disappeared before a new fixity of purpose.[20]

Two points may be drawn from this text. First, the adoption of imperial office is seen to produce a change in Basil. He has to refashion himself in line with the changing circumstances of his situation. He changes from a dissolute figure to a resolute one. Such a shift is in line with the expectations of self-mastery implicit in the imperial office and introduced above.

My second point is that Psellos has revealed that this conception of office was a potentially gendered one. Basil is described as being 'averse to all that is delicate'. For Psellos this aversion is a part of the positive reading of Basil's new imperial character. This 'delicate' quality is opposed to the 'virile' expectations of imperial office.[21] Such a reading was widespread in Byzantium, where the entry of women into imperial office was represented as problematic. In the sixth century, the empress Theodora can be seen in both verbal and visual media as a problem in imperial representation.[22] In the ninth century, the empress Irene is offered praise in language imbued with virile terminology and criticism in language that condemns her status as a woman in power.[23] In the eleventh century, Psellos struggles to account for Zoe in his biographies of the emperors.[24] In the thirteenth century, Nikephoros Blemmydes exploits the notion that the feminine is alien to the imperial office, in order to pin the blame for the fall of Constantinople in 1204 upon what he terms the effeminacy of the emperors at that time.[25] Through these various examples it can be seen that the imperial office is constructed as a masculine office and that the feminine lies outside of this.

The emperor fashions himself in the image of another man, Christ. Through this act of self-mastery, fashioned after a male paradigm, the emperor is fit to rule over other men. I would therefore argue that the exclusively male construction of the image of imperial power in the frontispiece to the *Psalter of Basil II* is no accident. Further, I would suggest that this is a coherent image of power produced by a society that identified the imperial office with masculine discourse and that could express power only in terms of male values. The vertical, 'upward gazing'[26] relation that the imperial self has with Christ, its model, writes a partial and homocentric discourse on to the body of the emperor.

My second text is the *Precepts and Anecdotes* written by Kekaumenos to his son in the 1070s.[27] This text plays an important part in Kazhdan's construction of *homo byzantinus* and for all its peculiarities it takes the reader into the more private world of the Byzantine 'man in the street'. The somewhat fearful views of the world expressed by Kekaumenos appear to support Kazhdan's reading of Byzantium as a society marked by 'individualism without freedom', such that 'the final aim of *homo byzantinus* was, in principle, a solitary, eremitical life, free from any form of social relationship'.[28] This somewhat misanthropic reading of Byzantine society and of its construction of the individual can be found in

Kekaumenos's text. Rather than placing its origins wholly in the political, ideological and physical worlds of Byzantium, as Kazhdan does, I would like to ask whether we might not also place its formation within Byzantium's masculine discourse?

The section of the *Precepts and Anecdotes* that will be discussed below includes chapters 88–160 and consists of the advice written by a father to a son on the ordering of his household.[29] A telling passage in this text (chapter 101) introduces the gendered world that Kekaumenos hands down:

> If you have a foreign friend and he comes through the city where you live do not put him up in your house. Let him stay somewhere else and send him the things he needs there – that is a better arrangement. If he were to live in your house then let me tell you of the difficulties. Do not let your wife, daughter or daughter-in-law leave their rooms and look into the house proper. If it were to happen that they should have to come out then your friend would immediately notice and fix his eyes upon them. If you are present then he will let his eyes drop, but he will find out their movements, their dress and their eyes, in short he will know them from head to toe. If he is alone with your people then he will chat them up and make them laugh. He will undermine your servants, your table, your household. He will ask your people whether you have this or that. Why don't I spell it out? If he has the opportunity he will make signs of love to your wife, looking at her with unchaste eyes, and if possible misusing her. And this isn't all, when travelling he will tell of these misdeeds.[30]

Within this text Kekaumenos's main point of reference is the other man. This friend is treated as an object of fear. Kekaumenos will not let him stay within his house. If the man does gain entry to this space, then Kekaumenos warns that the male householder must attempt to control the movements of the women within his household. They are not allowed to leave their rooms while the other man is present as Kekaumenos is afraid that this other man will disrupt the householder's control over his own household. In this attempt to police the people and spaces within his household, Kekaumenos demonstrates that the domestic space has come to serve as the battleground for the construction of masculine identity. It is the site that empowers the male and supports his masculinity. This is expressed through his control over the women in this place. That this is the product of a masculine discourse of empowerment is suggested by the source of Kekaumenos's potential disempowerment, the other man. Kekaumenos is here caught within a patriarchal paradox, whereby that which empowers him (male values) can also ensnare him.

In defining a role and identity for his son, Kekaumenos largely rejects the traditional public stage, instead urging his son to devote himself to his household. This, then, becomes the site for the construction of the son's (masculine) identity.[31] Such a strategy appears to be predicated on Kekaumenos's belief that everyone, including himself, simply works for themselves.[32] This is demonstrated in our text from chapter 101, in which Kekaumenos cannot bring himself to entertain his friend for fear of the disruption that this man might cause. For Kekaumenos, within the house the father was the model for all and the judge of all.[33] He was the focus of respect, and it was for him both to reward and to punish. Fear is introduced as a part of this paternal control.[34] In order to exercise this authority, the familiar notion of self-mastery is brought into play:

> Your sons and daughters ought to honour you; but handle them with great care and do not be negligent even when they are still small. They will behave according to what they have learned from you. So have regard to yourself! Who does not regard himself will not be able to watch over another.[35]

The master of the household is empowered by his own self-control, a constraint that is defined in terms of masculine discourse and that is manifested through his control over the others within his home.[36]

The masculine identity that empowers the father within the household also causes him problems. These are embodied in the man who enters into the household. What Kekaumenos fears is the stranger taking possession of Kekaumenos's women by usurping his place as the dominant male or mocking him because of them before the outside world. Such a challenge would threaten Kekaumenos's identity. This domestic model is then projected into the wider world. Its most obvious manifestation is Kekaumenos's rejection of the public life. His son is warned against corruption, debt, the holding of public office, and even public advocacy for one point of view or another.[37] He is told to offer respect to those in authority over him, and also to fear them.[38] The public world beyond the household is thus represented as a threat. Within the household Kekaumenos represents the male as sovereign, controlling the exchanges that take place within this particular economy. Beyond these walls this autonomy crumbles, now constrained by the challenge of other men practising the masculine discourse of empowerment.

In giving his advice, Kekaumenos is fashioning a masculine model for his son. The son is empowered by the practice of self-restraint. In adopting this role, he represents the public (homocentric) discourse to his household. Within this space he is dominant. The problem lies outside. There other men practise the same discourse and so present alternate sources of power. This threat to the son's autonomy suggests that Kazhdan's 'individualism without freedom' is generated both by the abstractions of institutions and of nature and *also* by the gender roles prevalent in Byzantine society. Byzantine man's relationships within the household are shaped by his identity outside of it. Rather than constructing *homo byzantinus* primarily in terms of his public social role, it might also be important to analyse him in terms of this domestic identity. This, we have seen, is shaped by prescribed gender roles that make women an object of exchange between men. Throughout this text the father advises the son on his relationships with other men and his own masculine role within the household. The sources of the fear that Kekaumenos harbours about the outside world ironically serve to empower him as the male head of the household. Within that space his identity is secure; outside of it other men present a threat. He therefore both manipulates and is manipulated by a homocentric discourse that can express social negotiation only in terms of a competition between men.

Masculine identity in Byzantium was formed from a fusion of the man and the male values prevalent within that society. The imperial image provided a paradigm for this process. In the case of Basil II it became apparent that the notion of imperial power was expressed in a language that consisted exclusively of masculine signifiers. Men were constructed through such means as the 'natural' voice of power in Byzantium. Given this, it is notable that a fluid relation between men and male values could be posited within this masculine discourse, such that an identifiable language of gender difference was recognised and exploited for strategic ends. For example, in writings on the imperial office, the values associated with 'effeminacy' and 'virility' could be exploited to construct a critical apparatus for the assessment of the emperors and empresses who held that office. This implies an ability to distinguish between men and male values within masculine discourse such that they can be manipulated as a weapon within critical writing. As such, masculinity becomes a fluid, complex and potentially plural concept. Kekaumenos based his world view on the assumed dominance of the man and male values within this masculine discourse. The *homo byzantinus* that he represents in his text defines himself through his compliance with a male discourse that empowers him within his household. The text also indicates that this source of power can return, in the guise of another man, to threaten him within his domestic realm. In this way Kekaumenos underlines a paradox in patriarchy that becomes obvious once we begin to analyse the relation between men and the male values that empower them. This discourse both fabricates the subjectivity of the man, and subjects him to its terms.

At the heart of the analysis of Byzantine masculinity lies the issue of *our* reading of texts. *Homo byzantinus* is a product of a reading of the past that overrides gender difference. By not making the gendered nature of the text an aspect of its reading, the reader is in danger of reiterating the assumptions present in the homocentric discourse of the text. The result is that Byzantium continues to be represented in (hidden) masculine terms. To counter this, a critical and active reading is required of *us*. Feminist historians have developed a post-structuralist methodology for the clarification of feminine textual space. In this chapter I have attempted to extend this work. Such an extension has been hotly debated in recent years, largely on the premise of a clear distinction between men's studies and women's studies.[39] In this chapter, however, I (a man) have deliberately attempted to apply feminist methodologies to the examination of Byzantine masculinity. My intention has been to ask whether men can develop a critical relation to the gendered notions of power that construct them as individuals. This has meant proposing, and I believe demonstrating, the differentiation of men from male values, and their common production from within and dependence upon a fluid masculine discourse. In so doing, I hope to have shown that a discussion of masculinities can supplement the research into the interplay of power and gender in Byzantium.

NOTES

1 In *ODB* vol. 1, viii. Note the comments on gender in the review of the *Dictionary* by Robin Cormack in *The Times Literary Supplement* 4611 (16 August 1991), 25.
2 A. Kazhdan and G. Constable, *People and Power in Byzantium. An*

Introduction to Modern Byzantine Studies (Washington, DC, 1982), *passim*. Now *homo byzantinus* has made a telling appearance as the title of the Kazhdan *festschrift* in *DOP* 46 (1992). My intention in this chapter is not to deny the value of *homo byzantinus* for opening a 'low-level' history of Byzantium, rather I wish to build on this quasi-structuralist figure in order to examine the possibilities for the construction of post-structuralist histories.

3 Kazhdan and Constable, *People and Power*, viii–ix.

4 This is not to claim that non-positivists are necessarily not sexist in their assumptions.

5 This point is made by feminist analyses of Byzantium. Masculinist studies should be seen to supplement this work through a further analysis of men in relation to male discourse in Byzantium. The literature on masculinity is growing rapidly. Works found useful by this author were: P. Middleton, *The Inward Gaze: Masculinity and Subjectivity in Modern Culture* (New York and London, 1992); J. Winkler, *The Constraints of Desire: The Anthropology of Sex and Gender in Ancient Greece* (London, 1990); A. Brittan, *Masculinity and Power* (Oxford, 1989); M. Foucault, *The Use of Pleasure* (London, 1986); M. Foucault, 'Nietzsche, genealogy, history', in P. Rabinow, ed., *The Foucault Reader* (London, 1986), 76–100M.

6 For instance, analysis of the problematic masculinities of the eunuch could be developed further: see Theophylact of Ohrid's discussion in P. Gautier, ed., *Théophylacte d'Achrida, Discours, Traités, Poésies* (Thessaloniki, 1980), 281–331, esp. 291–5, on the critique of the eunuch as a feminised male; similarly, investigation of homosexuality should be deepened: see J. Boswell, *Christianity, Social Tolerance, and Homosexuality: Gay People in Western Europe from the Beginning of the Christian Era to the Fourteenth Century* (Chicago, 1980), esp. 156–7, 359–62, and now J. Boswell, *Same-Sex Unions in Premodern Europe* (New York, 1994), esp. 199–279.

7 I am thinking, in particular, of Catia Galatariotou's work on Neophytos the Recluse: 'Holy women and witches: aspects of Byzantine conceptions of gender', *BMGS* 9 (1984–5), 55–94, and '*Eros* and *Thanatos*: A Byzantine hermit's conception of sexuality', *BMGS* 13 (1989), 95–137, and Averil Cameron on Theodora in *Procopius and the Sixth Century* (London, 1986), 67–83, and also Cameron's 'Virginity as metaphor. Women and the rhetoric of early Christianity', in Averil Cameron, ed., *History as Text* (London, 1989), 181–205.

8 The implications of such a study as a part of gender studies will be discussed at the end of the chapter.

9 The definition of masculinity and its place in gender studies is a fraught issue. See the articles in A. Jardine and P. Smith, eds, *Men in Feminism* (New York and London, 1989), and Middleton, *Inward Gaze*, esp. 113–65, for the nature of the debates.

10 On the notion of bodily inscription, see Foucault, 'Nietzsche'. Note also J. Butler, *Gender Trouble: Feminism and the Subversion of Identity* (New York, 1990), 1–34. As will become clear, the 'natural' claims of the body are overwritten by the value-laden discourse of gender categorisation.

11 S. Heath, 'Male feminism', in Jardine and Smith, eds, *Men in Feminism*, 1–32; E. Grosz, 'Contemporary theories of power and subjectivity', in S. Gunew, ed., *Feminist Knowledge: Critique and Construct* (London and New York, 1990), 59–120; P. Rothfield, 'Feminism, subjectivity, and sexual difference', in *Feminist Knowledge*, 121–44.

12 A. Cutler, 'The Psalter of Basil II', *Arte Veneta* 30 (1976), 9–19; A. Cutler, 'The Psalter of Basil II (Part II)', *Arte Veneta* 31 (1977), 9–15.

13 A comparison can be drawn with the exclusively male representation of Justinian as emperor at San Vitale, Ravenna: see C. Barber, 'The imperial panels at San Vitale: a reconsideration', *BMGS* 14 (1990), 19–42. I read the archangels in the Psalter as sexless rather than genderless in their representation.

14 This translation is an adaptation of that in I. Ševčenko, 'The illuminators of the menologium of Basil II', *DOP* 16 (1962), 272.

15 The *Oration* text is translated and discussed in H. Drake, *In Praise of Constantine: An Historical Study and New Translation of Eusebius' Tricennial Oration* (California, 1976); see also T. Barnes, *Constantine and Eusebius* (London, 1981), 245–60.

16 The most useful text on the public manifestations of the emperor remains A. Grabar, *L'empereur dans l'art byzantin* (Paris, 1936). To this should be added: Averil Cameron, ed. and tr., *Corippus, In laudem Iustini Augusti minoris* (London, 1976), 60 and 178 f., P. Magdalino and R. Nelson, 'The emperor in Byzantine art of the twelfth century', *Byzantinische Forschungen* 8 (1982), 123–83, and R. Cormack, *Writing in Gold: Byzantine Society and its Icons* (London, 1985), 179–214.

17 The translation is from H. Maguire, 'Style and ideology in Byzantine imperial art', *Gesta* 28 (1989), 224. The text can be found in E. Kurtz, ed., Michael Psellos, *Scripta minora* I (Milan, 1936), 46–7, ll. 36–56.

18 On self-mastery, see: M. Foucault, *Use of Pleasure*, 82–4; A. Rousselle, *Porneia: De la maitrise du corps à la privation sensorielle IIe–IVe siècles de l'ère chrétienne* (Paris, 1983), 13 ff. The theme is repeated in Byzantine writing on the emperor: Agapetus, *PG* 86.1165AB; Photios, *PG* 102:674D; Nikephoros Blemmydes in H. Hunger and I. Ševčenko, *Des Nikephoros Blemmydes* Βασιλικὸς Ἀνδριὰς *und dessen Metaphrase von Georgios Galesiotes und Georgios Oinaiotes: Ein weiterer Beitrag zum Verständnis der byzantinischen Schrift-Koine* (Vienna, 1986), 122.10.

19 This point is made by Henry Maguire in 'The art of comparing in Byzantium', *Art Bulletin* 70 (1988), 93–4.

20 This translation is taken from E.R.A. Sewter, *Fourteen Byzantine Rulers: The Chronographia of Michael Psellus* (London, 1966), 29. The text can be found in Michel Psellos, *Chronographie* I, 4 (Basil II), E. Renauld, ed. and tr. (Paris, 1926). I have altered the reading of τὸ ἁβρὸν to 'that is delicate', although the 'effeminacy' translation in Sewter's text makes concrete the gendered implications of this term.

21 Psellos is fairly typical of Byzantine writing in his use of virility and effeminacy as means of evaluating the worth of an emperor. For instance, he introduces the failings of Constantine IX by pointing to his relative lack of virility in military matters: Psellos, *Chron.*, VI, 163–4 (Constantine IX). See also C. Chamberlain, 'The theory and practice of the

imperial panegyric in Michael Psellus: the tension between history and rhetoric', *B* 56 (1986), 16–27, and D. Russell and N. Wilson, eds, trs and comms, *Menander Rhetor* (Oxford, 1981), 84 (372.30 f.).

22 See Cameron, *Procopius*, 67–83, and Barber, 'Imperial panels'.

23 The praise is offered by Theodore the Studite in Letter 7 of his collected letters which dates from 801. The letter is available in G. Fatouros, ed., *Theodori Studitae Epistulae* I (Berlin, 1992), 26, ll. 78–9. One example of such a gendered critique is offered by the iconoclast council of 815, where the return to iconophile belief is blamed on Irene: 'Wherefore the church of God remained untroubled for many years and guarded the people in peace [following the council of 754], until it chanced that the imperial office passed from men to a woman and God's church was undone by female frivolity.' This text can be found at P. Alexander, 'The iconoclastic council of St Sophia (815) and its definition (*Horos*)', *DOP* 7 (1953), 59, texts 6 and 7. The translation is taken from that given in the Appendix to Anthony Bryer and Judith Herrin, eds, *Iconoclasm* (Birmingham, 1977), 184.

24 B. Hill, L. James and D. Smythe, 'Zoe: the rhythm method of imperial renewal', in P. Magdalino, ed., *New Constantines: The Rhythm of Imperial Renewal in Byzantium, 4th–13th Centuries* (Aldershot, 1994), 215–29.

25 Hunger and Ševčenko, *Nikephoros Blemmydes*, 123.17.

26 In I. Heikel, ed., Eusebius, *Werke* I (Leipzig, 1902), 201, ll. 19–20.

27 The text is available in two editions: B. Wassilievsky and V. Jernstedt, eds, *Cecaumeni, Strategicon et incerti scriptoris De officiis regiis libellus* (St Petersburg, 1896), and G. Litavrin, ed., *Sovety i rasskazy Kekavmena* (Moscow, 1972). My reading is taken from the Litavrin edition. A German translation is available: H.-G. Beck, tr., *Vademecum des byzantinischen Aristokraten. Das sogenannte Strategikon des Kekaumenos* (Graz, Vienna and Cologne, 1956). See also the discussion: P. Lemerle, 'Prolégomènon à une édition critique et commentée des Conseils et Récits de Kékauménos', *Academie Royale de Belgique. Classe des Lettres Memoires* 54 (Brussels, 1960).

28 Kazhdan and Constable, *People and Power*, 33 and 160.

29 See on this: P. Magdalino, 'The Byzantine aristocratic oikos', in M. Angold, ed., *The Byzantine Aristocracy, IX–XIII Centuries* (Oxford, 1984), 92–111; K. Inone, 'A provincial aristocratic oikos in eleventh-century Byzantium', *Greek, Roman and Byzantine Studies* 30 (1989), 545–69; and especially P. Magdalino, 'Honour among Romaioi: the framework of social values in the world of Digenes Akrites and Kekaumenos', *BMGS* 13 (1989), 183–218.

30 Litavrin, *Sovety*, 202–4.

31 As such the text complicates any simple division between public and private spaces in Byzantium. See E. Patlagean, 'Byzantium in the tenth and eleventh centuries', in P. Veyne, ed., *A History of Private Life I. From Pagan Rome to Byzantium* (Cambridge and London, 1987), 551–641, and the review article: J. Nelson, 'The problematic in the private', *Social History* 15 (1990), 355–64.

32 Litavrin, *Sovety*, 192.

33 Ibid., 212 and 240.
34 Ibid.
35 Ibid., 212.
36 An echo of the emperor might be read into this. An appreciation of the emperor's role in Byzantium is a major feature of Kekaumenos's text.
37 Litavrin, *Sovety*, 194–202.
38 Ibid., 198 and 240.
39 See the contrasting views: S. Heath, 'Male feminism', in Jardine and Smith, *Men in Feminism*, 1–32, P. Smith, 'Men in feminism: men and feminist theory', ibid., 33–40, and A. Jardine, 'Men in feminism: odor di uomo or compagnons de route?', ibid., 54–61.

SELECT BIBLIOGRAPHY OF FREQUENTLY CITED SOURCES

PRIMARY SOURCES

Anthologia Palatina, ed. P. Waltz (Paris, 1928). English trans., W.R. Paton, *The Greek Anthology*, Loeb Classical Library (Cambridge, Mass., and London, 1916)

Nicetas Choniates, *Historia*, ed. J.L.van Dieten (Berlin, 1975). English trans., H. Magoulias, *O City of Byzantium* (Detroit, 1984)

Kartlis Cxovreba, ed. S. Q'auxcisvili (Tbilisi, 1959). English trans., K. Vivian, *The Georgian Chronicle. The Period of Giorgi Lasha* (Amsterdam, 1991)

Kekaumenos, *Strategikon*, ed. G. Litavrin, *Sovety i rasskazy kekavmena* (Moscow, 1972). German trans., H.-G. Beck, *Vademecum des byzantinischen Aristokraten. Das sogenannte Strategikon des Kekaumenos* (Graz, Vienna and Cologne, 1956)

Anna Komnene, *Alexiad*, ed. and tr. B. Leib, *Alexiade*, 4 vols (Paris, 1967). English trans., E. Sewter, *The Alexiad of Anna Comnena* (Harmondsworth, 1969)

Michael Psellos, *Chronographia*, ed. and tr. E. Renauld, *Chronographie*, 2 vols (Paris, 1926–8). English trans., E.R. Sewter, *Fourteen Byzantine Rulers* (London, 1966)

Theophylact of Ohrid, ed. P. Gautier, *Theophylacte d'Achrida. Discours, traités, poésies* (Thessaloniki, 1980)

SECONDARY SOURCES

L.J. Archer, S. Fischler and M. Wyke, eds, *'An Illusion of the Night'. Women in Ancient Societies* (London, 1994)

C. Barber, 'The imperial panels at San Vitale: a reconsideration', *BMGS* 14 (1990), 19–42

J. Beaucamp, 'La situation juridique de la femme à Byzance', *Cahiers de civilisation Médiévale* 20 (1977), 145–76

—— *Le statut de la femme à Byzance (4e–7e siècles)* I–II (Paris, 1990, 1992)

J.M. Bennett, 'Feminism and history', *Gender and History* 1 (1989), 251–72

P. Brown, *The Body and Society: Men, Women and Sexual Renunciation in Early Christianity* (New York, 1988)

G. Buckler, 'Women in Byzantine law about 1100 AD', *B* 11 (1936), 391–416

C. Walker Bynum, 'Women's stories, women's symbols: a critique of Victor Turner's theory of liminality', in R.L. Moore and F.E. Reynolds, eds, *Anthropology and the Study of Religion* (Chicago, 1984), 105–25

Averil Cameron, *Procopius and the Sixth Century* (London, 1986)

—— 'Virginity as metaphor', in Averil Cameron, ed., *History as Text* (London, 1989), 184–205

—— 'Early Christianity and the discourse of female desire', in Archer, Fischler and Wyke, eds, *'An illusion of the night'*, 152–68

Averil Cameron and A. Kuhrt, eds, *Images of Women in Antiquity*, rev. ed. (London, 1993)

A. Weyl Carr, 'Women and monasticism in Byzantium', *Byzantinische Forschungen* 9 (1985), 1–15

G. Clark, *Women in Late Antiquity. Pagan and Christian Lifestyles* (Oxford, 1993)

K. Cooper, 'Insinuations of womanly influence: an aspect of the Christianization of the Roman aristocracy', *Journal of Roman Studies* 82 (1992), 150–64

R.S. Cormack, *Writing in Gold* (London, 1985)

J.W. Drijvers, *Helena Augusta: The Mother of Constantine the Great and the Legend of Her Finding of the True Cross* (Leiden, 1992)

J. Dubisch, ed., *Gender and Power in Rural Greece* (Princeton, 1986)

C. Edwards, *The Politics of Immorality in Ancient Rome* (Cambridge, 1993)

S. Elm, 'Evagrius Ponticus' *Sententiae ad Virginem*', *DOP* 45 (1991), 97–120

C. Galatariotou, 'Holy women and witches: aspects of Byzantine conceptions of gender', *BMGS* 9 (1984–5), 55–94

—— 'Byzantine women's monastic communities: the evidence of the typika', *JÖB* 38 (1988), 263–90

L. Garland, 'The life and ideology of Byzantine women: a further note on conventions of behaviour and social reality as reflected in 11th and 12th century sources', *B* 58 (1988), 361–93

J. Grosdidier de Matons, 'La femme dans l'empire byzantin', in P. Grimal, ed., *Histoire mondiale de la femme* III (Paris, 1967), 11–43

R. Guilland, 'Les eunuques dans l'empire byzantin. Etude de titulaire et de prosopographie byzantines', *Revue des Etudes Byzantines* 1 (1943), 197–238

M. Harrison, *A Temple for Byzantium. The Discovery and Excavation of Anicia Juliana's Palace-church in Istanbul* (London, 1989)

S. Ashbrook Harvey, 'Women in early Byzantine hagiography: reversing the story', in L.L. Coon, K.J. Haldane and E.W. Summer, eds, *That Gentle Strength. Historical Perspectives on Women in Christianity* (Charlottesville, 1990), 36–57

J. Herrin, 'Women and the faith in icons', in R. Samuel and G. Stedman Jones, eds, *Culture, Ideology and Politics* (London, 1982), 56–83

—— 'In search of Byzantine women: three avenues of approach', in Cameron and Kuhrt, eds, *Images of Women*, (London, 1983, rev.edn. 1993)

—— '"Femina Byzantina": the Council in Trullo on women', *DOP* 46 (1992), 97–105

—— 'Public and private forms of religious commitment among Byzantine women', in Archer, Fischler and Wyke, eds, *Women in Ancient Societies*, 181–203

B. Hill, 'Alexios *I* Komnenos and the imperial women' in M.E. Mullett and D.C. Smythe, eds, *Alexios I Komnenos* (Belfast, 1996), 37–54

B. Hill, L. James and D.C. Smythe, 'Zoe: the rhythm method of imperial renewal', in P. Magdalino, ed., *New Constantines. The Rhythm of Imperial Renewal in Byzantium, 4th–13th Centuries* (Aldershot, 1994), 215–30

K. Holum, *Theodosian Empresses. Women and Imperial Dominion in Late Antiquity* (Berkeley, 1982)

I. Kalavrezou, 'Images of the mother: when the Virgin Mary became *Meter Theou*', *DOP* 44 (1990), 165–72

A. Kazhdan, 'Constantin imaginaire. Byzantine legends of the ninth century about Constantine the Great', *B* 57 (1987), 196–250

—— 'Byzantine hagiography and sex in the fifth to twelfth centuries', *DOP* 44 (1990), 131–43

A. Kazhdan and G. Constable, *People and Power in Byzantium* (Washington, DC, 1982)

A. Kazhdan and A.M. Talbot, 'Women and iconoclasm', *Byzantinische Zeitschrift* 84/5 (1991/2), 391–408

R.S. Kraemer, ed., *Maenads, Martyrs, Matrons, Monastics. A Sourcebook on Women's Religions in the Greco-Roman World* (Philadelphia, 1988)

—— *Her Share of the Blessings* (New York and Oxford, 1992)

A. Laiou, 'The role of women in Byzantine society', *JÖB* 31/1 (1981).

—— 'Observations on the life and ideology of Byzantine women', *Byzantinische Forschungen* 9 (1985), 59–102

—— *Mariage, l'amour et parenté à Byzance aux XIe–XIIIe siècles* (Paris, 1992)

B. Leyerle, 'John Chrysostom on the gaze', *Journal of Early Christian Studies* 1 (1993), 159–74

C. Mango and I. Ševčenko, 'Remains of the church of St Polyeuktos at Constantinople', *DOP* 15 (1961)

S.I. Oost, *Galla Placidia Augusta, A Biographical Essay* (Chicago, 1968)

E. Patlagean, 'L'histoire de la femme déguisée en moine et l'évolution de la sainteté féminine à Byzance', *Studi Medievali*, ser. 3, 17 (1976), 597–623; repr. in Patlagean, *Structure Sociale, Famille, Chrétienté à Byzance* (London, 1981), XI

K. Ringrose, 'Living in the shadows: eunuchs and gender in Byzantium', in G. Herdt, ed., *Third Sex, Third Gender* (New York, 1994), 85–110, 507–18

A. Rouselle, *Porneia: On Desire and the Body in Antiquity* (Oxford, 1988)

S. Runciman, 'Women in Byzantine aristocratic society', in M. Angold, ed., *The Byzantine Aristocracy* (Oxford, 1984), 10–23

H. Saradi-Mendelovici, 'A contribution to the study of the Byzantine notarial formulas: the *Infirmitas Sexus* of women and the *Sc. Velleianum*', *Byzantinische Zeitschrift* 83 (1990), 72–90

J. Seiber, *Early Byzantine Urban Saints* (Oxford, 1977)

B.D. Shaw, 'The passion of Perpetua', *Past and Present* 139 (1993), 3–45

B. Ward, *Harlots of the Desert* (London and Oxford, 1987)

W.L. Westermann, 'The castanet dancers of Arsinoe', *Journal of Egyptian Archaeology* 10 (1924), 134–44

V.L. Wimbush and R. Valantasis, eds, *Asceticism* (New York, 1995)

F. Winkelmann, 'Das hagiographische Bild Konstantins I. in mittel-
byzantinischer Zeit', in V. Vavrinek, ed., *Beiträge zur byzantinischen
Geschichte im 9–11. Jahrhundert* (Prague, 1978), 179–203

A very full bibliography of primary and secondary sources dealing with
Byzantine women has been compiled by Thalia Gouma-Peterson and is
available from Donna Warner, The Art Department, The College of
Wooster, Wooster, Ohio 44691.

INDEX